THE MIDLANDS & THE EAST OF *England*

Edited by Allison Jones

FORWARD POETRY REGIONALS 2010

First published in Great Britain in 2010 by:
Forward Poetry
Remus House
Coltsfoot Drive
Peterborough
PE2 9BF
Telephone: 01733 890099
Website: www.forwardpoetry.co.uk

Book Design by Ali Smith

SB ISBN 978-1-84418-559-7

Foreword

We at Forward Poetry have now spent an impressive 22 years in the publishing industry and retain our enviable position of being the largest publisher of new poetry in the world. Our founding belief is that creativity is something that should be accessible and enjoyable to all, and with more than two decades worth of experience, we remain just as committed to breaking down the barriers to elitism.

For this anthology we have selected verse from our talented writers that, while varying in style and content, each express and communicate thoughts, feelings and ideas to the reader. As a result this imaginative collection is one bound to inspire just as much as it entertains.

Contents

Barbara R. Lockwood (Norwich) 1
Ian Davey (Orpington) 1
David Speed (Stoke-on-Trent) 2
Kevin Cobley (Romford) 2
Foqia Hayee (Bromley) 3
Samuel Grizzle (Ravensthorpe) 4
Joan Fowler (Outwell) 5
Pam Penfold (Rainham) 6
Geoffrey Speechly (Bridgnorth) 8
Brenda Butler (Leiston) 8
Jennifer Ann Alcock (Tamworth) 9
Patricia Green (Norwich) 9
Margaret Lee (Oundle) 10
Daphne Foreman (Cambridge) 11
Stephen Whitehouse (Tamworth) 11
Gwilym Beechey (Peterborough) 12
Joanna Jayne Bucknall (Isleham) 13
Liz Davies (Papworth Everard) 14
Stan Downing (Cambridge) 15
William E Clements (Grays) 16
Tom Cabin (Beckenham) 16
Brian Clark (Gunthorpe) 17
Jimmy H (Walton-on-the-Naze) 18
Gladys Burgess (Great Cornard) 19
John Jones (Great Baddow) 20
Reginald E Gent (Kemsley) 21
Jean Hazell (Ramsgate) 22
Pam Hammocks (Whitstable) 23
Elaine Day (Romford) 24
Dorie Williams (Birchington) 25
Philip David (Colchester) 26
Kay Purkiss (Strood) 27
Robin Robinson (Sandhurst) 28
Fredrick West (Chelmsford) 29
Daphne Cornell (Saffron Walden) 30
Joan Erskine (Norwich) 30
Barry Dillon (Canterbury) 31
Susan Parr (Gainsborough) 31
Joan Croft Todd (Chislehurst) 32
Alan Compton (Tunbridge Wells) 33
Geoffrey Elgar (Canterbury) 34
Jean Everest (Gravesend) 35
Ms Elaine Neous (Coventry) 36
Aleene Hatchard (Hutton) 38
Brian Grace (Gillingham) 38
Gordon Miles (Brightlingsea) 39
Elizabeth Bruce (Teynham) 40
Liz Dicken (Tonbridge) 41
Fay Froud (Diss) 42
Frances Holmes (Whitstable) 43
Sheila Fernley-Benard (Northfleet) 44
Clare McAuley (Stanground) 45
Michael Larcombe (Stock) 46
David A Sheasby (Daventry) 47
Caroline Isherwood (Frinton-on-Sea) 47
Henry Disney (Cambridge) 48
Patricia Cannon (St Leonards-on-Sea) 49
Christine Flowers (Walsoken) 49

G L Glanville (Braintree) 50
Dorothy Gould (Dartford) 51
Geoff Foster (Sidcup) 52
Caroline Buddery (Gorleston) 52
Jayne Walker (Wolverhampton) 53
T Cobley (Romford) 53
Patricia Harris (Martlesham) 54
G Birke (Lowestoft) 55
Celia Law (Pembury) 56
Pauline Anderson (Cambridge) 56
Allan Bula (Bexhill-on-Sea) 57
Irene Kenny (Beccles) 57
Margaret Cowling (Trumpington) 58
Sue Whitehead (St Leonards-on-Sea) 58
Lesley Gill (Leigh-on-Sea) 59
Lauren Brazier (Romford) 59
Daianna Pinto (Peterborough) 60
Christal Medcalf (South Witham) 60
Joanna Lewis (King's Lynn) 61
Terrence St John (Pembury) 61
N Lemel (Westcliff-on-Sea) 62
K M Hook (Peterborough) 63
Latoya Maynard (Sudbury) 64
Judy McGregor (Burwash Common) 65
Alma Brace (Chilton) 66
Anne Cotton (Colchester) 67
Gerald Walden (Stanway) 68
Denis Griffiths (Ely) 69
Andy McMaster (Retford) 69
Daisy Carr (Walton) 70
Peter Davies (Fressingfield) 71
Steve Waterfield (Rainham) 72
Shirley Joy Dean (Eaton Rise) 73
Jill Stedman (Fordham) 74
Audrey Lay (Oulton Broad) 74
Daphne M Brady (Ormesby) 75
Jackie Hinden (Brighton) 75
George Coombs (Hove) 76
Beryl Sigournay (Grays) 77
Margaret Dack (Horning) 78
Holly Payne (Kings Hill) 79
Paul Green (Wisbech) 80
Anita Walker (Maldon) 80
Janet Jannaway (Stanford-le-Hope) 81
Stuart Springthorpe (Harlow) 82
Elwynne Willson (Walderslade) 82
Barbara Finch (Chapel St Leonards) 83
Tim Sharman (Eastbourne) 83
Jean Dickens (Rushden) 84
Sandy Randall (Bretton) 85
Nikki Robinson (Folkestone) 86
Joyce Memory (Gt Glen) 86
Hilary Jill Robson (Westcliff-on-Sea) 87
Maureen Williams (Attleborough) 87
Geoffrey Perry (Hainault) 88
Anthony David Beardsley (Alford) 88
Elsie J Sharman (Ipswich) 89
P W Pidgeon (Romford) 90
G F Snook (Benfleet) 91
Alistair L Lawrence (Oakham) 92
Jennifer Withers (Orton Malborne) 93
Julie Boitoult (Rochford) 93
Silvia Juliet Millward (Willenhall) 94
Norma J Bates (Warwick) 95
Rachel Todd (Wickham Market) 96
John W Brown (Ormesby St Michael) 97
Tricia Morgan (Paulerspury) 98
Brian Eley (Horncastle) 99

Anne Bailey (Telford) 100
Elizabeth Haworth (Burton-on-Trent) 101
Lizbeth Cooke (Oakham) 102
Leslie Dennis Pearce (Bexhill-on-Sea) 102
Irene G Corbett (Hammerwich)............................. 103
Kevin Davies (Solihull)... 103
Ann Dempsey (Sutton Coldfield)........................... 104
David Donaldson (Orcop) 105
Betty Bramma (Worcester).................................... 106
H Griffiths (Market Harborough)........................... 106
Doreen Gardner (Shirley) 107
Pauline Burton (Beccles)....................................... 108
Richard Bonfield (Leicester).................................. 109
Lucy Mary Dean (Horncastle) 110
Veronica M Brown (Wigston) 110
Tony Cashmore (Hartshill).................................... 111
Pluto (Oakington)... 112
Carl Kemper (Lichfield) 113
Susan E Roffey (Longfield).................................... 114
Angie Farrow (Ipswich)... 115
Calvin Madin (Chesterfield).................................. 116
Cynthia Fay (Maidwell) 116
Marie Wood (King's Lynn) 117
Dennis Field (Tamworth)...................................... 118
Alison Jackson (Pershore)..................................... 119
William Birtwistle (Market Harborough)................ 120
Lizzy Usher (Boyton).. 120
Dorothy Boulton (Tonbridge) 121
Pamela Javes (Winshill).. 121
Pam Gravett (Leigh-on-Sea) 122
Shirley Beckett (Bishopstone)............................... 123
Sally Babiker (Peterborough)................................ 124
Belinda Eddy (Earith) 125
Carolyn Reed (Lewes) 126
Paget Aisling von Wedel (East Sussex).................. 127
Don Amis Warin (Colchester)................................ 128
Frances Russell (Dovercourt) 129
Lorna Tippett (Hailsham) 130
Geraldine Frances Sanders (Leigh-on-Sea) 131
E Thompson (Hastings) 132
James David Holland (Bignall End) 133
Nora M Beddoes (Kidderminster)......................... 134
Kerri Moore (Keresley) 135
Patricia Mary Gross (Blisworth) 136
Freda Baker (Halesowen) 138
Riffat Nazir Ahmed (Sparkhill).............................. 138
Pamela Buckle (Alcester)...................................... 139
Lorraine Sheldrake (North Lopham) 139
Merlin B James (Oadby)....................................... 140
Elin Lewis (Wellesbourne) 141
Fliss Edwards (Rugby).. 142
Gael Nash (Northiam).. 143
Sue Cockayne (Burntwood) 144
G Bryant (Humberston) 145
Glan Grey-Jones (Northampton) 145
Karen Morgan (Corby).. 146
Denis Martindale (Gedling)................................... 147
Megan Hughes (Moulton) 148
Dave Brough (Southam) 148
Michelle Austin (Beaumont Leys) 149
Mark Moulds (Kimberley) 150
Walter Mottram (Hednesford) 151
Betty Mealand (Upton-upon-Severn) 152
Doreen Cook (Sutton at Hone) 153
Jim Lawes (Hereford)... 154
Dennis Thomsett (Dartford) 154
Nigel Lloyd Maltby (Fishtoft)................................ 155
Lynn Scatcherd (Mansfield).................................. 156

Lady M (Bowthorpe)....................156
Eileen Combellack (Loughborough)....................157
Pauline Hill (Littleover)....................157
Pearl Burdock (Whittlesey)....................158
Sid (aka Steve Allen) (Stockingford)....................158
Eddie Owers (Stanford-le-Hope)....................159
Vivienne Blanchard (Harlow)....................159
Patrisha Reece-Davies (Orton Longueville)....................160
Edward Ashmore (Burslem)....................161
Edna Harvey (Whitstable)....................162
Christine Michael (Blidworth)....................162
Christine Rands (King's Lynn)....................163
Jenna Goodwin (Stoke-on-Trent)....................163
Vaifro Malavolta (Maidstone)....................164
Susan Devlin (Epping)....................165
Jim Bell (Chatham)....................166
Bill Schaeffer (Sevenoaks)....................168
Marie Leppard (Leigh)....................170
Thomas Baker (High Halden)....................170
Peter Lee (Rusthall)....................171
Cynthia Shum (Yoxall)....................171
Sylvia Smallman (Tamworth)....................172
Jonathan Rhodes (Chesterfield)....................173
Barbara Russell (Tuxford)....................174
Maggy Harrison (Mansfield)....................174
Angela Allen (Weston Coyney)....................175
Lucy Green (Burgh-le-Marsh)....................176
Judith Mary Drinkhill (Redditch)....................177
Patricia Bisbey (Stourbridge)....................177
Angela Maguire (Smethwick)....................178
B M Greenwood (Barton-on-Humber)....................178
E Corr (Corby)....................179
Margo Rondell Storer (Dronfield Woodhouse)....................179
H D Hensman (Sibbertoft)....................180
Mavis Fry (Walsall)....................181
David R Smith (Longnor)....................181
Keith L Powell (Ashford-In-The-Water)....................182
Cal Pearson (Kingshurst)....................182
Hazel Palmer (Swadlincote)....................183
Craig Stanley (Manton)....................183
Stan Trent (Coventry)....................184
Percy Walton (Leek)....................185
Graham Saxby (Wolverhampton)....................186
Christine Frances Williams (Loughton)....................186
Lesley Paul (Irthlingborough)....................187
Colin O'Reilly (Ipswich)....................187
Ed Watts (Knowle)....................188
Nicholas Aris (Nottingham)....................188
Pat Williams (Wellesbourne)....................189
Patricia Whittall (Codsall)....................189
J E Winfield (Chaddesden)....................190
Colin Griffiths (Kettering)....................190
Teresa Whitfield (Weston-under-Lizard)....................191
Elizabeth Timmins (Wall Heath)....................192
John W Skepper (Burton-upon-Stather)....................193
John Brian Watkinson (Chesterfield)....................193
David M Walford (Cleobury Mortimer)....................194
David Wright (East Hunsbury)....................195
Sam Shingler (Maidstone)....................196
Irene Dodd (Northfield)....................197
Diana Stopher (Peasenhall)....................198
Andrew Fisher (Skegness)....................198
Diane Elizabeth Maltby (Clifton)....................199
John Mitchell (Thurlaston)....................199
Clive Bowen (Hampton-in-Arden)....................200
Trevor Beach (Birmingham)....................200
John Hewing (Spondon)....................201
Ron Dove (West Heath)....................202

Barbara Brown (Chesterfield) 202
John Cockburn (Bottesford) 203
Peter Alvey (Forest Town) 204
Joan Marrion (Oakham) 205
Jane Day (Barrow-upon-Humber) 206
George S Higgs (Birstall) 207
June Oliver (Leiston) 208
Jenny Amery (Scunthorpe) 209
S Jacks (Shrewsbury) 210
Margaret Meadows (Burbage) 210
Emily Cotterill (Alfreton) 211
Laura Dobbins (Lower Broadheath) 211
Lisa Burton (West Bromwich) 212
Barry Scott Crisp (Grimsby) 213
Trevor A Napper (Peterborough) 214
Jacqueline Claire Davies (Dudley) 214
Owen Davies (Horninglow) 215
Shirley Longford (Somercotes) 215
Derrick Wooding (Moulton) 216
Iris Covell (Sleaford) 217
T Raymond Stuart (Skegness) 218
Janet Angela Bendall (Alford) 219
Jim Wilson (Westcliff-on-Sea) 220
Kenneth Lynn (Dunholme) 221
Peter Brammer (Shireoaks) 222
Paul Holland (Stoke-on-Trent) 224
Stephanie Lynn Teasdale (Tattershall) 225
Carol Templey (Harlow) 226
Sylvia R A Southgate (Felixstowe) 228
Barbara Wilkinson (Longfield) 228
Lindy Roberts (Worlingham) 229
Sue Reilly (Kings Cliffe) 230
Laura Gordon (Benfleet) 231
Lyn Sullivan (Chatham) 232
Dinah Williams (Ludham) 233
Jeanne Yvonne Simpson (Sutton-on-Sea) 234
Colin Hubbert (Sutterton) 236
Chris Todd (Peterborough) 236
Juliet C Eaton (Allestree) 237
Joan Burgess (West Heath) 238
Mary Lefebvre (Stafford) 239
Don Nixon (Albrighton) 240
Joan Moore (Grantham) 241
Christopher Rothery (Uttoxeter) 242
Steven Pearson (Hempnall) 242
Joan Wheatcroft (Stourport-on-Severn) 243
Robert Walker (Shirland) 243
Jessica Heafield (Kegworth) 244
Jack Le C Smith (Ockbrook) 245
Lady Sandie Smith (Meir) 246
Diane Young (Spalding) 246
David Robinson (Belper) 247
Caitlin Kovacs (Ettingshall) 247
Christine Ward (Colchester) 248
John Pegg (Meir) 249
Rachel Taylor (Winthorpe) 250
Ralph A Watkins (Wellesbourne) 251
Albert Watson (Hodge Hill) 252
Victor William Lown (Loughborough) 253
Ivy Gee (Oadby) 254
Zena Brown (Radford) 254
Bakewell Burt (Bakewell) 255
N Brocks (Gedney Dyke) 256
Philip O'Leary (Redditch) 257
Veronica Twells (Groby) 257
Carol Ann Elsmore (Oldbury) 258
Dean Buffin (Nuneaton) 259
M Simpson (Oakwood) 259

Jane Air (Mablethorpe)..260
M Lovesey (Stone Cross)..262
Mary Lacey (Shrewsbury)..263
Pauline Vinters (Tattershall)..264
June Hickabottom (Scunthorpe)..265
Tyrone Dalby (Boston)..266
Thelma Robinson (Clarborough)..267
Michael Cotton (Kettering)..268
Josie Rawson (Selston)..268
Brenda Charles (Sherwood)..269
Yvonne Powell (Thorpe Satchville)..269
Wesley Alcinder (Dudley)..270
Sister Gregory Feetenby (Matlock)..271
Betty Johnson (Derby)..272
Goldah Jankiewicz (Mansfield Woodhouse)..272
Marilyn Bloomfield (Glascote Heath)..273
Eileen Henderson (Nottingham)..273
Donald Linnett (Wigston)..274
Margaret A Stonier (Kidsgrove)..275
Jacob Parker (Rugby)..276
Dorothy Buyers (Oswestry)..277
Carole A Cleverdon (Northampton)..278
R L Cooper (Radcliffe-on-Trent)..278
Nathan Thompson (Warrington)..279
E Riggott (Holmewood)..279
Ranjit Singh (Derby)..280
Ian Proctor (Biddulph)..281
Adele Rawle (Rugeley)..282
Barbara Young (Hereford)..283
Freda Searson (Ripley)..284
Brenda Reville (Whaley Bridge)..284
Linsi Sanders (Barton Green)..285
Daniel Song (Arun Budhathoki) (Northampton)..285
Theresa Richmond (Winthorpe)..286
Diana Walter (Calverton)..287
Shirley Ann Smith (Cleethorpes)..288
Anthony Weedon (North Somercotes)..289
Theresa Hartley-Mace (Calverton)..290
Violet Sinclair (Beachdale)..290
Roy John Humphreys (Rusden)..291
Olive Bedford (Burton-on-Trent)..292
Naomi Portman (Worcester)..293
Doris Bailey (Sheepy Magna)..294
Ruth Warrington (Cheadle)..294
Linda Jennings (Bilton)..295
Jayne Sanders (Belper)..295
Barbara Fletcher (Tipton)..296
T McFarlane (Wavertree)..297
Shelley Whitehouse (Kettering)..298
Sheila Taylor (Kingswinford)..299
Ann Thompson (Ledbury)..299
William Thirkettle (Draycott)..300
David E Anderson (Walcot by Folkingham)..301
Paul Norris (Kenilworth)..302
Dickon Springate (Gillingham)..302
Ronald Martin (Bulwell)..303
Enid Hewitt (Grantham)..304
Garth (Cranwell)..305
Paula Johnson (Wickenby)..306
Keith Deeley (Solihull)..307
Jeff Hobson (Lutterworth)..308
Sharon Atkinson (Stanford Le Hope)..309
Anna Elliott (Faversham)..310
Brian C Gamage (Southborough)..311
Jennifer Reeves (Rushall)..311
Fiona Holman (Ashford)..312
Bernard Newton (Chesterfield)..313
Olivia Kellas-Kelly (Stamford)..314

Joanne Manning (Hawkinge) 315
David J Hall (Birmingham) 316
Anne Morgan (Tunbridge Wells) 317
Andy Biddulph (Burton-on-Trent) 318
Tim Kitchen (Beeston) 319
Ambreen Akhter (Birmingham) 320
Mary Shepherd (Nottingham) 320
Elaine A Brocklesby (Brigg) 321
Susan Roffey (Longfield) 322
Joan Margaret Waller (Sidcup) 322
Carl Kemper (Lichfield) 323
Gloria Smith (Canterbury) 324
Alan Smith (Bromley) 325
Marion Webb (Bromley) 326
Maria Moller (Rochester) 327
Gwendoline Woodland (Gillingham) 328
Meg Nellist (Upminster) 328
Rhowen-Margot Brown (Scunthorpe) 329
Kevan Taplin (Thuxton) 330
M Turner (Bury St Edmunds) 331
J Hubbard (Diss) 332
Lyn Sandford (St Germans) 333
Gwen Dunn (Hadleigh) 334

The Poems

HEARTLAND (A PLEA)

A voyage of discovery
On a scene is all I see,
Life has been rather tough
Earnings very rough,
Denying us coordinated respect
A heart with little joy and much regret,

Our UK island once our home
Devoured by power
Capitalising where we roam,
Ruled with incompetence
Instead of confidence,
Let England's heart return again
To help us all regain
Independence and less restraint
To rule our own domain.

BARBARA R. LOCKWOOD (NORWICH)

CLOUD

Through the non-flaming hoop
Flying in the pouring rain,
Flying a solo loop-the-loop
That acrobatic aeroplane.

The pilot, no parachute,
Waves to the clapping crowd;
Then vanishes with a whoop
Behind a dripping cloud.

IAN DAVEY (ORPINGTON)

La Roque Gaeac en Êté (In Summer)

An angel of serenity falls upon the boat
Did she coolly fall from the crisp blue skies
To sit tranquil beside me silently on a chair
Generously accepting, I do not know she's there?

Was it from down below she rose to join our company?
Did we sense her breathe a deep river calm?
Perhaps from lofty caves, she stoops to conquer our alarm
Dwelling above roofs to mix the potion of her charm

Which through the atmosphere we drink, then swoon
Out of time and space, no ifs and buts, this place
Solely seems what is real, everything in collusion
Makes us foreigners to strain, work is the illusion

Her finger touches tongues, not a word is heard,
Even the chugging engine is oarstruck to our minds,
She concocts a silence, craft it once again.
Would you have me transported to the world of men?

DAVID SPEED (STOKE-ON-TRENT)

Moonstruck

Come coy moon hidden behind cloud
Tiptoe to open sky
For below
Drunk amidst the flowers I raise my glass
Inviting you to join me
To dance and spin across damp meadow
To chase between the sleeping trees
You, me and my shadow

Hurry princess of the night
Your suitor grows impatient
For already the owl is restless

KEVIN COBLEY (ROMFORD)

Summer (Silent Blessing)

where we live summer is celebrated every year
we can feel but cannot hear
soundless sizzling sun
brings so much fun
quiet warmth puts a glow
in hearts, which show
on faces, which smile
bodies become alive
where we live summer is celebrated every year
we can see but cannot hear
seeds planted underground
shoot up without a sound
scented colours collected
come up unexpected
in diverse shapes as flowers
with a little help from showers
where we live summer is celebrated every year
no room for sad tear
smell of shiny rays
fresh fruit, barbecues, birthdays
playing with wet mud on riverside
fishing, picnics, kite flying, donkey rides
these silent blessings cause loud cheers
a lot to share
where we live summer is celebrated every year

FOQIA HAYEE (BROMLEY)

Many Places Where We Could Go

There are so many places where we could go,
Places where we do not know.
We could go by sea or by air.
There are so many things that could take us there.

Perhaps we could go by motor car,
But it would not take us very far.
We could go by ships.
But so many places that we would miss.

We could go by bikes,
But we could not cross the dykes,
Or we could go by bus,
But it could not take many of us.

We could go on our feet,
But we may not reach,
We could go by coach,
We would miss the coast.

There are so many places where we could go,
Many places where we do not know
We could go by air,
But we cannot pay the fare.

There are so many places where we could go,
Places where we do not know,
So many things that could take us there,
But who will pay the fare?

SAMUEL GRIZZLE (RAVENSTHORPE)

My Garden

(INSPIRED BY SISTER MERCY)

My garden is a noisy place
The wind which howls across the fen
The clucking from the broody hen
The dove cooing in the tall beech tree
The buzzing from the bumblebee
The cat strolls lazily across the grass
A blackbird watches with a beady eye
But goes on singing as she passes by
When the sun has left the sky
And stars are shining way up high
My garden becomes a different place
The rabbits all come out to play
And start to chew my trees away
Then Charlie, the crafty fox appears
The cubs roll around like balls of fluff
The vixen says now that's enough
You must catch your dinner for tomorrow
But the rabbits have all gone back to their burrow
The owl has taken up his place
We hear his hoot but do not see his face
The foxes scream, the pheasants cock up
The guard dog starts to growl
The fox has woken him as well
But now the sky is getting brighter
The dawn chorus begins to swell
The air has a clean new smell
All these gifts come from above
To turn my garden into a place of love

JOAN FOWLER (OUTWELL)

His Enemy, His Friend

(BOXLEY IS A VERY SMALL VILLAGE NEAR MY HOME IN KENT. LIKE A MIRACLE IT IS TRANSFORMED EVERY JUNE BY ITS FIELDS OF POPPIES)

Have you never seen in June
The claim to fame that's Boxley's?
The meadows and the fields in bloom
Transformed by humble poppies?

They make me think of Flanders fields,
(Though I have never been)
And of the wars that shamed mankind,
I'm sure you all agree.

I want to share this poem
I wrote about a war,
And two enemy soldiers
Who aren't with us anymore.

The air was thick with smoke,
The smell of death and more,
In the muddy, bloody trenches
Half-full with body parts and gore.

Guns had fallen silent,
Young soldiers left to die
With dead and dying comrades
In putrid mud they lie.

Two dying enemy soldiers lay
In the stench and pouring rain,
They would not see another day
Nor see sunrise again.

Each knew that soon his life would end
In the tragic, bloody war,
With no one there to tend their wounds,
In the mud on the trenches' floor.

One man watched the other,
A young man in his prime,
Lying in a pool of blood,
Shallow breathing, little time.

The other man, his stomach bare,
Lay with innards everywhere,
He too knew that he would die,
And gave a choking, sobbing cry.

Both men thought hazy dreams of home,
Of family and friends,
How precious were sweet memories
To lives about to end.

One soldier felt inside his vest
For a crumpled photograph
Of the blonde-haired girl that he loved best,
And held it to his heart.

The other soldier reached to get
A photo from his pack,
Of a brown-eyed girl that he had met,
Promised to marry when he got back.

Each knew he hadn't very long,
The Reaper wouldn't wait,
There was no point in wasting time
On anger or on hate.

Faces etched with fear and pain,
Each one held out his hand,
And passed his precious photograph
To the other man.

Eyes closed, each waited for the end,
The fears of each were one,
No matter whether friend or foe,
They didn't want to die alone.

The sun went down, they passed away,
The Reaper came, they could not stay,
Each found his own peace in the end,
And in his enemy - a friend.

They were found in days to come,
They'd fought their bloody war and won,
What passing soldiers never knew -
And would not understand
Each died with the other's snapshot,
Still clutched in his hand.

PAM PENFOLD (RAINHAM)

Grass

The softness of the grass against my little finger
When, both fifteen, she and I in summer linger
On a tartan rug; the friendly sun smiling on her skin
And mine, not quite touching hers; ours not the bittersweet of sin

For we were young, and strange though now it seems
That enough for us was the sweet innocence of dreams:
The world we saw was full, not empty
Anything could be; its name was plenty.

Fifty years later, an older sun still shines
And I still rest on that same rug, but now alone.
I move my hand onto the grass, and memory floods back
My body quivers despite its muscles slack

And overgrown, like weeds among the grass.
Where is she now? Is her hair, like mine
A far, far paler hue; and are her lips as soft
As once I knew? And is for her

The grass still green; lives still that scene
When we were both fifteen?

GEOFFREY SPEECHLY (BRIDGNORTH)

Last Summer's Love

Last summer I sat near the gentle sea,
You were by my side.
Two sets of footprints
Showed on golden sand,
As we jumped and splashed
In the retreating tide.

This summer I sit beside the sea again
And watch the foaming waves
Break gently and softly on the shore.
One set of footprints
Lie on the golden sand
Because you are there no more.

BRENDA BUTLER (LEISTON)

SEASON OF LIFE

Oh how I love the summer,
Longer days and lighter nights
Packing for our holidays,
Speeding trains and long-haul flights,
Exploring brand new places and making lots of friends
Having so much fun, never wanting it to end.
Lots of new beginnings rising up, all around.
Seeds falling from the trees and bulbs up from the ground,
The grass is green, the sky is blue, the rivers running clear,
An ideal place for a picnic
It's the best time of year.
Baby birds are tweeting
Whilst their mothers search for food,
Then returning to the nest to feed the hungry brood.
Nature is very beautiful, helped by the burning sun,
The colours of the rainbow
No one knows where it begun.
We used to try and find it,
Went for miles, had so much fun.
Just like the phoenix from the flame
The summer begins, it's here again.

JENNIFER ANN ALCOCK (TAMWORTH)

MY SUMMER LOVE

The waves gathered
In the deep blue sea
Where we paddled and
Soaked up the sun
We felt wild and free
Together we were one
Happy lying on the sand
With the radio on
My summer love with hand in hand
While the sun shone all day long.

PATRICIA GREEN (NORWICH)

Summertime

Summertime is here at last
And schools have closed their doors
All the kids are happy
To catch up with their chores
Out comes the suncream
To stop you getting burnt
Greasing your arms and legs
And back so you don't get burnt
Mum packs the picnic hamper
And off they all go
Down to the picnic park
With the kids in tow
Down in the meadow
See the river flow
Watching the wildlife
And see the flowers grow
A walk down by the river
On a sunny day
Keeps you fit and healthy
In the bright sun ray
Some are really lucky
They go shopping in the town
Looking all around the shops
With the sun still shining down
Some prefer to stay at home
Instead of having fun
Lazing in their deckchairs
In the garden, in the sun
Mum gets out the paddling pool
For the kids to play
They are really happy
On this lovely summer day
When the sun is shining bright
And is a real hot day
Sunshades are out everywhere
As in the sun they lay
Then another day has passed
And the sun goes down to rest
All hoping they have another day
Just like all the rest

MARGARET LEE (OUNDLE)

THE SUN'S DEFEAT

An English cottage garden,
Steeped in the hazy silence of a July noon
An azure pool reflects in limpid depths
The fiery golden ball whose rays
Attempt to rob it of its gathered nectar;
All nature holds its breath
As the sun beats down.

But now a distant rumbling in the hills
And jagged lightning streaks across the sky;
The flowers lift their drooping parchèd faces
In grateful respite as a breeze wafts by;
The pool becomes opaque,
Pitted with fairy argosies,
As the rain comes down.

DAPHNE FOREMAN (CAMBRIDGE)

TO LOVE ONCE MORE

As we walked along love's golden shore,
We gave an oath to walk once more!

On golden sands,
We kissed the sun;
Hand in hand,
We walked as one.

Sailed a sea,
Surfed the tide;
Bathed our love,
We swam with pride.

We saw the moon kiss the stars,
Made our love;
Time was ours!

As we walked along love's golden shore,
We gave an oath;
To love once more!

STEPHEN WHITEHOUSE (TAMWORTH)

CHANT D'ETE

In France there always is a glass of wine
To cool the summer heat,
Relieve the feelings in the air
That weary walking feet.

The shady boughs that spread their leaves
And aid the gentle breeze
Are homes to birds that softly sing
And dwell among the trees.

The colours of the countryside
All spread an air of calm,
The streams and rivers gently glide
In silence, quietly warm.

The many crops of flowers and fruit,
The dahlia and the grape,
Enrich the hiker in his way
And help him to escape

The cares of life and work and toil
And crowds in every town.
Il pense - c'est bien s'attarder
Sur un repas
Et un verre ou deux de vin.

GWILYM BEECHEY (PETERBOROUGH)

MY NEEDING

Dank darkness envelopes the delicately latticed embers of sunlight
Swirling, it congeals each precious glowing finger
'Til the blackness couches over the Earth like an enraged god.

Laid low in death's icy sleep
Broods the lord of Heaven's unrequited love
Sprung from misery's tears and heart's black discontent.
Mortal flesh clothes his ancient bones
Abhorrent.

Only stillness echoes in his chest
His mouth a purple swollen bruise
Conceals the gift of theft
Savage in his lust
A blood quest.

She is his only witness
Her cold silver stare blinking through the dark
Her lullaby the murmuring of the sea
In her cool radiance
He sips on life.

He draws my tears
Full weeping for my succubae
Salt tracks run to wash him clean
Damned
I am ever seduced by his need of me

JOANNA JAYNE BUCKNALL (ISLEHAM)

THE HORSES OF AFTERNOON

See them float above the green and gold,
Suspended in an aspic of sunlit dust.
Leaf shadows shake, chestnuts gleam bronze,
And the greys move like galloping ghosts.
They press the ground so lightly in their flight,
To meet for a second their fleeting shadows,
And then arc again and again into the blue.
Elegant ears swivel to catch the turbulent air,
And the shouts of their bright silken riders,
And the swift horses of afternoon still run,
As they have always run down the centuries
Before Man, the saddle, the whip and bridle,
Before Man and his will, his leather and iron.
They run for joy, because they know no other;
Their fine heads rise and fall, large eyes glow,
Their long limbs stretch and bend, necks low,
Nostrils flaring, and foam-flecked shoulders
Ripple and heave with the power of speed.
Tails undulate like banners, neat hooves thud,
And the horses of afternoon will always run,
Together down the long hallowed green avenues,
Run with the great ghosts of their past,
The foals of the future, the horses to come,
Stampeding down the grass of all time.

LIZ DAVIES (PAPWORTH EVERARD)

SUNDAY AFTERNOON ON PARKER'S PIECE

I might have died here, sixty years ago,
As a cricket ball came fizzing over my head
Just as I bobbed down once more into my pram.
Another second and my skull would have been dented
By a hard and shining lump of leather,
And I would not have lived to tell the tale,
Or at least recount it as my mother told it
Years later when I was old enough to understand.
They're still here now, the white-clad cricketers,
Just leaving the pitch for tea in Hobbs Pavilion,
Watched by other mothers with babies in their buggies.
(Perambulators have long-since disappeared).
The couples are here, as they have been every day
For the last sixty years - but what is new
Are the men who are lounging with their laptops
Catching up on their work or getting ready
For the working week ahead? The pace of life
Is more hectic now than sixty years ago.
Some of the trees around the Piece have been replaced
Unlike my mother, dead now for forty years.
At least she fulfilled her womanhood
Just like the other women pushing buggies
Past the shaded bench where I have come to rest,
Returning to this familiar scene, after journeying far
On a lifetime's voyage of exploration,
And knowing the place, not for the first nor for the last time.

STAN DOWNING (CAMBRIDGE)

Smile Thru Life

The youthful days are gone
And my days are nearly done,
I have but many memories
Of all the years long gone.

Memories, some good, some bad,
Fading memories of when I was a lad,
Brighter ones as the years slip by
Some still bring a twinkle to my eye!

Memories are like a melody,
Some you love, others you hate!
Melodies of the earlier years,
Others of a later date!

As you pass along the road of life
You will meet trouble and sometimes strife!
But if you can pass it all and smile,
You will find life's still worthwhile!

WILLIAM E CLEMENTS (GRAYS)

Sea Birds

Far out to those rolling waves
Whipping a stormy sea,
Where the plight of skerries are shaken,
Buzzards zoom on rock ledges across the lea
And formidably an endless sky will awaken.
When sweeping gannets mark the cliffs
Chilling that formidable flight scavenging,
To the doom of small birds and swifts
The night falls to black kites avenging.
The gigantic waves hover, then halter,
And those stormy seas abate,
Fortuitously as in the island of Malta
A calm countenance can make.
Alone, and so alone, our rock birds wing
To strike those raging buffeting seas,
Where only our dearest rock birds
And their evening stars will sing.

TOM CABIN (BECKENHAM)

A WINTER MEWS 1962

Suburban landscapes,
distant trees,
old brick buildings under
blue grey slate.
A red provincial town,
backdrop of my life
and witness of my fate,
sleeps under November skies
as autumn closes late.

How still, how quiet.
how soft the space between
attic roofs and parkland trees.
Mid-afternoon yet lamps are lit
in lonely rooms under the dark and brooding sky
and ragged birds in desolate branches
search for food in winter's meagre store

Hushed and muffled,
distant footsteps on the paving
as winter pansies peep from corporation tubs.
Corduroy trousers, Rayleigh bicycle.
as the library closes, the last member leaves.
The flickering glow from his humming dynamo
fades in the distant melancholy light

A glass of sherry and the Light Programme.
Then a modest dinner, a mutton pie,
the electric bar of the fire reflecting
a reluctant warmth on the patterned linoleum.
A 'Book Before Bedtime' the wireless
addresses the stuccoed room, empty, save for the cat
reclining in somnolent lethargy.

The pageant stops, the eyes close
And the mind moves on to distant land.

The past is a locked room.

BRIAN CLARK (GUNTHORPE)

Fungi Delicacies

Gathering like mushrooms in a wood of words,
little fungi delicacies
damply undisturbed.
Red with spots, grey with spores,
fairy-dressed or castle-cragged.
Whole sentences of variety, elfishly stored.
Like secret love songs of my heart.
Varied kisses, sweet lip pressed.
Hopeful dreams shaped and formed
in a mind by heartthrob warmed.
Daydreams planned to win a love
smouldering in a glade of chance,
wanting love to last forever,
in that childhood place,
where fairies dance.
Frog-prince toadstool, endless changes,
one kiss could weave a magic spell,
make the merry love-songs knell.
One bitter bite, rejection given,
could drive this lovesick heart to Hell.
These secret fungi dreamed alone,
hidden in woods of the mind.
Short-lived beauty, food or folly,
to pluck your heart from its home.
By moonbeams grown for endless searchers
where the wandering gypsies roam.

JIMMY H (WALTON-ON-THE-NAZE)

BALLINGDON HILL (SUDBURY)

If only I could show you,
The beauty seen from this hill.
The morning mist just risen
And the valleyed town so still.

The blue sky up above me,
The sun so clear with dew,
Little town so beautiful,
You're such a peaceful view.

The Stour like a blue ribbon,
That winds from here to there;
The church spires they are scattered
Looking so tall and square.

The rooftops are so numerous,
Surrounding winding streets,
Smoke swirling from the chimneys,
Town not people sleeps.

The train puffs in the distance
Its carriages are two,
Through the meadows green and flat
Where cattle lie and chew.

No wonder Gainsborough painted,
These landscapes years ago.
I would stand here for ever
But homeward I must go.

GLADYS BURGESS (GREAT CORNARD)

Moments in July

The man sat on his back step
His mind misted with the virgin scent of a white lily
Misted with the brown scent of warm moist earth
He saw a seagull floating across the smooth blue of the sky
It was paradise in July
He heard a hidden bird giving music to it all
And then
Giving more
So much more
Flowers were fondled by the golden hand of the sun
A butterfly
Just one
Settled and flattened its wings
One butterfly said it all
The man sat on his back step
He heard a distant call
A feminine call
Cat
Cat
Can Heaven
He sighed
Be better than this
Better than these moments in July
Can it?

JOHN JONES (GREAT BADDOW)

SITTINGBOURNE TO ELMLEY REACH

New walkway to Swale at Elmley Reach,
Along Milton Creek, our history to teach.
Bring Saxon Shore Way into Sittingbourne town,
Turn area green, no longer brown.

Lovely park from town to Swale,
Here the islanders we can hail.
Although we are facing bird reserve,
See ducks, waders we wish to preserve.

Gone now are brick fields and the like,
Make way for pram, bike, ride or hike.
For visitors, resident to enjoy more,
Everything from town to shore.

See trees grow nice and tall,
See plans into life fall.
Watch girls, boys enjoy,
Climbing net, playground joy.

Rejoice when train running again,
Different outlook is quite plain.
Instead of rough ground country park,
Be so nice when everything off the mark.

REGINALD E GENT (KEMSLEY)

Cherish The Love You Have

We should cherish the time we have together
For little do we know when it will cease
When trouble and calamity break out
We should enter the Lord's peace

Do not take each other for granted
But with praise and gratitude
To love, honour and adore
That should be the attitude

Be always there for one another
Whatever comes your way
Greet each other with a kiss and a smile
At the start of each new day

Learn to bear with one another
Even with the things that irritate
For when you can love each other that way
That's the start of something great

Look out for one another
Bring little pleasures of joy
Be it through a flower, a card
Or even a cuddly toy

When you learn the secret of loving
From the bottom of your heart
Help to nurture and let it flourish
And from it never depart

Make your mark upon this world
So when you go to God in glory
Others who remember you
For you, will always have a story.

JEAN HAZELL (RAMSGATE)

SEASCAPE

Last night I walked by the sea,
She was angry and I was afraid,
There was no comfort for me
In the wild, roaring noises she made.

Her face was grey,
Her lip was curled,
I was wet with spray,
From the waves she hurled.

Today I walked by the sea,
And she was gentle and mild,
Bringing back sweet memories to me
Of lullabies, sung to a child.

Her glistening smile,
The lap, lap of the surf,
Made me stop for a while,
To enjoy her mirth.

If I walk by the sea tomorrow,
What then will be her mood,
One of joy or one of sorrow,
Will she mind if I intrude?

Oh such a challenging force,
This great, mysterious sea,
How can I but chart my course,
When she pulls, like a magnet, to me?

PAM HAMMOCKS (WHITSTABLE)

Ramblers' Walk

We go anywhere
Doing the ramblers' walk
From Land's End to John O'Groats
We are everywhere
Today we're walking the Pennines
Maybe see some wildlife
Sheep, foxes and the like
Mud in your eyes
Sweat on your brow
A happy smile
Conversation with the others
A bit to eat
In a pub maybe or a sandwich
Drink in hand
Toilet not in view
Maybe just around the corner
There will be a loo
Must get walking
Conversation is very good
The summer sun shines through
Warming my clothes
And my brow
Nearly finished the ramblers' walk
Tomorrow is another day
In the sunshine and the rain
I've enjoyed the walk
Tomorrow another walk
Not for me,
I'm having a rest
Maybe in two days time
I'll go a'rambling
Doing the ramblers' walk again.

ELAINE DAY (ROMFORD)

SEA

Footsteps in the damp sand
Tide receding into the sunset's
golden cape. Slowly spreading
its hues over a dark green sea.

I once swam here long ago
with sisters and cousins
in the lacy sunshine of
those summers past, as we
bathed away the smell of school.

We paced our strokes further
and further from the sandy shore
without fear.
Joe Rigden's eagle eye followed us
as he rowed over the waves
calling out like a squalled gull.

I want to repeat that long past memory.
Disrobe and swim into the golden rays.
But I am aged, Joe has gone,
rowing and saving souls in Heaven.
No one now to call over the distant sea.

Or row out to a lone grey head
bobbing over remote waves.
So I walk, retrace my footsteps
along the damp sandy shore.

DORIE WILLIAMS (BIRCHINGTON)

An Ode To 'Carbolic'!

What a wonderful word is 'carbolic',
Just roll it around on your tongue
It's more famous than 'Oxo' or 'Hovis'
For the incredible work it has done.
Florence Nightingale oft' sang its praises
And used it wherever she went
For it came into its own in Crimea
Where the doctors thought it heaven-'scent'!
It helped to get rid of infection
That war wounds are apt to conceive
And many a man thanked carbolic
For saving his life in the field.

For

Tables and floors - and quite often doors -
Were scrubbed 'til they shone pristine white
And aprons starched - tight - were soaked overnight
To kill germs as the soldiers fought Boers:
The whole world soon found - with carbolic around -
The hospitals and homes were germ-free,
If with sluices and drains they took the greatest of pains,
From carbolic the bugs would soon flee!

But

The trouble was - well - carbolic's strong smell
Offended some sensitive noses,
Thus - folks with diplomas researched new aromas
And came up oft' smelling of roses -
Or 'pine' from the wood - which smelled rather good -
As did 'lilies' and rustic 'impatiens',
So - it came to pass - to the bottom of the class
Went carbolic and all its relations!

And odours galore from nature's great store
Erupted all over the nation -
But with evocative smells - do they really work well
And kill all the germs in a trice?
Or do all the bugs give all their friends hugs
With 'You can tell it's Chanel' - isn't that nice!
Mind - it's just a suggestion - but perhaps cross-infection,
That appears in a way to plague us today,
Returned - cos it's true - that some things we do
Are done better the old-fashioned way!

PHILIP DAVID (COLCHESTER)

SUMMER IN ENGLAND

England in the summer? - Well!
Thunder and lightning and rain!
Not the gentle summer kind -
And - it's coming down again!

So

What happened to country walks
- And picnics in the park?
Cosy evenings and late night talks
- And the sweet clear song of the lark?

Then

Now the sun is shining
The sky is blue and clear
Let's hope the storm has gone away
And summer's really here.

Now

Typical English weather
Sunshine - then - showers again
Still as old gardeners say -
'We could really do with the rain!'

KAY PURKISS (STROOD)

A MAN IN LOVE WITH A WOMAN

Others can do all they can,
But a woman has the greatest effect on a man;
It can be a blessing or a curse,
It can be for better or worse.

From that day on, his life will change,
He will never be the same;
It is love you can see it in the eyes,
The chemistry is moving his body to a new exercise.

The wonderful thing of falling in love,
It can happen when you are old, middle-aged or young;
From now on his life takes a direction,
He longs to please her with affection.

He constantly looks out for her,
She is his only desire;
For love is stronger than death,
Many waters cannot quench its fire.

When a man loves a woman,
It takes control of his life;
It brings him to his knees.
He is stripped of all his pride.

He is addicted to love that is his lot,
Spending his last penny holding on to what he has got;
Not in the future or in the past,
Enjoying love while it does last.

ROBIN ROBINSON (SANDHURST)

SUMMER MODIFICATIONS

Summer mornings buzz with the sounds
of mower, sander, saw.
All the 'modernisers'
are out in force, once more!

As soon as the sun begins to shine
out come the pots and the paint,
the tubs of plants and trellis-work
to make things 'what they aint'.

The old coal hole is rebuilt
and labelled 'utility'.
The porch is now extended
so that it's 'conservatory'.

No end of time is taken building
walls for wrought-iron gates!
And there are built-in wardrobes,
cupboards, shelves for pots and plates.

It's taken weeks of perspiration
to produce a 'Tudor' gable
and tons of sand, cement and stones
for patio and bird table!

I don't complain. I must confess
I update things myself.
The irony: as soon 'tis done,
they want it something else!

FREDRICK WEST (CHELMSFORD)

Summer Gold

Grains of sand between your toes
in your hair and up your nose
bellyache from too many sweets
had enough to last you weeks
ice cream and sarnies on the sand
didn't have time to wash our hands
chasing crabs in tiny pools
splashing about like crazy fools
making castles and playing ball
didn't go home until nightfall
those were glorious days at the beach
they now seem so far out of reach
in those summers there was always golden sun
and trips to the beach were so much fun
no worries of sun damage to our skin
and eating chips wasn't a sin
but gone are those innocent days of old
those carefree days of summer gold.

DAPHNE CORNELL (SAFFRON WALDEN)

A Norfolk Summer's Day

Clouds drift aimlessly across the vast blue sky,
Where heat haze lingers above the marshes
Where cows drowse, tails swishing,
Where dragonflies and damsel flies
Hover over the waterways.
Where fishermen doze along the riverbanks.
Where bees browse in the flowers
Where a lone farmer tills the soil
Where gulls grouse as they follow the plough.
Where over all rests a dreamy languidness.

JOAN ERSKINE (NORWICH)

Silence

Appointed to sit on a city council committee
I listened to learn perhaps something to say
Of some importance
Not to waste the day
But the members spoke so quietly
Whispering in voices barely audible
My hearing has been tested and it's fine
I've never liked loudness
But why talk so softly, no one can hear?
Perhaps the reason is all that very small print around
Extended to the verbal range
If answering be careful of what you're saying
Don't be ashamed if it's something strange
You are most likely not to blame
No need for shame
In what appears to be a talk game
Maybe this is why some odd decisions are made
No one truly understands the way
Or what to actually say

BARRY DILLON (CANTERBURY)

Broken Friendship

Our broken friendship plays on my mind,
I sometimes wish I could press rewind.
Summer '08 is my best memory of all,
my favourite picture of us will always hang on my wall.
I tried to save our friendship,
but neither of you bothered to call,
you obviously thought our friendship wasn't worth fighting for.
Now months have passed and I'm completely drained from it all,
I give up the fight,
we're strangers once more.

SUSAN PARR (GAINSBOROUGH)

Elizabeth and Essex

Elizabeth loved Essex
('Twas whispered through the town)
Yet knew that given half an inch
Essex would wear her crown

Essex knew well Bess loved him
For she gave him her ring
And being egotist and male
His aim was to be king

Now good Queen Bess
Champion of chess
Always one move ahead
Well her plans laid
Well her game played
He followed - while she led

He bent the knee impatiently
Waiting to seize his chance
While queenly skills
Disguised by frills
Checkmated each advance

Then suddenly - misguidedly
He felt his hour had come
Made his false move
Which was to prove
Lord Essex was undone

Too proud to seek forgiveness
He shivered in The Tower
Awaiting execution
All for the lust of power

The day that Essex
Met his hell
It's said the Queen's heart
Died as well

Her crooked spine
Bowed deeper now
England had tolled her health
No true love dreams
For despot queens
What man could love her for herself?

Elizabeth loved Essex
Yet dared not let him rule
For well she knew
That so to do
Would be England's downfall

JOAN CROFT TODD (CHISLEHURST)

ENGLAND - THROUGH AUSSIE EYES

I love this land of winding ways
Of hedgerow'd fields whose golden greens
Touch heaven's blue, pale-edged in haze;
A land of pleasant rural scenes

That fragile waking in early spring
When nature stirs in woods and heath
Now hoary winter its course has run;
And lowly February's fair maids drooping
As their mantles melt beneath
The gentle, warming, length'ning sun

That dazzling riot of gold and blue
When later flowers carpet the hills
With a radiant beauty to delight, and imbue
The heart with a joy that quickens and thrills

I love her balmy summer days
Those lovely lazy days when bees
Go buzzing by; when swallows sweep
The sky in sunset's hues ablaze
And blackbird calls from leafy trees
His constant mate her tryst to keep

Autumn blusters with strong insist
And sheds its garb as nights grow chill,
And cottage eyes glow soft through mist
While Earthlings nestle, and all are still

ALAN COMPTON (TUNBRIDGE WELLS)

PASTORAL

(AN INTERPRETATION OF THE PROGRAMME FOR BEETHOVEN'S 6TH SYMPHONY)

Joyous feelings on arrival in the country

I flee the city's sordid streets,
One early morning, summertime,
And swiftly to the country wend,
With happy feelings so sublime.

My senses feel the perfumed breeze,
See countless flocks of birds in flight,
As natural life begins to wake,
My weary mind fills with delight.

In tune with every blade of grass,
Enchanting views now greet my eyes,
The last few wisps of cloud depart,
The warming sun shines from the skies.

By the brook

I sit by gently flowing stream,
Which hurries down from mountain high,
And murmurs softly on its way
It's own incessant lullaby.

Reclining on the grassy slope
It seems all nature's gifts surround,
Above the purling of the stream,
I hear a myriad of sounds.

At once are rising song-like tunes,
As tiny waves break on the banks,
The cuckoo, nightingale and quail
All start to sing their special thanks.

Peasants' merry-making

Now comes to me the distant strains
Of merry-making country folk,
As they enjoy their rustic dance,
My magic spell's abruptly broke.

The noise of dancing rises more,
The oboe makes a lively tune,
While one old yokel plays alone
A mere two notes from his bassoon.

Storm

The distant growl of thunder's heard,
Foretells the outbreak of the storm,
The peasants' revels soon must end,
And raindrops their own dance perform.

The tempest now begins to rage,
And dancers all are put to flight,
The squalls of wind are growing strong,
The summer day becomes as night.

Thanksgiving

The storm begins to fade away
As rainbows paint the clearing sky,
The air's serene, the peace returns,
The close of summer day is nigh.

The shepherds call their scattered sheep,
Give thanks for the return of calm,
Commune with nature is restored,
All safe again and freed from harm.

GEOFFREY ELGAR (CANTERBURY)

ENGLISH SUMMERS

English summers are unique
Often hidden in mystique
Poets rave of golden days
Skies of blue, warm sun's rays

Swallows circle in the sky
Fledgling birds learn to fly
Skylarks sing, high on the wing
Their song, breathtaking

Colours burst from every flower
Perfume scents every hour
Gardens alive with bird and bee
Children play safe and carefree

Every year the truth's the same
Summer brings both sun and rain
But it's the happy days we remember
In the darker days of December

JEAN EVEREST (GRAVESEND)

You Are The One

Balmy fields of bright red poppies,
Blue sky bequeaths the sultry summer sun.
My voracious heart is beating wildly,
For I have found the one.

Encircled by bright colours,
No shadows hang around
Many rainbows rise to show us
Where pots of 'love's gold' can be found.

Shared thoughts and deepening feelings
Are unified by our dreams.
Souls travelling, merging journeys,
Riding high on love's moonbeams.

Wanting, ever needing
Each other and always
Fantasies during cosy nights
Inspire our fervent days.

Hands holding, warm lips kissing
Bodies lovingly combine.
There are no demands forthcoming
In the knowledge that you're mine.

Conferring all of our wishes
Seeing many of them through,
Our bond forever strengthening,
Fused by respect for me and you.

A vivid future lies ahead of us
Experiences of which there will be many,
Fears allayed and put to rest
Together, there just aren't any.

Love's trials, disagreements
And differences, resolved.
Fallouts, misunderstandings;
All of them absolved.

All voyages have destinations
Our relationship is about to come in
But I'm not ready for disembarking
My heart is heavy and sinking, for him.

I am begging; 'Please don't leave me'
Desperation takes its hold
Rainbows once bright, now translucent,
Pots emptied of 'love's gold'.

My tears as you are leaving
My cries, 'Please, please don't go!'
Warm lips that brush a cold cheek
Whisper, 'I love you so.'

Black clouds! Black clothes! Black coffin!
Bleeding heart, now broken in two.
Teary eyes search the dark sky for a message.
No sun nor sign is filtering through.

You name rests softly on my quivering lips,
Until I hear it ride away on the breeze.
Chased by tearful anguish.
Carried by heartfelt pleas.

A white dove soars into vision.
Supporting the weight of my heart
Flying on the intensity of this message
Confirming we'd never be apart.

A gentle wind hums its soothing tune,
I absorb the words of your tender song;
'My darling, I will be with you always,
For my precious sweetheart,
You are The One.'

MS ELAINE NEOUS (COVENTRY)

The Blind Mole

The blind mole penetrating his subterranean mazes,
All other senses poised, in blankness gazes,
Hears the sonic ring of dying daisies,
Feels the pneumatic thomp of falling leaves
And in his sightless search conceives
The fall began . . .
Heedful the pulse and throb . . . the stomp of Man.

The Silent One in astral worlds receiving,
Vibrates the soundless void, perceiving
The individual aura lights of Man - no God deceiving,
Reflecting the tarnished self. He sets each flight
In time, before its groans grunt over vacuumed night,
Sensing each yearning soul,
There in the darkness heedful . . . like the mole.

ALEENE HATCHARD (HUTTON)

Blackberries

Sunlit in shades across a leaf fallen
Lane, autumnal breezes rising to the lift
And fall of your name.

Berries swaying to a natural caress
Move over me, like the swirl you
Made with your dress.

Lost in everything that isn't mine,
Blackberries, hawthorn and haw lay
Sunkist in sunshine.

While in black purple and darkest blue
I stretch where I stand, to hold another
Memory, to fill an empty hand.

BRIAN GRACE (GILLINGHAM)

Our Town

We don't know we're born in our town
There is barely a frown in our town
We look after each other,
your father, your mother, your sister, your brother,
That's how it is in our town.

We have the sea, which is blue and the grass, which is green
the most beautiful countryside you've ever seen.
We have banks of flowers in the town to enjoy
and a pond filled with goldfish, which would please any boy.
We have no graffiti and little crime,
you can walk our streets, late, at any time.

You don't have to drive many miles to a shop.
We've got it all here, we've got the lot.
We have a wet fish shop and fried fish with chips that are great,
with all shops so friendly you don't have to wait.
A beautiful lido where you can swim in the sun.
A skate park, a bike park, you don't need your mum.

We have dances and shows at our community hall,
we don't miss a thing here, we all have a ball.
Our harbour will welcome a visiting yacht,
keeping them safe in a nice quiet spot.
You don't have to fork out a massive fee,
the name of our town is Brightlingsea.

GORDON MILES (BRIGHTLINGSEA)

Messages of Summer!

There is more to a beautiful garden than trees and flowers and birds.
In the midst of such beauty is hidden the truth of God's holy word!
There is comfort for those who listen to hear His still small voice
That drifts into realms of contentment, causing the heart to rejoice!
There is wonder in colours blending, rich greens of every hue,
And the peace of His giants of splendour, teach a lesson found by few!
Could Man but learn the secret of His sentinels that keep
Their watch, secure, though storms may roar, because their roots go deep!
There's serenity flowing through water, and reflections upon a lake
That mirrors trees that bend to please, easing mind from mundane state.
There is pleasure in watching wildlife that is free from all life's care,
Swans, squirrels and dragonflies. 'Tis paradise they share!
There's delight in the perfume of blossom that wafts on the gentle air,
Each plant and tree has its own, set free to mingle, enhance and share!
And their colours blend together like a rainbow covering the Earth
Each lifting their face towards Heaven, knowing their place of birth!
There is sweet harmony in birdsong as they hide in the green canopy
Worshipping their Creator in the alter of ecstasy!
Without God's grace we could never enjoy all the blessings we see,
For He sends the rain and the sunshine in equal capacity!
So much we can learn from a garden as we wander and seek to be shown
The miracle of creation in the fullness of nature's own.
We can mirror the life of a garden when our roots go deep into God!
Reflecting His ways when lived in praise for the wonders of His love!
Allowing the perfume of His grace to spread and do its part.
Then every day, if sunny or grey, is summertime in the heart!

ELIZABETH BRUCE (TEYNHAM)

THE CALL OF THE SEA

The long-awaited journey to the sea,
strange how it brings humility
yet can spread havoc in its wake.
Now calm, gentle ripples lapping, washing
sandcastles clean away
with the welling of the waves.
Paddling, screwing up my toes for fear
of objects that lie below
pulling at my feet, sinking ever deeper in the sand
with the turning of the tide.
Children playing with their buckets and spades
reaching into rock pools for treasures
they cannot see
little crabs and pretty shells,
jellyfish with tiny fish darting to and fro.
The sun high above glistens on the sea
reflecting peace and tranquillity,
worries blown away with fresh sea air.
People on the rocks awash with waves that come and go,
bringing tangled seaweed forming patterns in the sand.
Seagulls circle high above searching for their prey,
following the fishing boats, as they do each day.
Now the time has come to part and say, 'Goodbye'
To this idyllic scene.
My face covered in sea spray
the sun slowly sinking, slipping away
I leave with heavy heart, my bag of seashells swinging at my side,
until such time, the sea once more calls out to me.

LIZ DICKEN (TONBRIDGE)

'Diss' is It

'Diss' appears from nowhere,
'Diss' appears from out the blue,
You wouldn't know 'Diss' exists
Unless someone told you.

'Cause 'Diss' is my country town,
Where no one feels alone
This bustling, hustling market town
Is what I call my home.

The endless traffic flowing
From nine o'clock till five,
But the sounds of this little town
Makes me feel alive.

Calm tranquillity of the Mere
The park where children play
And all the country folk
Who shop on market day.

From the church there on the hill
To the quaint old-fashioned street,
The twisting little alleyways
Where past and present meet.

Some folk yearn for city lights,
Others love to roam,
But 'Diss' is where I belong
'Diss' it is my home.

FAY FROUD (DISS)

MRS GREEN MAN

(WITH APOLOGIES TO CAROL ANNE DUFFY)

I know he has a job to do,
spreading his lusty seed throughout
the virgins of the land
While I wait here in this forgotten wood
fretting away my fruitful years.
I lie here on my bed of moss
naked to the sky
I feel men roam my sensual thigh
and think, if he can, why not I?

Once winter's storms have ended
He trims his shaggy beard
his press-ups are impressive
and his manners next to none.
He talks about his duty
how he must be getting on,
So I'll wave him off quite sadly
and phone the gardener's son.

When he returns one August day
Complaining that his back's done in,
I'll shake my comfy bed of moss
and throw his sleeping bag at him.

FRANCES HOLMES (WHITSTABLE)

Burning Embers

A red glow rises where the forest burns
To make a livid scar across the skies.
The air that once was sweet of smell, now turns
To irritate the nostrils, mouth and eyes.
A black offensive smoke, first billows high
Then covers all beneath in choking cloud,
And trees once voiceless can be heard to sigh
Or tremble, as they stand with heads now bowed.
This once was England's green and pleasant land
Here, where the sap has dried within the heat.
'Tis but the work of someone's careless hand
That brings untimely death to all around

Another time, another place, we find
A country stream no longer bubbles free,
Polluted by the chemicals that bind
Each atom as it struggles to the sea.
We give so little to our heritage
But rather feel the need to devastate
That which support sour lives through every stage
Let us draw back now, before it is too late.

SHEILA FERNLEY-BENARD (NORTHFLEET)

SOUL OF THE SUMMER

Like a phoenix out of a flame
I am born and rise again
Protected by fire and heat
Fresh meadow earth at my feet

Sweet drops of summer dew
Gently glisten and shine
Dampening my bare toes
Under green blades so fine

The heady scent of flowers
Burst in glorious blooms
Open up to the sunlight
And close to the moon

Orange dawn early and bright
Silver stars will appear tonight
Hazy purple pollen air
Breathe me in and glaze my stare

The honeybee and dragonfly
Peacefully play in the evening sky
Yellow fields and carpet green
Waiting every morning this beautiful scene

CLARE MCAULEY (STANGROUND)

Silver and Gold

The silent, cooler, deeper fragrance;
Enchantment of the evening air;
How my heart is so light and happy
As the souls pass so joyously there.

Where are they venturing, tumbling now,
The passing young children of Heaven;
Joined in much deeper limestone structures
When the elements were uneven.

Through the woodlands they all whirl along,
Happy, excited, breathless and gay;
Threading the long journey before them;
'We'll love you always,' they seem to say.

I follow the path they are taking,
Down the hillside, through the bed of stone;
Where are they going, the happy throng?
As I stand here, in love, not alone.

Prisms spreading light and pure colour,
Crystals and sparkling, dashing white spray,
Chattering, racing, turning bubbles,
Under the bridge, then down and away.

They journey down through enchanted scenes,
Where long branches are by magic cast;
O'er waterfalls, then down past the oak
Bound in the lovely woodland's clasp.

Perhaps I may see them yet once more,
On a fine morning after the storm,
When the sun is peeping through the trees;
Then joy and much love my heart will warm.

In my mind I can trace their journey,
Across rich green countryside and plain;
Joining then, in purpose, to the sea;
Tiny, pure, silver droplets of rain.

MICHAEL LARCOMBE (STOCK)

HOLIDAYS

We are off today on holiday,
We are going to the sea,
But we are very careful,
That we are in time for tea.

At last we get there,
And find our caravan,
We want to make the most of it,
And get in all we can.

As we gaze out on the water,
We may see a ship or yacht,
And the wife wants to go for a walk,
And I say, 'Yes, why not!'

Then at last it's all over,
We each have a little moan,
But we all have to agree,
As there is no place like home.

DAVID A SHEASBY (DAVENTRY)

UNTITLED

The wind sighs, I sigh,
The rain pours, I cry,
The sun shines, I smile
Happy for a little while.

The sea roars, I quiver,
The frost glitters, I shiver,
The birds sing, so do I,
One day I will learn to fly.

The Earth turns, I too,
The moon hides, I'm blue
The stars gleam, I reply
I too will blaze across the sky.

CAROLINE ISHERWOOD (FRINTON-ON-SEA)

NATURAL SELECTION

In times of shared restrain in war,
And aftermath, we mostly scorned
A spiv or two and often shared
As needs arose. But since has spawned
A swarm of cons and email spams
And monster frauds. And even firms
Of some renown resort to spin.
We're made to feel like lowly worms
If we complain of shoddy goods,
Or service falling short of least
One might expect as basics due.
Perhaps they think I'm stupid beast!
An enterprise is sheet of cloth.
One corner's held by worker band.
Another's meant for we who buy
The goods. One's fixed by post to land
On which it all depends. But those
Who own the shares contend their show
Of profits means the costs along
With wages must be kept as low
As greed can go, while price is hiked
As long as sales increase. And as
For land that's held in trust, they call
Concern a waste of breath that has
To be ignored if market god
Is given freedom's right to sort
The strong from weak. Support for poor
Is not allowed to enter thought.
They treat the market like a dose
Of weather dealt by chance and just
Ignore the fact they're safe inside
Exclusive car, while others must
Endure the storms and winds on way
To work on foot. So why complain
When credit crunch disrupts the scene
And floods, along with torrent rain,
Demolish all their cunning plans?
They've joined the ranks of also-rans!

HENRY DISNEY (CAMBRIDGE)

BESIDE THE SEA

Little bare legs and shoeless feet
They play in the sand, a summer treat
Ice cream cones and minty rock
Tones of cream, the sun to block
Buckets and spades, castles to make
Perhaps fish and chips, some cod or a hake
Squeals of delight as waves splash toes
Sweet candyfloss stuck to a nose
Penny arcades with bright shiny lights
Burger bars with smells that delight
Salty air on tongue and lips
A rock pool crab, your finger nips
Seagulls floating on summer breeze
Trousers rolled up above the knees
Nap in a deckchair in the afternoon sun
Then crawl into bed when the day is done
These are the sights I see each year
I live by the sea, I think that's clear

PATRICIA CANNON (ST LEONARDS-ON-SEA)

HONEYSUCKLE-ROSE

Honeysuckle on the vine smelling as sweet as ruby wine,
Lightly composed, delicate and captivating the eye
With such a sweet fragrance which directs a sigh,
Ivory in colour as the petals unfold,
Opening with alacrity, as if sounding a bell,
The timing so perfect as the petals do swell,
Entwined with a garden rose over an archway you see
Growing in my garden and kempt by only me,
So to love it and tend it, as I invariably do,
With each passing day and all weathers too,
I'd send you a photograph, but instead there's just prose,
Like the captivating wonder of magenta in rose!

CHRISTINE FLOWERS (WALSOKEN)

My Secret Garden

My garden gives me so much pleasure,
I never mind whatever the weather,
Although the weeds keep on growing,
I just keep on hoeing.

Through winding paths I wander,
A secret waiting round every corner,
A new plant appearing, now what can it be?
We'll just have to wait and see.

Bright red poppies nod their heads as I pass by,
And the buddleia is full of bees and butterflies,
Golden marigolds are a sight to see,
Rambling roses and of course sweet pea.

Hard work is rewarded I'm sure you'll agree,
For there are no short cuts to gardening you see,
You dig and you hoe, feed, water and sow,
And don't forget also there's the lawn to mow.

All looks bare now winter's here,
And Jack Frost will do his worst I fear,
But still through winding paths I wander,
To see what secret lies around the corner.

G L Glanville (Braintree)

Mother Nature

Nature is like a naughty child
Wanting her own way
Some days we feel cold and miserable
Then giving us a sunny day.
We've all made silly mistakes
Mostly in the past
But give nature a life she will treasure
Make her seasons last
Ignorance is bliss and folly to be wise
But remember Earth can destroy us
And nobody will survive
Give a thought to nature
Make sure that she'll approve
Then perhaps one day we'll be given back
Our havens where we live
Earth is like a cauldron, always on the boil
When pressure comes it's too intense
And she penetrates the soil
Have you ever felt Earth tremble
And then begin to shake
Well, you know devastation will follow
With one almighty *earthquake.*

DOROTHY GOULD (DARTFORD)

Lakeland Beauty

I sit here in this land of poets,
Where for centuries, men wrote such beautiful words,
Where splendour and beauty in great measure abound,
Perfect peace, except for the song of the birds.

Dry stone walls, weathered with moss,
Have flanked fields for many a year,
Streams run down from lofty green hills,
Into lakes that are so deep and so clear.

Trees serene, in shades of green,
Soar gracefully into a sky of blue,
The lakes have a beauty of their very own,
Round every bend, between the trees, always a stunning view.

This lakeland beauty is ours to cherish,
Every stone, every lake, every tree,
Relax in its beauty, enjoy its peace,
It's the nearest thing to paradise, that you will ever see.

GEOFF FOSTER (SIDCUP)

Summer Sonnet

On cleaving, soaring wings, scything swiftly
Through the scudding cloud, glides the graceful bird
And forsakes the sea-lapped, pebble-strewn shore
And wave-dashed dunes of sand and rippled green grass.
There frisks the wind, torment of yesterday,
Whipping the foam-flecked waves into fury.
Ruffling the papers clasped in the fingers
Of summer sunbathers seeking slumber.
But the wind has ceased its frenzied clamour
And now takes rest on seafront swing hammocks
To await the sun and the snow-white bird
That may return when winter walks the shore
Cloaking the coast beneath an icy pall
Until spring sunshine gilds the sands again.

CAROLINE BUDDERY (GORLESTON)

TRANSITION

(DEDICATED TO SYLVIA ELLIS)

My children have become all they can be
I watched them grow and watched them leave me
In the blink of an eye my job was done
And the romance in my marriage had gone

Left alone I felt cold and scared
I could not even face the world

Then I woke to see that this is not the end
I built a new life and made new friends
I now realise there's so much to do and see
And I now revolve the world around me

Going new places, don't know where
Meeting new people, so much to share!

JAYNE WALKER (WOLVERHAMPTON)

SITTING IN THE GARDEN

An old man waiting
His thoughts but memories confused
His respite
Untroubled sleep, an easy pipe, a place in the sun
Where to sit and listen
To neighbouring noise
Blending harmonies
Filtering thru a sunken head

All things ignore him yet he knows them
Sees a child play
The mother tends the clothes line
Stretching skywards as Pavlova
Nude nuptial thighs
Paradise

Once I wandered the temples of Babylon
Insatiable, scorning the gods
. . . So long ago

T COBLEY (ROMFORD)

AT THE END OF DAY

The sun is setting in the west
the sky, all golds and reds
and flocks of birds start flying home
each tree and bush their beds.

The rooks flock home to roost each night
their soft caws fill the air
as day turns slowly into night
to rookeries they repair.

The starlings too collect in groups
like chattering crowds they search
they squabble and they fight for space
all wanting the same perch.

Then geese fly home in skeins of grace
like threads of yarn in flight
their calls carry down to earth below
a signal that it's close to night.

A lonely blackbird's lovely voice
signals the end of day
the last worms collected for the babes
now dusk once more holds sway.

And now the magic of the night begins
a nightingale in song he starts,
that liquid voice in quiet of night
brings joy and peace to hearts.

PATRICIA HARRIS (MARTLESHAM)

IN THE SUMMER GARDEN

I rest in dabbled light and shade under the trees.
Wood pigeons cooing up above
Make me feel lazy, and I love
To watch the seagulls circling high
As butterflies settle nearby
On phlox, delphiniums and poppies red;
The cat is sleeping near their bed,
Safe is the blackbird, wings outstretched
Beak half open as it says,
'Gosh it is hot!'
'Time to be lazy'
Says the daisy
The bumblebee murmurs
'I'm in clover'
As it flies over
To the pond
Where damselflies in streaks of blue
Flit over water lilies who
Shelter the frogs watching for flies.
Though weeds are quietly growing high,
I will not leave this pleasant chair
When warm and scented is the air,
When all is quiet, all is at peace,
When joy is all around; just be at ease.

G BIRKE (LOWESTOFT)

Opera in the Open Air

My birthday treat was a little bit late
But it was really good, well worth the wait
Bayham Abbey was the setting, a beautiful sight
We settled down for our picnic and the sun shone bright
As we had a glass of wine, the sun began to set
When low in the sky a better sight you could not get
As it shone on the ruins the broken walls turned red
You could almost think you somewhere in the Med
Amongst the ruins we could see the stage
Many people were there of varying age

Opera was what we were all waiting to see
Out in the open air, where the birds fly free
Then the stage lit up and the sopranos began to sing
The tenor and baritone their voices began to ring
They sang their way through many a composer's score
Arias by Puccini and Verdi, my favourites for sure
There were many others, they were enjoyed by all
And when they had finished 'more' went out the call
A summer evening, good company, such times are rare
It just seemed so perfect, opera in the open air

CELIA LAW (PEMBURY)

The Deck Chair

Along a windswept promenade in a little seaside town
I came across an old deck chair by wintry winds blown down.
Lying on the pathway, lost and soaked with rain,
Warped wooden frame and faded stripes, never to be used again.

In great demand in summer by all the family,
Children eating ice creams, fat ladies drinking tea.
Many a red-faced gentleman, knotted kerchief on his head
Has sat and dozed while on his lap his paper lies unread.

Sandcastles built around it until the sea creeps near,
Hired out for fifty pence a day, underneath the pier.
Now listlessly stirring in the wind, forgotten and forlorn,
It lies there lost forever, its companions stacked and gone.

PAULINE ANDERSON (CAMBRIDGE)

QUITE FREE WITHOUT A FIGHT

My summer hopes are on a beach hut pinned.
It's my defence against the sun and wind.
The simple wooden structure carves from space
A home where all takes place at slower pace.
From there, I scan the seascape straight ahead
And stretch on deckchair like an outdoor bed.
As people come and go, the pebbles crunch
And hungry terns and gulls arrive for lunch.
On both sides, neighbours tell of what they've done,
Review the weather, face or dodge the sun.
We ferry tea from seafront kiosk near,
And sometimes ices, then gain weight I fear.
And lastly, let me frankly just make plain,
A hut can be a refuge from the rain.
But soon, September comes around again
And energy suppliers bring back pain,
By selling captives costly heat and light,
Just now received quite free without a fight.

ALLAN BULA (BEXHILL-ON-SEA)

SUMMER

What can be said about summer?
It's warm and sunny and fun
Long lazy days at the seaside
Are the dream of everyone
The gardens are full of beautiful flowers
Blossom now covers the trees
Butterflies flit from flower to flower
But the pollen makes some people sneeze

Days have grown quite long now
Evenings are longer and warm
A nice evening stroll at the end of the day
Walking home again arm in arm
To wear pretty summer dresses
Is every woman's delight
The best thing of all about summer
Is it makes everybody feel bright

IRENE KENNY (BECCLES)

After Milton's Serpent in Paradise Lost

Long, long ago I was a charming snake
more lovely than Harmonia and Cadmus,
more potent than the healing serpent
coiled round the Rod of Asclepius,
until Satan inhabited my silken skin
with lustrous golden neck.

As I slithered in the leaves,
Eve heard a soft rustling,
watched me encircle the
Tree of Knowledge from which
slyly I inveigled her to disobey God,
tempting her to eat its flavoursome fruit.

As she bit into its juicy flesh,
smirking and self-satisfied,
I slithered into the shade
of a nearby shrub and
slept.

MARGARET COWLING (TRUMPINGTON)

In Praise of Sussex

Sussex, jewel in England's crown.
Forest, sea, majestic down,
Hamlet, village, market town.

Sussex, tourists' hunting ground,
Antiques, cream teas, horse and hound.
Follies, battles, burial mound.

Doomsday Book, historic tome,
Castles, churches, Brighton's Dome.
Sussex: gentle . . . tranquil . . . home!

SUE WHITEHEAD (ST LEONARDS-ON-SEA)

DISAPPEARING GARDENS

What's nicer on a summer eve when flowers raise their drooping heads
and the air is slowly cooling their sun-baked flower beds.

To take an evening saunter, without the scorching heat
and the pavements are not burning under lightly sandalled feet.

As dusk is slowly falling to peep over garden walls,
to see what folk are growing to grace their hallowed halls.

Hollyhocks tall in stately rows nodding to the scented stocks,
antirrhinums, delphiniums, lupins, rose and brightly coloured phlox.

Their glowing colours pleased the eye and perfume teased the nose,
such simple pleasures as they were, you couldn't better those.

Now in this greedy modern age these treasures nearly all are gone,
no grass so green, no leaves, no bees and flowers there are none.

Instead they have front gardens full of multicoloured bricks,
on which to park their many cars and leave the odd oil slicks.

Can't even leave a patch of soil so our precious earth can breathe.
My senses are no longer pleased, these times just make me grieve.

LESLEY GILL (LEIGH-ON-SEA)

SIMPLICITY

I have to say I have been hypnotised
And now I am mesmerised by your tries
To keep me close
To hold me tight
To keep me forever and after, our last night
I have to say I'm in a daze
Since I caught your gaze, I'm not afraid
To fall in love
To fall in deep
To lie in your arms and fall asleep

LAUREN BRAZIER (ROMFORD)

The Dreamer's Dream

The sky was as blue as crystal,
With clouds as white as snow,
With beautiful green mountains and clear blue sky shining upon the rainbow water passing by.
You can even see the beautiful clear green land.
Posing with red, white and yellow flowers where you can see for miles.

Upon the village stoned road,
Where the brown and white houses still stand
Looking innocent with growing age.

With clean blue windows,
You can even see the mountains through them
Where the clear blue crystal sea stands still.
You can even see the sunset and sunrise with the colours of the rainbow shining upon the sea.

The villa is as quiet and as calming as the bright green trees and dark shadows
Forming upon the green grass
Looking so cooling and relaxing.

The place I describe is called a dreamer's paradise.

DAIANNA PINTO (PETERBOROUGH)

Low Pressure

The rise of field against the sky
Wind on my face - I should be 'high'
But nothing cheers me - grey and brown
have taken over.
'Find someone who's worse than me - and having done
bring them some change,' a smile - a laugh -
a prayer perhaps - for nothing's half
as good as that to help redeem
a soul that's sad - renew life's dream.

CHRISTAL MEDCALF (SOUTH WITHAM)

DARK DAYS

The albatross wraps its weighted wings
Around my taut body and the panic of suffocation
Rises in lurches like cramps.
Its feet almost break my skin
In the heaviness of its descent.
Diving down, drowning in feathers
Grey, monotone, nulled of colour,
Like a rediscovered photo
Of some distant frozen moment
Of an old forgotten family feud.

In brief moments as my head pulls away
I breathe easier
And the absorbing crushing of my inner beat
Is relinquished - fleetingly.
But its sensations linger on like
The aura of a passing migraine,
Painless but pressing tight in its seeming absence,
Suggesting it dwells like an undefeated threat.

JOANNA LEWIS (KING'S LYNN)

FIFTH DIMENSION

Cascades the computed logic
Electronically nourished
Spewing out its torrential
Floods into the oceans
Of crisis-thinking . . .
Rivers of detail
Equating the fountain heads
Of real elements like time
And space, negative or positive
Idea or inkling . . .
Blissfully the wild goose chasers
Seek to establish an identity
In the seas of infinity.

TERRENCE ST JOHN (PEMBURY)

LOVE SEEPS THROUGH - SO TRUE IN VIEW

Time will tell fairly
And truly, if squarely
Two persons together,
In a unison tether.

No encumbrances, divide us along or less
Or elude us for tenderness
No excuse for dilly or dally
Or true feelings in trust on rally

As bitter loneliness fades,
Lose it - we meet, it wades
Measure ourselves, alone together,
With thoughts only of us to measure.

Pure heart, how can I please you?
Is it not a case of me too?
Someone likes you, who comes along,
To signal a sign in song.

Ever closer, loud and clear
Ever sweeter, without fear
What owes it to be so wholesome,
Up and coming to a 'Fore' some.

So for what it seems again
Nearer time clear, not in vain,
Clarity - when we meet,
Just again, another treat!

Evoke in us both, not only
Semblance of romance and love, lonely
But true feelings of rapprochement
Intermingling mental and physical resource, sent
To turn to
A partnership for two in one couple, to do.
Falling in love again, is a 'Sweet' beyond compare!

N LEMEL (WESTCLIFF-ON-SEA)

WARRINGTON - OUR TOWN

Far-off places now out of our reach
but we're not really people who lounge on the beach.
No more the hassle of cancelled flights.
We will stay in our town and discover new delights.

So what really do we need from our town?
Somewhere to go when feeling down.
A place to sit silent in open space
to enjoy a meal out in a friendly place.

Shopping is great with a market and square
a stone tableau of 'Alice in Wonderland' is there
also a museum - a gem to see
steeped in the town's great history.

King James 1st came to stay
here for one night when passing this way.
Battles and sieges have taken place
the statue of Cromwell looks out across space.

The Borough Town Hall with the Golden Gates
have seen many visits of the 'royals' to date.
So much to see and so much to do
whether here to stay or just passing through.

We have it both, the old and the new
with a welcome for all - the many or few.
Through all the years it has been known
we are proud to call this town our own.

K M HOOK (PETERBOROUGH)

The Scream

I just wanna scream!
I don't think you know what I mean
I need to scream,
I want to wake up and pretend it's a dream
Warm salty tears
Are streaming down my face,
The strain reflects the years
And life's fast pace

I just wanna jump
So you might hear a thump.
Or maybe you can see the lump
In my throat, like mumps.
My throat is throbbing with uncontrollable pain
It makes me wanna scream!

But it's just my heart's been broken again
I feel I need to scream!
I suppose I'm not ready for love
I wanna push . . . scream . . . shove . . .
I need to get above
This feeling, this feeling of love

Let me scream! Let me scream!
Let me heal and let me cry
Let me walk the wooden beam
Let me look to the stars in the sky

I just screamed
With emptiness in-between
I screamed and screamed
I didn't wake out of a dream
I don't know
How much heart I've got left
I can't show
The emotion in my . . . inside my breast

I'm screaming until I wanna stop
Screaming to show my emotions . . . *not*
To seek attention . . . *not*
Because I'm young . . . just
Till I wanna stop.

LATOYA MAYNARD (SUDBURY)

THE OAKS

Outside my window
two colossal oaks, so high, so wide
you cannot penetrate the depth of them
or their canopies leaning over the flowers.
How dark the barricade of branches,
how quiet it is, even the jackdaws
have flown elsewhere.

Gazing out, I am a time traveller
floating free skyward,
skimming fields and valleys, where farmers
grind long years away, toiling night and day
a mode of life as ancient as the oaks.

On this April day, oak and silver birch
are bursting into leaf, heaven-sent
for squirrels, as round the trunks
they scrabble in the thick greenery.

Winter sings of snow and ice.
the branches stripped bare rake the sky
like iron lattices, planes flying
in the spaces, crammed with people
chasing dreams elsewhere.

But I am here, beside the old oaks,
Mother Earth's living beings,
English hearts of oak, long may they flourish
in this lovely country garden.

JUDY MCGREGOR (BURWASH COMMON)

My Teenage Daughter

'It's such a nice day out there
Shall we go for a walk
We can stroll along the river
And maybe have a talk?'

I could see that my daughter
Was not too keen
So I decided to go on my own
And photo the summer scene

There wasn't a soul anywhere in sight
And the birds were singing their song
Then a little canoe came round the bend
With the water rippling along

I finally came to a nice clean bench
I sat for a while and looked across the fence
The horses in the field over the way
Were munching at their feed of hay
Oh what peace!

Then my mobile ran
And it gave me a start
'There's a man in the garden
He's pushing a cart'

My daughter sounded quite upset
I said, 'Lock the door and stay inside pet'
I turned and increased my pace to a run
So much for my hour in the sun

I quite forgot the riverbank was soggy
Over I went and shocked the local moggy
Clothes all wet with mud and muck
Frightened to stop in case I got stuck

The man in the garden was Charlie next door
He's not very rich, in fact he's quite poor
So I let him borrow some of our things
But forget to tell Serena, cos he usually rings

I fell in the chair with quite a hard thud
Serena said, 'Mum, did you know you're full of mud?'
'By the way,' says she, 'I don't want any tea
I'm going for a bike ride, will you leave me out a key?'
What peace did I mean?

ALMA BRACE (CHILTON)

SUMMER LOVE

My summer love began in spring
With woodland bluebells that did bring
A sudden, sensual flowering.
Then all the world was brighter even
Than the winter stars in Heaven
And I could then begin to sing
A thanksgiving.

My summer love went into June;
It led me to the solstice moon;
Then I could sing a summer tune
With new-fledged birds and cattle herds
And go to gather tall, pale grasses,
Wafting, whispering in breezes
Without words.

My passion's quieter in July -
Familiar as the estuary.
It wakens in my memory
Again a semi-century
Of love I've had, of love to give,
Of love bestirred, of love bestowed,
Of loves inherited, endowed -
Loves diverse and manifold.

Some are secret
Some are told.

ANNE COTTON (COLCHESTER)

KINGS MEADOW TRANQUILLITY

Material, mechanistic sounds - muted, distant, not too far though
Semi-silences, birdsong, laughter, picnics, not too distant, riverbank, other side though
Materialists need and greed, rushing, tearing past to and fro
Rushing and tearing, not caring, sweating, swearing no tranquil place to go
Near the opulent lush and green signs of nature's life
A sad contrast - an abundance of death's contempt for life
Sadly, so sadly it seems trees in parts more dead than those alive
The hacked and chopped remains of trimmed beside outright dead or dying those half alive strive
Yes, dying ones strive to stay alive either stricken by storm's furious excesses
Or endured to a great old age and seem many suns have weathered strains and stresses
Life and death contrasting living side by side the survivors will future man deride
As the eternal river Colne does unconcerned unhurriedly flow and slide
Yes, the river Colne sliding and winding like a vast unfettered snake
For the water before me, I think by boating to the North Sea how long would it take?
At last on this day - heat haze, blue skies and flies and over-breeding ants
Unaccustomed to high temperatures Colchester and other Essex folk puffs and pants
Many, many parents, grandparents, a sister, a brother
Enjoy the many and various personality variations of each and one another
And make the most of what a rare high pressure trough of weather brings
And sun themselves in glorious abandon with personal belongings and things
Now I the rambler passing sunbathers here and there
See gorgeous half-clad ladies but have no time to stop and stare
Entering Colchester's adjoining lower Castle Park
Wishing I were decades younger and with the youngsters enjoying a lark
Found myself amidst a joyous scene of joyful fun and pleasure
A fair of sales folk, side shows, stalls of much variety and measure
And a lovely young girl selling strawberries and cream
Elysian fields of delight, laughter, peace, perfection, friendship - every person's dream.

GERALD WALDEN (STANWAY)

WIMBLEDON

I am the umpire and I called it out.
I nodded and affirmed in a civilised way.
You should not behave like a street corner lout.

I make the decisions and there is no doubt.
There is no one else and no other way.
I am the umpire and I called it out.

You may stand and quiver and stride about
But I am aloof to what you might say.
You should not behave like a street corner lout.

You may throw your racket or give it a clout.
You may demonstrate your obvious dismay.
I am the umpire and I called it out.

For you, of course, it might have been a rout.
Perhaps you concluded it was not your day.
You should not behave like a street corner lout.

High up in my chair I govern the game
And leave it to players to grapple with fame.
You should not behave like a street corner lout.
I am the umpire and I called it out.

DENIS GRIFFITHS (ELY)

SUMMER

All is content now, at midday with a sky of long-awaited blue.
A mouse cuts the kernel of a nut, hazel here already.
A blackbird scolds he who dares to greedy-eye her nest;
Quiet, the interloper gone. Train bound for human things
Passes through and allows back the silence.

Trees full-leafed rejoice by a keening thank you to the wind and rain;
A summer song for the good trading between incandescent insects and flowers.
Blackbirds wet and sun wood sing full throated happiness after showers.
Field lark fountains a hover of trilling joy.
God looks on, and forgets his sadness

ANDY MCMASTER (RETFORD)

Blessings

To stroll in a field of daisies
On a lovely summer's day
While in the air there lingers
The smell of new-mown hay.

The tinkle of a cow bell near
The song of a bird in my ear
The solitude of a peaceful summer's day
While up above the white clouds play.

The gentle stirring of the trees
In the warm summer breeze
I am more than content
For God gave me these

A sky of blue and grass of green
Silver fish in a rippling stream
A wild bee upon the wing
All of these make my heart sing

Stars shining in the night
And a lovely rainbow bright
But best of all - He gave me life
He gave me all my senses

So I will give praise to him
To thank Him for all blessings
So generously given by Him.

DAISY CARR (WALTON)

TRANSIENCE

An ordinary Suffolk summer scene
of church and pub reflected in the pond,
of worthies sitting on the village green,
of thatch-roof, lived-in cottages beyond;
and I sit here and slumber.

The sign - a donkey - where old pilgrims met
and where, today, new fortune-hunters meet
to catch the bus to join the Ipswich set,
who think they have the whole world at their feet;
and I sit her and ponder.

Old barns where now the glitterati feast,
the Mace where you can buy most anything,
the village hall, named after pious priest
who long ago refused to bless a king;
and I sit here and wonder.

Wild poppies blaze against a sea of corn
and sad, less transient, flowers speak of war.
As men all stand in line and look forlorn
the bells ring out across the land once more;
and I sleep here forever.

PETER DAVIES (FRESSINGFIELD)

Titanic

The stars shone cold. And I gazed spellbound,
back across the ocean's dark, silken plain,
that lay drowsed, subdued by ice, to silence.
No clouds veiled the sky. Nor wind, nor sound
of nature's voice masked the cries of pain
and terror fading, dying in the distance.

'We must go back! Go back and help!' I said.
But then the ship thrust its colossal tail
a hundred feet into the air, to wheel
like Poseidon rearing his wrathful head
out of the deeps, drowning our little wail
with his thunder - the drum of shearing steel.

Our blood ran colder than the ocean's heart
and we wavered, aghast before the doomed;
riven between humanity and fear.
But from life to death, taking now our part,
we faced the proud, majestic stern that loomed
above us - a monument to despair.

We faltered forwards as the stern reared high
shivered and slunk into the hungry depths.
The lights trembled - and then oblivion.
Only the moon, amidst the crystal sky
lit our way, like Death's pale lantern that keeps
its flame forever on a distant shore.

And so we stole on, through the emptiness,
slipping through the dim solitudes of space.
Through the silent voids our calls resonate
unanswered still; except for the grim press
like spectres, drifting past - with upturned face,
and white eyes glaring as if in hate.

Time shall not fade the horror of that night;
The eyes frozen in harsh reproach,
The unmouthed words of bitterness frost glazed
On chill lips; dead faces, cast in leprous light,
Thronging ever nearer around the boat,
And from the deeps, accusing fingers raised.

Such was the downfall of outrageous pride;
we styled ourselves the masters of the main;
the air, the earth, the ocean were our slaves.
But in a stroke, the ocean justified
his claim with guiltless blood. But one domain
he ceded there: the dark, eternal graves.

STEVE WATERFIELD (RAINHAM)

SUMMERTIME 2010

Oh summertime how I love you
You bring to me such hope anew.
Away with ice and frost and snow
And the cold north winds that blow
The warmth it makes me so at ease
That I forget dark winter's freeze.
There's long warm days of lengthening light
With star-filled skies and warmth at night.
The happy sounds of summer fun
As all enjoy the warming sun.
There's birdsong and the buzz of bees.
With the gentle murmur of the breeze.
Off with the layers of winter things
Oh! The freedom that it brings.
To feel the sand between my toes
As I happily discard my hose.
To run into the calm blue sea,
This is certainly the life for me.
Such happy days to put in store.
To have in my memory for evermore.

SHIRLEY JOY DEAN (EATON RISE)

Almost One
(An East Anglian Coastal Experience)

Contented at its perceived margin,
until the sly tidal sea divided;
channelling unexpectedly behind
our backs, almost stranding our
togetherness.

Warning shouts and laughter
saved us from disaster and we
waded through cold, murky depths,
as the children we once were.

Warm, welcoming sand dunes,
laced with toughened fronds,
became a sunshine backdrop
for our resting.

JILL STEDMAN (FORDHAM)

July

Mad, crazy days of summer.
Butterflies dance in the buddleia tree,
and fishes leap from a calm blue sea.
Birdsong wakens us at dawning.
Greets the sun a warm good morning.

Mad, crazy days of summer.
The scent of roses fills the air.
The water lilies bloom so fair.
The old oak tree give cooling shade,
to a lover and his maid.

Mad, crazy days of summer,
when otters bask by rivers' side
and jellyfish swim with the tide.
These crazy days so soon fly by.
Before we know, the autumn's nigh.

AUDREY LAY (OULTON BROAD)

My Prayer

Let the deaf hear the music of kindness
Let the blind see the true Christian's light
Let the dumb speak of caring and sharing
To those in despair bring delight
To the poor a hope of the future
And courage for those who are ill
May frightened folk feel more secure
And acknowledge thy 'Peace be still'
Perhaps there is something that I can do
With this small humble being of mine
To dispel all the gloom and make the clouds go
Rainbow promises soon then will shine
Take me and show me and use me
Give me the right words to say
May I be their inspiration
This is my prayer Lord today

DAPHNE M BRADY (ORMESBY)

Mushrooms

Here in the lower meadow,
feet caught in milky mist -
mushrooms my grandmother picked.

Up there the farmhouse -
smokeless chimney,
B & B on a swinging sign.

No cats, no ducks, the pond
filled in and fumigated,
horseflies, mayflies puffed away.

Dandelions, nettles killed,
hedgerows given the chop,
yellow rape stains the land.

Caravans squat in the lower meadow,
smothering mushrooms no one picks.

'Here's your milk. Have a good day.
The mist will clear.'

JACKIE HINDEN (BRIGHTON)

Then the Children

then the children
running, laughter
dancing on the summer air
happy as moments are precious
bodies gilded
with kindly summer light

joyful in creation
their refuge is in innocence
as a breeze moved through
pausing, looking
music for the eyes from
the golden harp of feeling

I walk on slowly
away from their area
I hear a child laughing
down the years
running into
the arms of time

still I move along
my path in life
then the real freedom
bathing in memory
slowly quietly
entering the waiting light

GEORGE COOMBS (HOVE)

TREES - BEAUTIFUL TREES

From those beautiful trees
The soft green buds begin to sprout,
Heralding springtime without a doubt,
Bringing colour to brighten our days,
Shelt'ring us all from the sun's hot rays:
Just trees - beautiful trees

Elijar fled from the scene with fright,
He ran and ran, out of Ahab's sight;
'Neath a juniper tree, and ready to die,
Exhausted and weary - the Lord drew nigh,
With food and water his needs were met;
A future pathway most clearly set.

Zacchaeus desired a view that was clear,
Knowing that Jesus was now quite near,
Climbing up high, so that he could see,
Sat on the branch of a sycamore tree:
Called from his perch to receive a guest,
A teatime encounter of the very best.

Trees - just beautiful trees
Stately; majestic; and proudly they stand
When autumn comes they look simply grand,
Leaves aglow with brown and gold,
A vista of colour, a joy to behold:
The fun of climbing - or picnic mood,
A place of rest, and of quietude.
Just trees - beautiful trees.

BERYL SIGOURNAY (GRAYS)

A WALK THROUGH BROADLAND

On a bright and sunny day, or even when the skies are grey
A world of wonderland awaits as Broadland opens wide her gates.
The birds above, the fish below with insects, all their colours show.
The trees, the reeds and flowers too, join in to add a further hue.

With geese and swans, the grebe and duck - to see these does not take much luck -
Kingfisher and bittern are far more shy, with other birds which you might pass by.
The natterjack and the common frog can be found hiding by a log
Whilst otter and the water voles would be on banks or in their holes.

The roach and bream, the perch and pike all live in river or muddy dyke.
Upstream, to breed, returns the eel, when cooked they make a tasty meal.
Skipper, tortoiseshell and peacock, of these the Broads have quite a stock.
The swallowtail and dragonfly flash jewelled colours in the sky.

The alders and the guelder rose along the riverbank still grows
Whilst willowherb with flowers a-bobbin' join cuckoo flowers and ragged robin.
Bulrush and iris can't compare with many orchids, some quite rare,
Frogbit and lily cannot match the common reed we use for thatch.

Now through this Broadland walk you've been and many things I'm sure you've seen.
Perhaps you'll come again some day. *Let's hope it will remain this way.*

MARGARET DACK (HORNING)

A MEMOIR

Favourite Minnie Mouse swimsuit adorned, I remember shuffling laboriously through cinnamon sand;
You, grappling to keep hold of my hand
As I ambled further from the safety of the shore's gentle surf
Towards mighty, thrashing waves.

You saw the world differently back then; it blossomed from your love of art I think.
You seemed to notice things that went ignored.
I caught you once staring at an old, weather-beaten stone pot, teeming with weevils.
I hurried you along . . . typical. I was bored.

I mourn those lost moments now, am left reeling with regret the precious hours, minutes, seconds I could have spent with you, but didn't.
What for?
I watched you lie butchered in the foul-smelling ward for months and couldn't wait until they rang the bell.
Their voices calling visiting hours over were like honeydew. A wicked temptation, laced in sugar-coating that I anticipated.

I go back to our beach now in solitude and recall with affection the nineteen years spent with you guiding me along.
I wish I'd never struggled to break free of your nurturing hand: the sun never feels so warm now; the waves are not quite so blue.

HOLLY PAYNE (KINGS HILL)

Wishing It Would Rain

The smell of grass is raw and sweet
But asphalt's burning both my feet
And sunburned shoulders are a pain
I wish to God that it would rain

The Cornish winds whip you dry
As seagulls go flying by
This endless sun is such a drain
I wish to God that it would rain

The sky is stretched out like a sheet
All parched and dried out in this heat
And we who live here are insane
I wish to God that it would rain

I can't believe that people pay
To come here! Me, I'd run away
If I could just hop on a train
I'd find a place where it would rain.

PAUL GREEN (WISBECH)

The Promenade Park

There is a park across the road
Which is a lovely place to be
There're ducks and swans on the lake
And it's a sight to see.
The barges are on the river
Their sails so high they go along the river
Black water day, tide night tide
It's also a sight to see
I'm very proud to live here
It's an amazing place to be
Any day you can go for a stroll
And you're sure to see some friends
To meet who also share the same feelings as me.
In Maldon, Essex, that's the place to be.

ANITA WALKER (MALDON)

SHANKLIN BEACH

Distantly along the beach,
Two outlines can be seen,
One tall, one small,
Hand in hand they go,
Along the beach to the rock fall.

Stopping, bending, looking, listening,
All around the rock face exploring,
Anything new since last year?
The rock fall perhaps to explore,
Maybe dinosaur bones will be there.

Sometime maybe, something to find,
To bring back home, to remind
Us of the beachcombing on Shanklin beach.
Coming back year after year,
The best beach in the world.

The happy times that we had on holiday,
Waiting on the waves to wash up a fossil or two,
Whilst stopping, bending, looking, listening,
Paddling in the rock pools at the same time,
On the edge by the sea again.

Walking back with all the finds,
Carefully placed in a special bag,
Being careful to take notice of the tides,
Remembering the suntan cream,
Sunglasses shading the sun from view.

Showing all the treasures to Mum,
Waiting seated on a deckchair,
She has been reading a good book,
She gives a little wave to you,
To acknowledge her interest.

Once home put them on view,
For everyone to see,
What a good holiday you had,
Looking for the things others don't want,
They are treasures to you.

JANET JANNAWAY (STANFORD-LE-HOPE)

Cow Clapping

Hardened by the estuary breeze,
Houses are made as a cluster of clouds and dung streets
Clap and pat an avenue parted by spring grass;

As herds pass to the sheds as fat bloated builders
Underpinning and cementing playgrounds
In a splattered moment of tail swish and sweet summer dairy stink.

Rock-caked statues patter as thatched roof cottages
Crisp over and contour as meringue pies,
To shelter something not yet decided upon -
A thistle spike maybe, to let in some air.

The farmer's boots do not connect with eyes ahead
And curse in a step upwards and backwards
As slap piles are trod upon and cracked open and spoilt,
That reveals the inner workings of a cow.

It is a field of cakes cooked by the sun,
Tested for quality by a hard rubber sole
As plant life will soon spring,
From its cleaved open sores.

STUART SPRINGTHORPE (HARLOW)

First Summer Day

With back against the trunk of my beech tree -
I sat, enjoying a warm, sunny day.
I listened to the busy buzzing bees
Attending blooms, then watched them fly away.
A welcome breeze blew gently through the leaves
I watched their dancing shadows on the lawn
Sun, heat and gentle breeze began to weave
Great satisfaction - summer's here - I yawned
Closing my eyes; I fell asleep, was peeved
When woken by giggling girls passing by
Glanced upwards through tree branches, saw blue sky
Thanked God that summer days were here at last.

ELWYNNE WILLSON (WALDERSLADE)

Thoughts of Summer

Let's sing the praise of summer
As no season can compare
With the beauty, warmth and colour
That is sent for us to share

The perfume of the roses
The humming of the bees
It portrays a pretty picture
Like the buds up in the trees

The sun shines down in all its glory
From its kingdom up above
Giving out a ray of sunlight
With an everlasting love

We shall savour all its beauty
For it's like a sweet refrain
And we'll remember it so, so clearly
Till it comes round again.

BARBARA FINCH (CHAPEL ST LEONARDS)

Sunny Daydreaming

Words can have a strange rhythm
Poured out from deep within
The sun shines off a cat's eye
Sea birds fly high and low in the sky
Sunny day in a blue clear way
Happiness rises and hits a ray
Colours shine so brightly
Then become darker nightly
Dreams of a daylight of gold
Daydreams to be sold
Warmness comes from my lady
No thoughts of the shady
Colourful scenes at the back of dreams
The sun shines on a happy scene.

TIM SHARMAN (EASTBOURNE)

Family Day Trip to the Sea

We collected up a lot of the family
For a bus trip to the sand and sea.
Children, uncles, aunts and Grandpa and Gran.
Teenager Mary with her nice young man,
Tommy, raring to go with his bucket and spade,
Jennie with her sandwiches and lemonade.

At last we arrived all eager and excited
Uncle Fred thought the trip was as good as visiting United.
Let's find a nice spot on the beach to call our own,
Henry can't wait for an ice cream cone.
Grandpa had some people stop and stare,
Giggled at him trying to put up his deckchair.

'Big' Basil so wanted a ride on a donkey,
the owner refused, thought it would make it wonky.
They suggested he went and looked at the ships,
But he decided he would rather go get some chips.
Then there is poor Florie, quite unhappy and moody,
Still unable to find the Punch and Judy.

Sally looks saucy in her hat with the slogan 'Kiss Me Quick,
But she's been on the big dipper and now feels sick.
Uncle Bert, in suit, waistcoat, tie cap and boots
Seems over-dressed near the girls with their teeny swimsuits.
Tommy's sandcastles with moat and flag look grand,
Soon some of us will be off to listen to the brass band.

We went for a paddle, trousers rolled up and skirts held tight,
Letting the waves chase us. Oh what a sight.
Unfortunately Henry was running and dropped his ice cream
Onto the sunbathing girl in the bikini, that made her scream.
Time is getting on, must keep an eye on the clock,
Before we go I must buy some rock.

Time to gather all our belongings and head for the bus,
Basil has a big candyfloss, if he takes that aboard there will be a fuss
All settled down and home we go, we all agreed to do it again,
Oh look, we have timed it right it is beginning to rain.

JEAN DICKENS (RUSHDEN)

MY PATCHWORK QUILT

My patchwork quilt is made from remnants
That tell the story of life's memories and special moments
The fabrics of childhood outfits discarded as one grows
Hobby horses, buttons and rosebuds, the patterns on my summer clothes

Next, the candy strip of my school uniform dress
And the yellow gingham apron I made myself in class
Mum's grey flower fifties' outfit, crisp and fresh
A tablecloth, seersucker, spread out for picnics on the grass

Then from my teens, I have added all my favourites, more or less
The psychedelic pattern of a sixties' mini dress
A yellow checked shirt and the purple blouse with a sheen
Paisley prints, blue denim and dare I mention, pink *crimplene?*

And in time I start to gather and mix
My own children's various fabrics
Little boys' shirts, cotton, one green, one blue
Red corduroy trousers and the pyjamas with the bright balloons

Duvet covers, various, one with a patchwork pattern of its own
Have joined the shapes being cut and sewn
Assorted scraps are swapped with friends and others
Themselves once children, teens, now mothers

My quilt is made of patches stitched together
Memories merged and secured forever
I have mentioned just a few
This is life's rich pattern . . . from my point of view.

SANDY RANDALL (BRETTON)

Summer Fun

Take a walk along the beach,
The one you love to know,
The frothy waves that try to reach,
The sand between your toes.
Put a seashell to your ear,
Listen to the sound,
Is it the sea that you can hear,
Or your footsteps on the ground?
Ice cream melting in your hand,
Chocolate flakes and sauce,
Punch and Judy on the sand,
And fairground rides of course.
Summertime is lots of fun,
It really makes you smile,
Let's enjoy the gorgeous sun,
It's here for just a while.

NIKKI ROBINSON (FOLKESTONE)

Am

A deathly hush hangs in the air -
Retired people everywhere
Are sleeping off the many pills
Which docs supply to cure their ills.

Blood pressure is the number one,
Although when all is said and done
Our aches and pains are lessened too
With drugs and creams - all 'on review'.

Gradually we begin to stir,
Resume our tasks and take the air;
Washing and shopping to be done;
Is it the same for everyone?

JOYCE MEMORY (GT GLEN)

WAR IN AFGHANISTAN - VILLANELLE

To engrave names of soldiers' smite
Since yesterday's communiqués,
Their loved ones left in fractured plight.

Heroes who fought and lost last fight
Crowds wait to pay homage this day,
To engrave names of soldiers' smite.

Cortege passes length darkens light,
Thoughts locked in sober sadness way,
Their loved ones left in fractured plight.

Pallbearers recall combat sites
Mates covered mates if foe waylay,
To engrave names of soldiers' smite.

These brave men are the modern knights
Freeing lands from despotic haze,
Their loved ones left in fractured plight.

Sorties save lives from sniper blight
Patrols lead locals to safe stay,
To engrave names of soldiers' smite,
Their loved ones left in fractured plight.

HILARY JILL ROBSON (WESTCLIFF-ON-SEA)

CREEPING

Creeping, dangling, spreading, flowering, fern-like,
vine-like leaves in pots, all shapes and sizes,
ivy twining round the stair rail.

Spider plants hanging overhead, overwhelming the china cabinet
are monster leaves, just like a jungle.
Cheese plants, praying plants.

Avocado taking over, cacti spreading tongues of fire.
Little shrimp plants, African violets, citrus trees, their thorns so sharp but
perfumed and beautiful are their flowers.

MAUREEN WILLIAMS (ATTLEBOROUGH)

SEASHORE BRAINWAVES

I have sat each year of my long life
On a seashore holiday beach
To watch the waves (along with my wife)
Roll in with surge; myself to teach.
Repeatedly returning unceasingly,
Gentle lap or roaring rage, amazingly.

Our young family also came to stare,
Going deeper as strength increased,
Without these deeper thoughts I could share!
Thoughts like waves never ceased -
Flowing as tides, high and low unfailingly,
Gentle thoughts alluding to eternity.

This year now an ageing pair at home,
No seaside trips on holiday.
No tides or waves or beaches to roam;
Our home address the place we stay
Ever dosing our infirmity -
Soon heavenly shore, joining God's fraternity.

GEOFFREY PERRY (HAINAULT)

LINCOLNSHIRE PRIDE

Lincolnshire present and Lincolnshire past,
Building a future and long may it last,
Lincolnshire folklore and Lincolnshire tales,
Lincolnshire custom and all it entails,
Lincolnshire farming shaping her land,
Carefully managed and cleverly planned,
Lincolnshire life with unique rural way,
Forging communities every day,
Lincolnshire fishing and her countryside,
Lincolnshire yellow-bellies so full of pride.

ANTHONY DAVID BEARDSLEY (ALFORD)

THE FOUR SEASONS

The log fire crackles with spits and sparks
It looks so cosy and bright
While outside the trees are heavy with snow
Our winter is at its height.
Then one day, the ground is coloured again
The brown earth dotted with green
And small flower buds come peeping through
Here signs of spring can be seen.
Soon summer arrives with its warming sun
With skies so constantly blue
And gardens so bright with flowers galore
In colours of every hue.
Then autumn is here (some call this the fall)
An extremely descriptive name
For this is the time when trees shed their leaves
And the weather is far from tame.
When winter is cold we long for the sun
Yet sometimes find summer too hot
And spring is often constantly wet
We're never content with our lot.
How dull it would be if each of our days
Was always the same as the last
With a scorching sun searing the earth
Or skies always so overcast.
Our land could always be white with snow
A scene we love for a while
It's great that our seasons alter so much
For changes we get - make us smile

ELSIE J SHARMAN (IPSWICH)

Songbird

The songbird in its little cage,
Is singing to the dawn,
The trilling notes both high and low
Enrich the early morn.

The people walking by all say,
'How merrily he sings,'
Do you not see this confined space
No space to spread his wings.

He cannot know why he is there
Cannot know the reason
Why he was snatched from out the sky
Put in this painted prison.

Above him he can only see
His fellows freely flying
Entrapped is he so far beneath
Alone and slowly dying.

One day soon the sun's harsh rays
Will end this life so grim
The body shaken from the cage
Replaced with one like him.

Oh gentle people passing by
Awaken from your dreaming.
The singing that delights your ear
Is not a song, but screaming.

P W PIDGEON (ROMFORD)

SATURDAY IN JULY

Light reflecting on the leaves of trees,

Passing by a misty sky,
Rain close by.

Leaves are fluttering in the breeze,
Their colours every shade of green.

Pink, white and red roses,
What a display.

The sky above grey,
Showing a little blue.

Light rain begins to fall,
A good day for the garden, but keeps people indoors.

The pine tree cones coloured green,
Growing between other trees.

Aerial on the chimney pot,
Used as a perch for birds.

Rain fell heavy in the night,
Keeping one awake.

Morning came with a cooler day.

G F SNOOK (BENFLEET)

SUMMER IN RUTLAND

A winding wide-verged lane leads through fields of ripening corn beneath azure skies
and sun-baked stone walls necklace the leafy rolling countryside
dotted with historic homes and cottage plots inviting all
under the 'open gardens' scheme to admire and be enthralled.
For these, summer is a garden deckchair, a lazy yawn
with accompanying book and afternoon tea,
perhaps admiring the view across herbaceous fringed lawn
from the spreading shade of a specimen tree.
Then there are village greens filled with fun-packed fetes -
tombolas, donkey rides and WI home-made cakes,
whilst Oakham, in its own summer festival partakes
with colourful carnival and jolly bandstand music in the park.
A cycle ride away, Rutland Water has its summer share of sailing regattas, osprey viewing and the popular annual bird fair.
Away from the bustle of summery human life nature slowly takes its seasonal course as the fading, sweet notes of nightingale tell,
fledglings fly and skylarks sing up in the heavens high
whilst cuckoo returns to Africa and bids farewell in July.
Amongst the foxglove spires a bumblebee whirrs and a red admiral flits over the ivied wall;
countless distant lawnmowers can be monotonously heard
as gentle breezes rattle the aspens and poplars tall.
Then brambles and sloes ripen under a late uncertain sun
and bales of harvested hay dot the landscape of this small shire;
September approaches, school term beckons after August fun,
migrating swallows gather on the village wire
as one realises summer in Rutland is nearly done.

ALISTAIR L LAWRENCE (OAKHAM)

SUMMER

Summer breezes drift by endlessly beneath a cloudless sky
While the sun is starting to sizzle as the scorching heat is nigh.
Schools are closed for the summer, now the holidays have begun
Seeing families go off to the seaside, hoping they'll have lots of fun.
On the beach there will be kiddies
building sandcastles with their hands
Or playing with their buckets and spades across these golden sands.
Take a stroll along the promenade on a lovely summer's day
Whilst licking a strawberry ice cream as the tide is ebbing away.
Have a picnic down at the river's edge, where boats go cruising by
As insects fly and buzz around
while the birds make their squawking cry.
Relaxing in the garden with a long, cool drink is grand
There may even be a barbecue on the next-door neighbour's land.
The weather is quite changeable, as summer lingers on
Thunderstorms with pouring rain we hope will not last long.
Summer is the season when trees and fields look green
From seaside towns to parks and lakes it makes a tranquil scene.

JENNIFER WITHERS (ORTON MALBORNE)

LAST OF THE SUMMER WHINE

It's now the end of summer where I live
and the kids go back to school,
the mothers breathe a sigh and the weather's getting cool.

It's the time I like the best, when the noises do quiet down,
the strimmers go to bed, my thoughts they do not drown.

Gardening frenzy is now over as people go inside,
but . . . oh no, is that a drill I hear?
It's time for DIY.

JULIE BOITOULT (ROCHFORD)

Johan's Vineyard

The air was moist and heavy scented,
and drinking in the honey sun,
wisteria cascaded over wood and metal,
a breeze softly persuading its falling petals
to whirl and capriole,
drowning my vision in blue-violet
and effervescent white.

I threw Johan's letter away,
with their kangaroo postage stamps.
His heartfelt words, too painful were
of a second home that rooted within me,
long walks through fields of vines,
scrunching bare toes in silt and yellow-red clay,
then bathing our feet in fountains of water
leaking from irrigation pumps.

My first taste of wine
was deep within Johan's vineyard cellar,
where we sipped its zesty lemon tang
that fizzed on our tongues and made our bodies giggle.
His mother said, 'The vines weep when they're cut now.'
I did not understand, as I listened
enthralled by her German accent
making music of English,
deep tones that vibrated in my ears
as if caught beneath the lid of a piano.

My hippie bracelets and bobble earrings
jangled in tune with the wind chimes
that were hanging from the terraces and arches
drenched in blossoms.
We held ripe grapes in our hands,
translucent green emeralds, swollen with juice,
pressed them between our sunburnt lips,
then crunched them on our back teeth,
a flavour more sumptuous than Chardonnay.

Johan and I walked between the vines
with armfuls of grapes for his mother's table,
then stepped into her home,
with its blue haze of curtains, red cedar boxes
and treasures placed in every empty space
as if they had always lived there.

We ate liverwurst on butterbrot
with thin slices of large red tomatoes.
This taste fermented in my mind
with all that I had consumed that year,
making a vintage wine
to be stored until my emotions calmed
and leaving Barossa Valley and Johan
no longer crushed my heart.

Now, ten years on, I uncork my memories.
The aroma of lemongrass comes first,
as I harvest all that my wine has to give,
savouring every zesty moment
and when I crave more
I'll weep vintage tears
for Johan's letters.

SILVIA JULIET MILLWARD (WILLENHALL)

TIME BY THE RIVER

Sitting by the river on a lovely summer's day
Watching the ducks and swans, swimming on their way.
A breeze gets up and the water ripples gently
And people with kids come to feed the ducks a'plenty

The ducks and swans enjoy being fed
Fishermen enjoying their days at the water's edge
Tales of big ones caught long ago
Unable to fish when winter brings the snow.

The river flows along with each day that comes
With the trees bowing gracefully, with the wind and rain
But even the rain brings its beauty too
And as it hits the water it makes a splash or two

Then the winter comes and with it brings the snow
The river looks lovely with its frosty glow
The sun comes out and it sparkles, its beauty to be seen
Then it melts away again, as though it's never been.

NORMA J BATES (WARWICK)

Just For A While

It goes so quick
one blink and it's gone,
the sun
because no sooner that it's out
the rain comes tumbling down
you have to race to grab your clothes off the line
wishing they could be dry, ready to iron
and everything is fine.
It's very quiet I think for summer holiday time
with the children home from school
mums must feel like drinking several bottles of wine.
Oh no,
it's time for summer fun
a good run
in the park
hear the wonderful sound of the singing lark!
Make the most of this treasured time
because very soon
the young children who run around free
will be like you and me
older and hopefully in work
thinking I wish I were young again
not living in a hard world that sometimes feels berserk.

RACHEL TODD (WICKHAM MARKET)

GREAT YARMOUTH

A sandbank formed on Norfolk's eastern shore
Fishermen were first to call it home
A wealth of herrings saved them from living poor
Never from their shoreland would the roam

A village on the sandbank came to be
Traders came to trade along the shore
All made their living from the sea
Where time and tide are subject to God's law

The village grew and prospered, selling herrings by the cran
And with passing time became Great Yarmouth town
Where people came to holiday all along the strand
And for holidays and herrings Great Yarmouth became renown

Scottish lassies came to work, to gut the silver darlings
Working in the wind and rain and sleet
And they all sang a cheering song, standing at the farlins
Their fingers bandaged, chilblains on their feet

From grains of sand to world renown
To holidays from the farlins
Great has become Great Yarmouth town
On miles of golden sands and shoals of silver darlings

JOHN W BROWN (ORMESBY ST MICHAEL)

Is it over yet?

I really can't remember
The new people that I've met
The fuss, the threats, the presents
Is it over yet?

What was it all about?
I have a stomach ache
I've eaten far too much
Is it over yet?

I think I'll sleep
A day or two, repair the stomach ache
Just get up and wash my paws
Is it over yet?

It seems to happen every year
The noise, the chaos, the mess
I really don't know why
Is it over yet?

My owners bring me in a tree
Then shout when up I climb
I am trying to say thanks a lot
Is it over yet?

I help by eating all the chocs
They'd hung about my tree
I think that's what caused me all the pain
Is it over yet?

Next year I think I'll have a trip away
No people, no trees, no noise, no mess
Somewhere that's just nice and warm
Leave them to the stomach ache

TRICIA MORGAN (PAULERSPURY)

OUR HOMELAND

This pleasant land whose varied clime
Likes to surprise us all the time.
Today it's fine, warm and sunny
Think it will last? Don't be funny!

Tomorrow may be dull and cool
As the children set off for school.
Then later sunshine and showers
Perfect for our hosts of flowers.

This land has so much to admire
Market town with high church spire.
The city with a hill so steep
Cathedral there, just take a peep.

Open country, do not miss it
Colourful place, worth the visit.
Ramblers come upon village inn
To pass it by would be a sin.

Cattle herds graze on grass so green
Brood mare with foal, a sight serene.
The forest ponies roaming wild
A stunning sight for any child.

A land of natural beauty
Vales from where peaks rise acutely.
Lakes for boating, caves to explore
Could we wish for anything more?

Little townships, cities so grand
Coastal resorts for sea and sand.
Pride and contentment hand in hand
Here - in this green and pleasant land.

BRIAN ELEY (HORNCASTLE)

My Summer Garden

Summer is calling,
From out of the blue.
Grass all a-shimmer
In the cool morning dew,
Flowers are lifting
Their heads to the sun,
For they know
That summer has truly begun.

Some, bend their heads low
As though reluctant
To be part of the show,
But their perfume belies
Their discreet little bow.

Colours are glaring
Clashing and daring
While others subdued
With a subtle glow.

Trees burgeoning
In various greens,
Helping to temper
These dazzling scenes.

The long summer days
Are a delight,
And a walk in the garden
In the late evening light,
As the vestiges of sun
Disappear from sight,
Leaving behind a warmth
And a glow,
Perfume and sights
To gladden our hearts
On warm summer nights.

Anne Bailey (Telford)

THE OLD OAK TREE

Oh mighty oak
How many secrets do you hold?
How many lovers have you seen bold?
How many summers have come and gone?
How many seasons keep moving on?
Springtime awakens new birth
From old to new
As the earth bursts forth its beauty
Exciting, breathless and new
Oh mighty oak that stands so proud
Lover's names entwined around
Wild flower and mushrooms
Collect at your feet
Your branches stretch out
As lovers meet
Oh mighty oak that shelters lovers
From sun and rain
Soon see the seasons changing
Once again
Autumn comes and you must rest
Now that you have given your best
Lovers will wait once again
For you to shelter them
From sun and rain
As their whispers of love
Reach your heart
Will they stay together
Or will they part?

ELIZABETH HAWORTH (BURTON-ON-TRENT)

Summer Is Here

Summer months, the sweetest time of the year,
Fragrant air assails the senses with uplifting cheer,
Attracting Nature's workers, as, from bloom to bloom they race,
Birdsongs abound as the proclaim their chosen space,
While youngsters flap their wings to ensure they are not ignored.

Time for living out of doors, forget the daily chore,
Bats and balls of sporting ilk in the gentle air resound,
Wrapped in fine weather warmth, a most welcome sound.
There are country strolls, stiles to climb,
Panoramic views gladden the eye, lush, sublime
On Sundays melodic sounds waft from a well-rehearsed band,
Old familiar tunes the passing years have spanned.
Now harsher times are but a figment of the mind,
Fading in the past, forgotten, as we unwind.
The joy to relax in a cushioned garden chair,
Such bliss indeed, freedom from every day care.

LIZBETH COOKE (OAKHAM)

So . . .

Summer's here
The sun's ablazing;
Cows and sheep
Are quietly grazing.
Children shriek!
The sound's amazing!
Praise the Lord
For double glazing.

LESLIE DENNIS PEARCE (BEXHILL-ON-SEA)

JUNE 2010

Strawberry teas, sitting on the grass
Farewell St Bartholomew's churchyard
Serene and peaceful
Sun shining, birds singing
Along with choir voices ringing
This our countryside, England
At its best
Friends around, all enjoying
Tea, cakes, stalls and sunshine
Rippling stream, lake and grazing cows
A view to remember and savour
When days are dark in December
You'll look back and remember
Strawberries and cream, sunshine, singing
In a country churchyard
Until summer comes again
With God's blessing
On this special place.

IRENE G CORBETT (HAMMERWICH)

ISLAND HOLIDAY

On this beautiful island of dreams
When the man sits and schemes
He lets sand slip through his hands
The starry sky at night in his eyes a delight
The hot sun by day bouncing off the sea at play
The waves singing out, this beautiful island we shout.

KEVIN DAVIES (SOLIHULL)

SLEA HEAD

So wild is the wind and so high is the sea
When our holidays bring me once more
Where the mighty Atlantic gathers its strength
As it thunders in on to the shore.

The seabirds are crying a hymn to the sky
As the gulls ride the milky white foam,
The flash of a dolphin there now - and then gone,
As the black shoals of herring head home.

I lay down my burden of trouble and care,
So my heart will find solace and rest.
At Slea Head I am one with the elements there,
In the wild, craggy jewel of the west.

In Ireland's vast coastline of myriad moods
That no hand of mere man sought to tame,
Find patterns of land, sea and sky that I love,
Ever-changing and never the same.

In nature's wild tumult my soul will find peace,
Then refreshed and renewed I will be
And Slea Head in Dingle will find me once more
Where the dark cliffs slope down to the sea.

ANN DEMPSEY (SUTTON COLDFIELD)

THOUGHTS OF A CONIFER PLANTATION

We've a lot to think about. Being brought close together
Has deepened our power of thought. It's discouraged
The birds and the sun's light and those tiresome tangles
That can arise at one's feet. Sheer concentration of spent
Thought-needles has put paid to that; it's the best mulch
For peace and quiet . . . You say we've grown too self-absorbed?
Well, thinking separates you out, means you keep some things
To yourself. It hardens you, it's true; the wood overwhelms
The flower. But we like it like that. Do you understand?
Keeping the sun in check, dimming it down. All that blazing
Ardour pouring out and everybody springing to attention,
Glorying in their perfumed costumes and giving thanks - it's
Just not us. We can't stand the rambling variety it creates
And as for those outrageous roses . . . No we prefer to stand
Apart, think our own thoughts. Keep your tinder dry, that's what
We say. And we've had a dream. Did you know? It's risen
Among us out of our silent depths. It speaks to our inmost
Self: we call it - Resin. It holds the flower-force back. Yes,
We've a lot to think about. We see now that we're different
From the crowd: our sun-juice, that's the difference: we
Can choose what our flower's to be. We think about it day
And night. Imagine: one spark - and we could set the world alight!

DAVID DONALDSON (ORCOP)

THE GIFT OF SUMMER

Welcome summer, halcyon days and azure skies,
Scented flowers and gentle breeze.
Multicoloured butterflies,
Sweet honeysuckle, bumblebees.

On leafy bough the blackbirds sing
And honeybees their nectar seek
And swallows swoop on velvet wing,
Whilst purple violets shyly peek.

Forgotten are bleak winter's days,
As Nature in oblivion
Soaks up the summer sun's warm rays
And once bare trees their green cloaks don.

And in the evening's heady balm,
When crimson sun sinks in the west
And all around is peace and calm,
Then Nature takes her well earned rest.

BETTY BRAMMA (WORCESTER)

SUMMER OF 2011

Summer 2011 begins on March 31st when 4 West closes.
I will be a slave worker no more
Earning disabled pocket money wages

Since age 18 in 1983 I worked at WDC
Wages £2.50 per week
Today they would be before the 'beak'

1999 moved to 4 West
Paid no better than at WEDC and the rest
Since 2011 I am better paid
Remainder of life to enjoy with a maid

Looking forward to the London Games
Next summer, 2012, more gold to gain
World Cup England, summer 2018
Fifty-two years of hurt ended on the green.

H GRIFFITHS (MARKET HARBOROUGH)

Summer Pursuits

Now at long last summer is here
Rays of sun through the clouds appear
The waiting fisherman, along with his mate
Seeks out his tackle, maggots and bait

The happy picnicker, out for the day
Children and dogs jumping for joy
Who's got the sandwiches, beer for Dad?
Soon polish that off, no more to be had

The hearty walker views the distant hills
Dons his heavy boots and Mac
He breathes afresh of Nature's air
On city life he turns his back

The crazy golfer in his bright attire
Dreaming of his hole in one
Flexes his muscles on the green course
To the 'nineteenth' when game is done

The sea-going man with his little boat
Challenges the waves as he gets afloat
This is the life and he feels fine
Dismisses thoughts of a gale force nine

The tennis pro with his kit so white
He and his racquet strung up tight
A contrary ball scatters chalk dust
Throws down his racquet in sheer disgust

The jolly jogger too can be seen
Hoping he'll soon be less in the beam
Sun beating down as he puffs with a will
Will he ever reach the top of the hill?

But not for me this hectic pace
Not caring now to join the race
It's here I lie on daisied lawn
Content to stay from early morn

DOREEN GARDNER (SHIRLEY)

Norfolk

For marshes, broads and wildlife,
For reed beds, ducks and drake,
Cottage thatch and gardens,
The sand and sea awakes
All that I love in Norfolk
And it brings to the seeking mind
Our ancient times when treasure unfolds
In stories Of Dane, Saxon and Norman.
Here in the whispering wind
A silence unknown
In castles, monasteries - lawmen.

Here is the harvest of the sea and land
Church bells and the toil of hand.
Landscapes rolling flat and free
As far on horizons the eyes can see.
There is Norwich city for a shopping spree
Horning and Potter Heigham for tea.
The National Trust is here to stay
Blickling, Felbrigg walk your way.

In Fairhaven Gardens
The wild flowers bloom
While Cromer singers fill it with tune.
Yarmouth races and Pleasure Beach
King's Lynn Pageants.
Thetford Chase
Making Norfolk a lovely place!

PAULINE BURTON (BECCLES)

FLOTSAM AND JETSAM

I'm nine again - beside the sea
The bladderwrack surrounding me
For now I have a one-track mind
With X-ray specs I hope to find
A mermaid's purse - a belemnite
A dragonfly that drowned in light
A shark's tooth from the Carib Sea
A clasp of Saxon jewellery
Sea glass pounded by the waves
A sabre tooth from long drowned caves
A rook lost from the Lewis hoard
A Viking sword swept overboard
King John's treasure
Narwhal tusks
Armadas sunk in gales of rust
With - here and there
The glint of gold
An Inca's ransom in the hold
A seagull wakes me from my trance
I gaze across the waves to France
I'm nine again - beside the sea
A small boy lost in reverie.

RICHARD BONFIELD (LEICESTER)

Sir Robin Dines With Us

Mother Nature knows wildlife she must feed
Sam Squirrel can't be sure and to all displays his greed
Back and forth, back and forth, searching for a nut
Stealing hoards from others to nurture his own gut.

Slowcoach, the tortoise, approaches a shed
Sleeps over winter, a cosy box for a bed.
Birds gathering on rooftops will soon start to swarm
Flying south over oceans where climates are warm.
Mr Robin Redbreast decides with humans he'll stay
When he sees snow and children riding a sleigh
Knowing gentle taps on the windowpane
Will bring out 'Mrs Human' with titbits again.

He's not staying far from his new-found friends
Not until spring arrives and winter ends
He has built a nest under the porch
Mr Human checks him nightly with the beam from his torch.

Like a five star hotel, in warm places he hides
Lucky Sir Robin gets toast buttered both sides.

LUCY MARY DEAN (HORNCASTLE)

August For Historians?

Henry VIII as Robin Hood -
No, he was thin then. Figs grow fat,
Fresh, beech-leaf glossy green, too good
For leaving, feeding finch, fox - rat?

Like Thomas Cromwell, painted fast
Swelling in black, the berries throng
With bramble-thorns. They will not last,
Need picking, eating - never long.

Monsters? Not now: these fruits are sweet
As marzipan, do no more harm
Than shrimps. Perhaps a chance to eat
Less chocolate, after scale's alarm?

VERONICA M BROWN (WIGSTON)

When I Look in the Mirror

When I look into the mirror, what do I see?
An old grey-haired man, staring back at me.
His body's gone quite fat, his hair is going thin,
He's lost his athletic prowess; he used to be so trim.

When I look into the mirror, what do I see?
A round and cheery face, staring back at me.
There's a depth in those eyes, of pain and understanding;
He's been battered and bruised by life, but he is still standing.

My work has given me such joy and satisfaction,
But latterly it gave more tension and disruption.
The pain and stress just took its toll till I could take no more,
I quit my job and turned away and walked out of the door.

The depth of pain, the stress of life, it makes its mark,
The big cloud that hung over me was very, very dark.
I am very lucky, I have God and a lovely wife;
Without them both, I'm sure, I would have given up on life.

The mirror sees but doesn't see the person it's reflecting,
It only shows the outer side, an image it's perfecting.
What if it could see the person that's inside?
Would we be so willing to reveal what we try to hide?

When I look into the mirror, what is that I see?
Is it just an image of the person I pretend to be?
What if that image showed the person I could be;
Or worse still if it showed the real inner me?

When I look into the mirror, what do I see?
The face of love and peace; a face that is line free.
Reflected in the glass it surely is my face,
But the stress is gone thanks entirely to God's grace.

TONY CASHMORE (HARTSHILL)

FACE-PAINTING - SAFFRON WALDEN'S SUMMER FÊTE WITH HAYLEY, JONATHON AND FLORENCE

And now that spring is spent
Clowned its way to the main event
And the high noon of summers crowned,
So the stressed crocus forgets its early frown.

When in purple mood, it fluted, over fields and down
To spread across the county wide,
To paint the face of bill and brook in saffron glow.
Imitate the glancing look that falls astride,
Espouse the sunny summer's rise.

All are friends and cheerfully acquainted for the fête
Coconuts fuzzily trying to make a stand, yearning for the awning
Far too late.
Pet dogs are held to judgement in a ring,
As to who will wear the widest grin.
Creaking, wooden boat-swings soar, as if in awe
That grovelling earth returns once more.

So all the lovely smells of summer that creep about at dawn
Are held this summer's day and on this afternoon.
Children's earnest faces, dedicated to the art of sitting still,
Eradicate the natural law of human status, for clownish flaw

And painted tears, whiskers, bright wide lips, snub nose and bunny ears, saffron cakes, china plates, cups of tea - the band plays -
Song surrounds this softened, tinted realm of enchanted fling
And like the infant crocus underplays the camaraderie of spring
So the Walden woods stand guard of little things.

PLUTO (OAKINGTON)

A French Summer Holiday

The solstice is today
When the sun is in its special place -
Today is also a very special day
We leave our homes for our special holiday
To France we fly, a place called St Cyprien
Where the sun shines from morning until night
The atmosphere is calm and right.
A small pied à terre we share with a friend who is very dear.
We walk to the boulangerie to collect our warm baguette
For early morning breakfast
With coffee which is perfect and right.
A stroll to the market, where stalls have goods so bright
La Plage is warm, the sea so still.
We plunge therein for a gentle swim
We spread ourselves upon towels
And dry in less than an hour.
Back to our pied à terre we go
For a siesta which is just so -
We awake now, full of go
Our evening spread for us is a delight
We eat and drink at our leisure
Into the early night.
The air is warm, the atmosphere still
We ascend the wooden hill
Our sleep is deep, but so relaxed.
When we awake we are not faxed.
Alas in seven days our holiday ends
We now look and hope we may go again
Long may this last until time with us is past.

CARL KEMPER (LICHFIELD)

Seagull

Oh chalky winged way up high
Why do you make such mournful cries?
You swoop and glide through sunny haze
Then dive to bob on lazy waves.

If I could attach to you a silvery string
You could fly like a kite; I could reel you in
We'd pretend that we spoke, what tales you would tell
Of the sea's many moods and the wind's fearful yell

The search for your food before folks awake
For your season's young, to the nest you must take
Tell me stories of the great ships you spy
Of the lives that left them, on the sea's bed now lie.

Have stories been told to you how the cannon balls fly
Or of pirates flags on masts flying high
With muskets and knife and the clash of steel
Man upon man - for what right did they kill?

Down through the years in books we have read
Of the wondrous creatures of the seabeds
I'll imagine you're a sentry as you bob on the sea
Trying to protect it from the people - like me!

SUSAN E ROFFEY (LONGFIELD)

Summer Miracles

When the summer sun begins to shine
Warming all hearts both yours and mine
Laying on the beach waves come and go
Sometimes fast, sometimes slow
Maybe they'll come gently with peace
Making in the sand a passage or crease
As I bathe in sun's warm glow from above
Gazing up to the sky and thinking of love
I am blessed in my life surrounded by kin
My husband and children, grandchildren in
Yes this love is a different kind for me
There is to be a new member in the family
He is yet to be born, nothing will he lack
A great grandson who is already named Jack
Whilst the flowers and trees have all grown life anew
The beautiful colours, reds, green and blue
So whilst we can watch all this wonder with
Our very own eyes that loom
Baby Jack's been safely growing and developing
Within his mum's womb
Nothing but miracles the sperm and the seed
Is sent from our Lord for all that we need

ANGIE FARROW (IPSWICH)

No Room

Alone
On a platform
She waits
Patiently
For the train to arrive
Seven fifty-nine
Guess she won't be home till late
So I'll just sit, relax and wait
And take everything that comes to me
There ain't no problem here
There ain't no problem here
They say it's tough in the city
Well Mr you ain't been up north
We got it pretty cushy these days
I'm kinda lucky I guess
There's no solution here
There's no solution here
As the tail lights slowly
Disappear . . .

CALVIN MADIN (CHESTERFIELD)

My Garden

My garden I would rather be
It is my place of sanctuary
There is always something different to see
And it never fails to draw me.

Its addictive therapeutic powers
Can keep me occupied for hours
Each day always something new to see
So many flowers and variety.

The birds sing merrily in the trees
Oh what, such creativity
The butterflies, frogs and the bees
What better place could one be?

CYNTHIA FAY (MAIDWELL)

A DAY IN THE COUNTRY

She gazed in wonderment and awe
She'd never seen the like before
A field of poppies gleaming red
'And no one picking them,' she said
A pheasant raised his head to see
This creature racing wild and free.
A city child from London way
Had come to Norfolk for the day.
The picnic spread, the meal begun
She laughed and thought it all such fun
To have our dinner on the grass
We vowed to make the magic last.
She stood before the gates so wide
And really longed to go inside.
'The Queen lives there, in that big house'
She whispered quietly as a mouse.
Taking her hand we led the way
The perfect end to a perfect day
And as she stood beneath the trees
'Pick as many as you please
The Queen won't mind, she lets us share
In all her apples hanging there'
The box was filled and true to rule
The largest apple went to school
And teacher told of this day in heaven
As seen by a little girl of seven.

MARIE WOOD (KING'S LYNN)

Excuse Me, It Is British Summertime You Know

Summertime, year to year, just the same
You put up with what you get.
July to August
Always very wet.
The wind picks up during the day
Dies down at night.
One good thing about it
You can always fly your kite.
British summertime
Is like living in a drain.
People who like sunny holidays
Spend holidays in Spain.
Well, this is Britain
Nothing will ever change I swear it,
If your holiday is spent here
You have to bear it.
If you go outside take you Mac
You won't need an overcoat.
Better still get some oars out
Keep fit with a row boat.

DENNIS FIELD (TAMWORTH)

PERSHORE TOWN

I've lived in this market town
For thirty years and more
With a splendid abbey and Georgian homes
And interests by the score

Tucked in the Vale of Evesham
Surrounded by field and farm
With a college of horticulture
I've been blessed with so much charm

Walk down by the river Avon
Take a picnic and watch the boats
Come and enjoy our carnival
With Morris dancers and floats

Pershore has a special festival
Named after its own fruit, the plum
Villages and pubs lie all around
Serving their own ale and rum

In the distance lies Bredon Hill
Gorgeous woods lie in between
Visitors come and go all summer
Saying, 'What a super town we've seen.'

ALISON JACKSON (PERSHORE)

ONCE UPON A SUMMERTIME
(HOMAGE TO CHET BAKER)

We might glimpse a gift unfolding as a
Cloud yet never register its form
Beyond the contrail where a wisp
Might drift or secretly declare with time -
Still believing what we know of Heaven.

The mellow afternoon is privy to
Its sigh - the passages of dappled shade
A veiled accompaniment - seeming idle
Yet where that instrument has audience
It finds that interval and whispering.

And further to that breath a time concedes
Anticipating every pleasure;
A perfect lip applies a tender pitch
Taking ease and subtle embouchure to
Play as nothing else and with profundity.

WILLIAM BIRTWISTLE (MARKET HARBOROUGH)

THE BUTTERFLY

Across the meadow, the butterfly dances.
High and low, how arrogant she prances,
her red and blue wings mellow
with the golden buttercup,
as she silently sits.
Hovering over the tall, serene, red-petalled poppy,
then floating down to the yellow-faced daisy.
The soft summer breeze gently lifts her
to the green velvet of the trees,
higher and higher she seems to fly.
Butterfly, princess of the summer sky.

LIZZY USHER (BOYTON)

BARBECUE

It is a lovely day
To be invited to a barbecue
To have some sizzling sausages
Sweetcorn too
Perhaps a chicken wing
As extra
Relish is a must
With toasted bread crust
Red sauce
Brown sauce
Mustard as well
Onions too with their gorgeous smell!
Aromas all around
Making a barbecue to be
A favourite of all
A summer outdoor feast
With nothing left at the end of the day
Stomachs full
To await the next invitation
To an outdoor barbecue!

DOROTHY BOULTON (TONBRIDGE)

AN ENGLISH ROSE

The wild rose of England
Seems as hardy as the county.
While tears fall like a shower of rain.
Nourishing new life
But the perfume is invigorating
As a warm summer's day.

PAMELA JAVES (WINSHILL)

Summer in Leigh

At last the winter is over and done,
We are eagerly awaiting the warming sun,
We, the inhabitants of Leigh on Sea,
The place where everyone loves to be,
Are looking forward to things to come,
For dear old Leigh is full of fun.

People from far and wide, come to see,
Our annual folk festival in old Leigh,
Dancing on the cobbles, passing many an ancient inn,
Secreting stories of smugglers within,
Welcoming day trippers, out for a spin,
The Peter Boat, Smack, and Crooked Billet,
To name but a few,
All affording a super view.

Morris, belly and folk dancers each,
Entertain us not far from the beach,
On the wharf, what a jolly dance,
Where one and all can up and prance,
Rounded off by a sing-around,
Before we go homeward bound.

But think not that this is all there is to Leigh,
Plenty more things to see,
Sparkling water when the tide is in,
Warms your heart and makes it sing,
Mud, glorious mud, when the tide is out,
Is also what Leigh is all about.

If, now you think it is time you were fed,
Then make a visit to Osborne's shed,
Cockles, winkles, prawns and crab sticks,
What a delightful seafood mix!

Or up in town, in the Broadway.
More delights, what can I say?
Shops and boutiques galore,
Everything you could want and more,
Cafes, bars, restaurants, plenty of outdoor seatings,
Perfect for your friendly meetings.

But all too soon the winter curtain will come down,
On this, our little seaside town.

PAM GRAVETT (LEIGH-ON-SEA)

SUMMER STORM

As I walked out one summer morn
Feeling happy, feeling gay . . .
Then suddenly a mighty storm
Took my merry mood away.

But then I spied a skein of geese
Flying high against the rain.
The sight of that 'V' did release
My merry mood to me again.

I paddled through a sodden field
Ablaze with dandelion and poppy
And corn once high with heavy yield
Now heads hung low and floppy.

Then all went warm and all went bright
And all around me I did spy,
Myriad drops - pearls of delight
Lit by a rainbow in the sky.

SHIRLEY BECKETT (BISHOPSTONE)

Reflection

And so I continue,
Down this long and narrow road . . .
The unfamiliar journey takes me by surprise!
Yet, still I find a glimpse of hope.

Over *shattered* dreams
And stories left untold . . .
Of futures built together.
Of friendships effortlessly sold.

Conditioned to forsake that which I believe in,
How can it be that I have lost hope?
Is this really *me?*
Or is it just a veil . . . waiting to unfold?

Exhaustion setting in . . .
How is it that we have reached this road?
No way out . . . *trapped!*
Waiting in anticipation . . . the verdict so bold!

Inevitably, the moment comes . . .
I struggle with despair . . . *silent* mode.
Courageously I accept the consequence
And ultimately surrender to that which is bestowed.

SALLY BABIKER (PETERBOROUGH)

SUMMER

I am the breeze on the sunlit sea,
The child on the sand, happy and free.

I am the joy of a summer's day,
The scent like honey of new mown hay.

I am the cricket match on the green,
Gathered together the village team.

I am the sound of the wind in the trees,
The shade underneath with foxgloves and bees.

I am the dog who basks in the sun,
Dreaming of games with a ball, having fun.

I am the bird in the fledglings' nest,
Flying and feeding without any rest.

I am the gardener pulling up weeds,
Tilling the soil and planting new seeds.

I am the summer fete, stalls and ice cream,
Bowling for pig, (now not often seen).

I am the peace at the end of the day,
When summer has gone and there's no more to say.

BELINDA EDDY (EARITH)

First Romance

As I sit gazing out of the window
With the rain running down the glass
I think of summers I used to know
Of romance that was in the past

Behind our house were fields of grass
And a river that flowed to the sea
I would disappear for hours on end
And nobody looked for me

I saw a nest of snakes writhing about
Heard birds that are now quite scarce
I fished in the river and caught, not trout
But minnows and eel and dace

The long summer holidays stretched ahead
As I changed and grew and dreamed
While the cattle lowed and chewed the cud
Of boys I thought and schemed

We sat by the river 'neath a grassy bank
Our arms became entwined
We kissed, then suddenly jumped apart
We heard voices that came from behind

We were so afraid of being found out
That we didn't meet again
This was my first taste of romance
In the sun, by the river, back then

CAROLYN REED (LEWES)

Us

Just the sound of your voice
And my soul breathes and relaxes
Into the moment of life that
I was born to live and to love.

What is this journey of missing each other
Time and time again?
Yet running parallel is the closeness of spirit
That knows without words and without meeting
So much is met.

Tell me, do you have any hopes,
Any dreams of time together?
Stepping into the moment that
So long ago we lost -
Innocence and good intention not knowing
How to seize the day.
Has it gone? Or is it ours but for the claiming?

Maybe it will look very different than
The fairy tale we believed in . . .
But who is to know
If it is not all the more
Through perils and thresholds
Taken right to the edge?
Do we choose to fly in daylight
Beyond dreaming?

PAGET AISLING VON WEDEL (EAST SUSSEX)

When Things Don't Work Out . . . Change

Living for the moment was my usual way
As I sit here with nothing to do
Thinking whether I change or stay
Yet can't decide if it's cos I'm blue
These feelings lingering and not fading away
All alone waiting for the phone to ring
Even if it's a cold call and a survey
To have someone to talk to and sing
Friends few and far between
Even the closest not close anymore
Almost as if I have lost my sheen
Becoming an almighty bore
I want to stand up and shout out
Wave my arms around with a laugh
Ending what has become a summer drought
Having fun again with the riff-raff
These sunny days, a dream comes true
Looking for love is the way for me
All I need is a nudge and a clue
Some advice that's for free
Hopefully that is all I need
Whilst I search for my own Venus
Pray for me so that I may succeed
And not fall foul of crimes a-heinous
Searching not just for beauty
Charm, kindness, warmth and a connection
With a hint of something fruity
And a sprinkling of some affection
To make a love cocktail supreme
Making new friends in the process
This is the plan and the dream
I need to get up and not stress
If this doesn't happen overnight
These things can take some time
But at some point I will see the light
Otherwise it's a waste and a crime

My way is beginning to change
Looking to the future, not just today
Though at first will seem so strange
Here's to tomorrow, bright not grey

DON AMIS WARIN (COLCHESTER)

THE VILLAGE

Small houses round a pretty green
A duck pond, no ducks to be seen
A little church upon a hill
A tower above; a graveyard chill.

A group of trees, a smithy too
Neighbours saying, 'How do you do?'
A lord within his stately hall
Surrounded by a lofty wall.

Horses trotting through the lanes
Jingling harness, tossing manes
Gardens flowering in the spring
Autumn crops the harvest bring.

A tiny school where children play
And learn to show the world the way
That Godly lives may yet improve
Mankind and teach him how to love.

So in the church upon the hill
Priest and people worship still
Asking for God's guiding hand
On England's green and pleasant land.

FRANCES RUSSELL (DOVERCOURT)

THE PASSING OF TIME

The passing of time happens so fast,
Looking back one wants to captivate moments to hold fast,
Moments through the years, that stirred memories,
Even at times to a discovery of extremities.

Extremities when news is conveyed with utmost care,
Knowing the news will instantly cause constant despair,
Longing not to disclose this heart-rending news,
Wondering what the outcome will be, bringing what issues?

Time is a constant mystery of happenings,
Sometimes one can only say extremely challenging,
For from the complexities of any given time,
Emerges a new understanding, elements of peacetime.

The joy when viewing the family tree, how it's grown,
As son was born, making a family of three, a stepping stone,
As time passes the son becomes a father figure,
Then if time allows a grandfather family anchor, a wise thinker.

Seasons are forever changing, how we welcome spring,
When new life is visible, a constant challenge for everything,
Summer arrives but at times we wonder just when,
But suddenly it's here, the sun glows and shines once again.

Colours are the constant appeal when autumn quietly arrives.
Displaying such artistry of creation, nothing of nature is deprived,
Winter brings artistry often with a quiet silence of design,
Revealing the most amazing landscapes, beautifully refined.

Christmas of course comes during winter's acceptance,
For it's the season when we rejoice in the gift of God's presence,
Acknowledging the light which shines brightly worldwide,
Light of the world which we use as our constant guide.

LORNA TIPPETT (HAILSHAM)

QUESTIONS OF SUMMER

How do you cast that first brush stroke
On a canvas so pure and clean?
How can you capture the silence that
Can neither be heard nor seen?
Visions of splendour, luminous auras,
Light up the globe like a lavish screen,
Flights of the geese, aroma of lawns,
Serenity captured, not simply a dream.

When do the first signs of summer appear
With its blossoming, scented impact?
When does the dew so silently form
Could we watch it perform its strange act?
Lament of the waders, call of the wild,
Solace leaves new life intact,
Palpable sunsets, fledging of infants,
Buttercup, clover, compact.

What is the basis for dragonflies' wings
Silky thin, yet mighty and strong?
What do we feel when a butterfly hovers
Perfection which cannot be wrong?
Finches dart aimlessly, or so it seems,
Swans protect young for so long,
Orchards of fruit trees, cuckoos and warblers,
Both dense in the morning song.

Why, when happiness comes from within
Do we not smile so much in the rain?
Why will we not see the balance we need
For the crops to produce ample grain?
Haze from the sunshine, happiness grows,
Basking in heat once again,
Hampers appearing, offspring elated,
Blessed, for the summer remains.

GERALDINE FRANCES SANDERS (LEIGH-ON-SEA)

THE SEASONS

The Lord works in mysterious ways
His wonders to perform
From the rain that falls to feed the trees
To the clap of the thunderstorm.
From the sun that shines giving warmth and light
To the stars and moon that shine so bright
To every flower and plant that grows
It's all a mystery that He alone knows.

From the seasons at the beginning of the year
Bringing snow and rain and fall
Snow that falls like bits of lace
Leaving everything white all over the place!
To the rain which washes it all away
Then comes the sun to dry it again
The gentle winds that come from who knows where
They blow the leaves and the trees are left bare.

Then comes the spring and young shoots appear
A new creation suddenly rears
Flowers show their beauty in every petal
And the sun returns to shine and settle
Giving life to all the living things on Earth
It's all a wonderful mystery! It's new birth.

Then comes the summer with its rays of heat
And the ground which is hot under our feet
The plants and flowers awake to greet the sun
And show all their colours, one by one.
The trees stand tall and strong and lean
Everyone has a different shade of green
And the branches reach up to the sky in splendour
All their magnificence to the Lord to render.

E THOMPSON (HASTINGS)

THE ANCIENT OAK OF STOKE-ON-TRENT

On this blazing day in May,
I remember Josiah as he shipped his clay,
On the canal below me the boats moved slowly,
The coal and limestone came the other way.
From the smoking chimneys choking the sky
To Reginald's birds fighting way up high,
I am the ancient oak of Stoke-on-Trent,
I've seen many of the ages that came and went.
Spent pages of a history booked turned
Tell of an industry spurned,
But what lessons learned?
Just a nickname earned from the kilns that burned.
'The Potteries', but what of it now?
Not a lot left, empty factories stand,
Our heritage survives on lottery grants,
Whilst industry thrives in foreign lands.
Each age marks a line in the sands of time,
Gets washed away as each new dawn chimes,
My branches still sway, my leaves still fall,
I cast my shadow on Etruria Hall,
But what do I see when I look out now
Over the hazy horizons of the Five Towns?
A leisure complex now stands where
The Festival Gardens once filled the air
With a fair scent of flowers, but it's no longer there,
Just the smell of oatcakes being freshly prepared.
Times have changed, things moved on,
The pot banks closed down, one by one.
But I'm the ancient oak, I'll change for none
And I'll be here long after you've gone.

JAMES DAVID HOLLAND (BIGNALL END)

I REMEMBER

A hessian sack was such a useful thing
To tie around your waist with thatching string
When blackleading the grate.
Now that is a job most people would hate,
But with the flues brushed clean and the hob shining bright
What could be more welcome on a cold winter's night?
Logs from the woodpile spitting and crackling
A spark to stamp out on the cosy hearth matting
Made from old clothes cut into strips
Then prodded into a hessian backing.
There was a draught from the cellar
Where cider barrels were kept
And also potatoes.
I would light a candle, step into the darkness
And in the flickering light
Delve into the rows,
My groping hand would touch something soft
And this something would jump
And more often than not
Frighten me witless.
Tiny frogs loved this cellar but I was told they were quite harmless.

I remember the threshing time
When hungry workers came in for a meal
And tackled a dinner with gusto and zeal.
Pieces of sacking tied round their shin
To stop scattering mice from scuttling in.
(A mouse once ran up a wide trouser leg
So the worker made use of a clothes line peg)'
I polished this table and was proud with the look
Of my hand-embroidered runner
And primroses I'd chosen from the banks of the brook.
There were cowslips in the meadow
Which I gathered for wine
But as I was young the wine was not mine!

I remember the cherry blossom bursting with glory
It could be seen from Clee Hill
Which overlooked Coreley.
Those were the days with no thought of the morrow
No thought of a war which could bring so much sorrow.

NORA M BEDDOES (KIDDERMINSTER)

BEAUTY AND BELIEF

May all your dreams come true.
Me, the summer and you,
Nothing to answer to,
But love and desire.

By the by, the resonant sky,
Nature's sun and breeze,
The birds fly free,
By the by is nature.

Beauty gets beneath the skin,
Skin deep, deep, the rhythms
Of nature, as resonates
Love as love.

Nothing more reassured,
The waking grace, the morning
Of the soul, is satisfied by love,
Comes day by day as belief.

From morning comes day,
Grateful of life and grace,
In love, vibrations of love,
The resonant summer skies.

Glad to be alive,
By the by, people smile,
Me, the summer and you,
Nature beating, his solar rays.

KERRI MOORE (KERESLEY)

Sabbath in the Sunshine Stoke Road, Northamptonshire

'Tis the Sabbath in the sunshine,
and the clouds are plump and white;
and the sky a perfect azure-blue,
where the sun burns hot and bright.

And the joyful congregation,
is a tiny feathered crowd;
and the glorious acoustics,
cast a sound, that's clear and loud.

They sing to the Son of Mary,
as they nestle in the trees;
and his blessings are abundant,
when the choristers he sees.

And as I listen to the choir,
the church bells start to chime,
and the Sabbath was never dearer,
that at these moments in time.

Peace is all around me,
tho' music fills the air;
and the bold, elusive cuckoo,
makes his mocking sound up there.

The fields that stretch beside me,
are where horses graze each day;
and these creatures in the sunshine,
are at peace in their languid way.

A feline in the hedgerows,
steps forth with stealthy tread,
and scampers after fieldmice,
through the many gaps ahead.

Folk extend their greeting,
as they walk along the way,
worshipping the sunbeams
on this extra special day.

A tree, tho' gnarled and ancient,
lends very welcome shade,
so once more I stop and marvel
at this rural esplanade.

A growling dog seems threatening,
when it sees me standing hear,
but a friendly pat, and some soothing words
make it see, there's nowt to fear.

I continue with my wandering,
for this road is rather long;
and I rejoice for the many sights to see
and sacred birds in song.

A fox appears - but briefly,
in its quest to find a meal;
but rabbits hide in burrows,
which the sun-kissed leaves conceal.

The imposing shades are many,
which dominate the scene;
like the colour combinations
in the splash of evergreen.

Wild geese make their raucous sound,
in the vast expanse of blue;
and the cause of much amusement,
in their groups of four-three-two.

Rodents forage in the undergrowth,
shielded from the summer glare,
and very much a part of this rural code -
one can hear them everywhere.

I salute the many songsters,
for a very splendid show,
and will be an avid listener,
when I return in the summer glow.

So thank you Lord for summer,
and the pleasure that it brings,
for the Sabbath in the sunshine,
is a day when my heart sings.

PATRICIA MARY GROSS (BLISWORTH)

Sunny Days

Long days, short nights.
Summer's come, turn out the lights.
Kids off school, there's lot to do,
Dig out your shorts for a barbecue.

Smell those sausages and burgers cooking,
See over there the neighbours are looking.
We are having fun and we don't care,
So invite them over to have a share.

There's music playing and lots of laughter,
So eat your fill and we will tidy up after.
Six hours later we quieten things a little,
Put the kids to bed, now we can have a tipple.

Long or short, soft or stronger,
Whatever you wish, this party's going on longer.
The stars have come out, so we turn the lights on,
Carry on talking till the last guest is gone.
Everyone has had such a brilliant day,
Thanks to family, friends and neighbours coming our way.

FREDA BAKER (HALESOWEN)

Aids Rebirth

The night's wearing shrouds of light
Perhaps the moon encumbers death
The hungry fangs dug deep in the throat
A grisly grope for feticide
This infant lay in arms astray
Umbilical cord fastened like prey
To greedy womb's incessant bray
Encysted boil of tumours bide
Concord of pain and dark descend
To chew and cheval the mugging chide
Deem it horror or night's attire
The robust pearl will poke a pier
Is life grotesque or farce or fear
It is condemned with death so near.

RIFFAT NAZIR AHMED (SPARKHILL)

SUMMERTIME

Exams finished, school's ended
Waiting for results
What will the future hold
University or work?

Day trips to the seaside
Digging in the sand
Sandy sandwiches to eat
Paddling in the sea.

Late night picnics at
Concerts in the park.
Music, dancing, having fun,
Fireworks and traffic jams.

Fields of golden corn
Waiting to be cut.
Farmers working day and night
To get the harvest in.

The days are getting shorter,
Summer's nearly gone,
The memories linger on,
Now the seasons change.

PAMELA BUCKLE (ALCESTER)

THE WEDDING

She floats towards him on a cloud of white,
Wedding veil hiding her face from his sight,
He turns, they smile, she stands beside him,
They exchange their vows, sealed with a kiss,
They sign the register,
Now she is his.

LORRAINE SHELDRAKE (NORTH LOPHAM)

Visitors to the PM

Late last night, around midnight, I left my room
And whilst looking up, in the sky the moon
I saw a bright light shoot out of the darkness into sight.
Then a spaceship like metal kite, landed as I stood in fright.

Though in my fear I turned away, I could not walk, I had to stay,
Then turning back I saw a doorway appear, from where an alien,
Appearing not unlike myself, came near. Who,
In unbroken English, spoke to me firmly and ever so clear.

'Please explain how you can treat unkind,
so many on Earth to whom you give no mind.
Why are weapons so important to your worlds few,
who control and dictate their own preferences over the fates
of the unequalled inhabitants of this godforsaken place!

Where we come from we protect all our young
in an ageless society that excludes no one.
And the planet we call home is free and safe to roam,
With little to no exclusion zones!

Our leaders have been chosen
because they've raised a family and worked the land,
they've felt the sting of sweat falling on bleeding hands.

Our leaders are educated about their world and its needs.
They are not perverted or grasped by greed.

Our leaders serve the people and eat from their hands.
They do not live in big houses, palaces
or any place equally so grand.

These observations of your planet have been, of little to no fun.
Our advice to you is to try to cure the things you have done.
And to change the things we guarantee are certain yet to come.'

With no time to go inside and write a manifesto detailing my plight
I stood composed putting together in my head
the answers I'd chose.
But before I could speak and give my political speech
To the right honourable gentleman,
appearing before me so discreet.

Without any warning or even a fall, I woke up from my sleep.
Then, getting out bed and looking up in the sky at the moon
I swear I saw a bright light shoot into the darkness out of sight.
As I stood deep in thought, dreaming about our next election fight!

MERLIN B JAMES (OADBY)

SONG OF THE BITTER ANGELS

Hear the bitter angels singing
Some mournful, moonlit cries
The melody, black-feathered, winging
Across the black hole of the skies,
Leaves to the dark canvas, clinging,
A thousand silver eyes
And a haunting echo ringing,
Like a thousand breath-dead sighs.

The blackened sky lies bleeding,
The silvered fissures run,
But bitter angels, unheeding,
Cry out chanting hymns begun.
The stars, their doom impending,
Now their silver rings undone,
Storm through heaven a dark stampeding,
To the throat of the blackened sun.

Bitter angels, now lamenting
The sky's empty, barren dearth,
From their dark eyes, resenting,
Roll reams of diamonds, newly-birthed,
Then flood the heavens, now cementing
Their endless kindling worth;
Unremitting, unrelenting,
On the starlit world of Earth.

ELIN LEWIS (WELLESBOURNE)

Sights and Sounds of Summer

Sheep bleating on a distant hillside,
Buzzing of the flies and insects, as they flutter in frenzy in the
Hot sunlight.
Dancing particles of weeds, white dandelion seed known as
Children's wishes.
Grasped eagerly by outstretched hands, caught and wished upon,
Then set free to lazily drift, blown by a gentle breeze to take root who
Knows where.
The sound of the leaves rustling and swaying in a warm summer
Wind.

Water flowing gently its stillness rippled, marred by jumping fish
Eagerly catching the flies that nestle on the surface of the water.
The flash of fishing lines as baited hooks hit the water.
Whirring sound of fishing reels as the empty baited line is wheeled
In and reset, re-baited to be cast out again and again.
Rattle of containers as the bait boxes are used time after time.
Excited cries, 'I've got one,' as man and boy pit their wits against the
Canny fish.

The drone of aeroplanes high in the sky,
The glitter of silver as the sun reflects on their outstretched wings.
The call of the cuckoo, its song competing to be heard amidst the
Drone of the giant silver bird.

Varying shades of green, light and dark and browns parched
Dryness of the summer grass.
Dry, cracked earth from lack of rain.
Peaceful stillness to rest the wearied mind in you.
Oh blessed countryside of my home, thou rolling green fields of
England.

Isolated farmhouses painted white, framed within green hedgerows.
Cattle grazing on sloping hills,
Slow, lazy flowing rivers, their quiet waters rippled, marred by the
Sound of jumping fish, eagerly devouring the flies that
Nestle on the water's surface.

Two gulls flying side by side, holding a heated conversation between
Each other. 'Caw, caw, caw, caw, screech, shrill, screech - shrill'
Swish of waves, muddy coloured waters, churned sandy-brown,
As the sea waters foam and creep ever closer to the sandy pebbled
Shore line.

Gleeful, excited cries of families of sea-worshippers, as the swim and
Play games amidst the foaming waves.
Families of different creeds, nations and social standings,
All in oneness, in unison, enjoying the waters of the sea.

Water's enfold the deserted sandy beach the tide has raised.
Darkness descends, only the roar of the wave's mares, the stillness
Of the summer evening, all is quiet.
Tomorrow is another summer day.

FLISS EDWARDS (RUGBY)

THE ROSE

A flower of beauty, resplendent to the senses
with fragrance that fills the nose and touches the taste buds.
The standard, the miniature, the climber, the floribunda,
The rose of celebration, the rose of remembrance.
The warmth and depth of the red rose of love
And the iciness and sharpness of the white, cognisant of death.
The imprint of humanity preserved in the name of a rose
living on in perpetuity in this perennial.
Delicate patterns of pink and lilac and those edged in lemon.
The strong crimson velvet and the Tuscan orange.
No flower surpasses its
beauty and variety.
Long before its time of fading
the petals linger like confetti in the soil,
blown gently by the wind or the recycling of Nature
and setting in mounds of perfection.

GAEL NASH (NORTHIAM)

THE MOMENT

When a sunny day tempts you
And you stop to sit and rest,
You look around
And see Nature at its best.

The beauty that surrounds us,
Is a wonder to behold,
A lovely field of corn,
Or a flower ready to unfold.

A majestic oak,
The horse chestnut tree,
What have they seen?
Far more than you or me.

For a hundred years
They have spread their canopy.
They have seen children playing
And laughing happily.

Lovers have kissed
And carved their names,
Rabbits and foxes
Have played many games.

Now your time is up,
It's back to work,
Things to be done,
Of which you must not shirk.

But just for a moment,
You took the time to see
And appreciated the pleasure in Nature
When you sat beneath that tree.

We are so lucky
That we share this beautiful world,
As Nature's seasons alter
And her wonders are gently unfurled.

No war at the moment,
To spoil all this peace,
Just the sun setting gently
And memories to keep.

SUE COCKAYNE (BURNTWOOD)

SIGHTLESS

I can't see the daffodils,
The bright blue sky or the rolling hills,
So I have a friend with me,
Who guides me where I can't see.
I can smell the scented air
And I sense the wild flowers there,
I can hear the tumbling brook
And the call of the big black rook.
Then we'll lay down on the soft, green grass
And let the long day gently pass,
With the summer sun on my cheek.
What greater pleasure could I seek?
Many hours we will stay,
Loth to go upon our way.
When meadow lark has chanced along,
And we're in tune with Nature's song.
Now time, as always, has come to pass,
Come on then, my canine lass,
For we must up and wend our way,
But haven't we spent a glorious day?

G BRYANT (HUMBERSTON)

IN MY GARDEN

I knew that God was in my garden,
for I felt His presence there,
in the birds, the bees, the apple trees,
I sensed Him in the very air.

He spoke to me in the whisper
of the gentle breeze around;
I knew that He was there beside me,
as I stood upon the ground.

The sun's bright rays seemed brighter
and His love filled my very soul.
That most wonderful morning in springtime
for such love had made me whole.

GLAN GREY-JONES (NORTHAMPTON)

TELL ME WHY

Tell me why I don't like summer
With the sun beating down on me
Tell me why I don't like summer
When I can be footloose and fancy-free
Tell me why I don't like summer
Watching kids playing in the park
Tell me why I don't like summer
Listening to owls hooting in the dark
Tell me why I don't like summer
People laughing, having fun
Tell me why I don't like summer
With barbecues and hot dogs in a bun
Tell me why I don't like summer
When you can be doing up your home
Tell me why I don't like summer
When you could holiday in Rome
Tell me why I don't like summer
When the funfair comes to town
Tell me why I don't like summer
When you go to the circus and see a clown
Tell me why I don't like summer
Seeing ducklings on a nest
Tell me why I don't like summer
When eating ice cream is the best
Tell me why I don't like summer
With the birds singing in the trees
Tell me why I don't like summer
Sitting outside having a cream tea
Tell me why I don't like summer
Whilst walking in a cool summer breeze
Tell me why I don't like summer
Can anybody, please.

KAREN MORGAN (CORBY)

KEEP ON DREAMING YOUR DREAMS!

(THIS POEM IS BASED ON CINDY HUMPHREY, THE SHOPPING TV PRESENTER, WHO SAID SHE'S A FIRM BELIEVER IN THE DECISION TO KEEP ON DREAMING YOUR DREAMS)

The wisest, kindest words of all,
'Keep on dreaming your dreams!'
Exciting, dreamy dreams enthrall
Beyond your well-planned schemes!
Let fancy thoughts fly through the night,
Like moths and angels do!
Like planes flown by Brothers Wright
Across the midnight-blue . . .

Each teensy-weensy human soul
Has faith the world can't see,
Yet there it waits to take control,
To set your spirits free!
Its childlike essence can't be rushed!
Its miracles take time!
It's well-protected, can't be crushed
And truly quite sublime!

Take time apart from worldly woes . . .
Refresh yourselves, dear friends . . .
Pray daily, for we know God knows
And on Him all depends!
So always wish upon a star,
No matter how life seems!
Heaven's above, here, near and far . . .
'Keep on dreaming your dreams!'

DENIS MARTINDALE (GEDLING)

Summertime

Summer was full of sunshine,
Birdsong and flowers,
Days by the sea,
Gentle waves and the taste of brine.

Summer now is cold and grey,
East winds and heavy showers,
Huddling in the conservatory,
Waiting for the sun to shine.

And what of summers yet to be?
Blackbirds and roses?
Stormy days and starless eve?
Who can predict? Wet or fine?

MEGAN HUGHES (MOULTON)

In No Time

In order to escape doorbell and phone
I ventured to my favourite garden seat
And there I settled down to lay back - prone,
Relaxed, allowed the summer sun to beat
Straight down from out a clear azure sky.
I felt there was no movement in the air
I heard no sound, no song, no bark, no cry,
While no branch swayed nor any leaf did stir
This peaceful scene becalmed me now until
I knew my stream of consciousness was blocked
I had no thoughts but yet awareness still.
It came to me that *time* itself had stopped.
I was at one with every shrub and tree;
Epiphany! . . . I sensed *eternity!*

DAVE BROUGH (SOUTHAM)

THE CHASM

There is a world inside my head
where other people scream.
Not me.
Voices and faces
not my own.
Ghosts
and relics of people unknown.
In my world,
my nightmare nocturne dream-world,
there are terrors
fit-to-frit.
I close my eyes and see
the lunatics in their dark abyss,
twisting and writhing and calling
for me.

I hear my name in a thousand tones,
a million inflections,
the urgency conveyed in decibels
from a desperate Hell.
My People.

In my world of dark and shadow
there are people crying.
Their shrieks, like jet-black needles,
pierce my ears.
Amazing no one else can hear.

The shrill sound splits my synapses,
taut strings fit to snap.
Severed
I spin away into the chasm
and I begin to scream.

MICHELLE AUSTIN (BEAUMONT LEYS)

Barbecue Summer

The ants are in the jam again
And I think it looks like rain,
But wait, is that a patch of blue
A ray of hope shining through,
The party's on, the barbie's out,
Chicken wings and rainbow trout.
I'll get the mower, cut the grass,
Perhaps these clouds will pass.
But no, what's that a'thunderin'?
Phew! It's next-door's wheelie bin.
I'll fetch the gazebo from the shed,
Oh God, I wish I'd stayed in bed.
The poles are missing, the cord is broke,
I think I'm going to have a stroke.
Light the gas, the bottle's empty,
That'll cost another twenty.
In the store I bump into Bob,
He says, 'I'm having a barbie, come join the mob.'
An antipodean day was had by all,
(As far as I recall)
So this is my advice to you,
Go to someone else's barbecue!

MARK MOULDS (KIMBERLEY)

GOOD OLD YORKSHIRE TEA

Yorkshire tea to me
Is pure enjoyment
It's utterly heavenly
It makes me content

It perks me up in an emergency
Because I love the taste
With Yorkshire tea
There's certainly no waste

For Yorkshire tea's a message
No matter what your age
It's enjoyed in many a home

It's of prestigious quality
It oozes excellence
There's nothing like Yorkshire tea
For its intense flavour has prominence

So if you visit my home
And knock upon my door
You'll have the best cup of tea known
Once you're in I'll pour

WALTER MOTTRAM (HEDNESFORD)

Summertime in Malvern

It's summertime in Malvern, a pretty hillside town,
Where people come and frolic on hillsides green and brown,
Proud bells of Priory pealing, resounding far and wide,
Call joyfully to travellers, to Malvern's green hillside.

How sweetly skylarks singing, notes echo in the air,
'Neath shade of leafy foliage, come rest and linger there,
By crystal stream descending, bright sunlit dappled pool,
A timelessness pervading amidst the emerald cool.

The hilltops high are calling, so rise and slow ascend,
A pathway steeply climbing winds upwards to the end,
The weary walkers thirsting, at last the summit reached,
Then round in wonder gazing lay splendour at their feet.

Fair vista before us the Severn Vale,
Blue hills of Wales westward, horizon growing pale,
Serenely time is passing amongst the hills so calm,
Until the day is fading find peacefulness and balm.

With lighter step tread downward, a star to guide the way,
As happy hearts go homeward at the closing of the day,
Sweet bells below still pealing, sound on the pathway down,
A farewell to the people bids Malvern's sleeping town.

BETTY MEALAND (UPTON-UPON-SEVERN)

Summertime

The warmth of the sun shining down on my back
and seeping right into my bones,
I'm sure it must have a detecting device
'cause on my aching muscles it hones.
I quickly forget the winter that's passed
with its snow and its frost and its rain,
I suddenly realise summer is here
and I start to feel human again.
Coats are discarded, cardigans too,
into cupboards and drawers they are packed.
Out comes the shorts, which enable my legs
to absorb the sunshine they have lacked.
Out in the garden there is work to be done
beneath a sky that is bright azure-blue,
The reward for this effort is colour that comes
from the flowers of every hue.
My skin is now turning a deep golden brown
and my hair is becoming quite bleached,
I suddenly realise with contentment and ease
that a state of well-being I've reached.
I wish this contentment could last all year through
the feeling is really sublime,
But that's unrealistic, I'm sure you'll agree,
so we'll just wait for next year's summertime.

DOREEN COOK (SUTTON AT HONE)

PASSING STORM

The clouds o'erhead were thunder-black.
A stinging rain came hissing down
Upon the parched and thirsty land.
Stream-waters turned a muddy brown.

Then lightning struck a tall, straight oak;
It split with mighty crack
As if by monster axe hewn down.
The storm went on its track.
The summer roads they couldn't cope,
And water streamed down every side.
And no birds flew and no birds sang,
Each found a place to hide.
Suddenly the sun burst through,
On moving clouds shone bright.
A rainbow end now blossomed forth -
Bold colours to delight.

The storm moved on; a peaceful calm
Embraced the gleaming hill.
As we emerged from shelt'ring barn;
Of sweet air had our fill.

JIM LAWES (HEREFORD)

ONCE WISHED

My eyes, you know, they look for you
My arms, though empty, wait for you
My thoughts, you know, are there with you
My heart, as ever, is full of you
My lips, you know, just speak of you
My smile, though bright, is shone by you
My thrill, you know, is to be near to you
And my wish, the wish, once wished by you.

DENNIS THOMSETT (DARTFORD)

Summer Treasures in My Garden

Sitting in the garden
Surrounded by shrubs and trees
I watch as the colourful flowers
Are visited by the bees

Then there's the family of bullfinches
Flitting from tree to tree
Suddenly they fly down
To eat food, left out by me

The buddleia attracts the butterflies
With its velvet purple fronds
And the family of bullfinches
Are drinking from my garden ponds

Where the sparkling goldfish
Leisurely take their time
To swim around the fountain's droplets
Dancing in balletic line

Does one ever wonder
What summer means to me?
Just sitting in the garden
With the flowers, birds and bees

To enjoy the world around me
And appreciate life's good
Who needs to wander far from home?
To see such treasures; I never would!

NIGEL LLOYD MALTBY (FISHTOFT)

SUMMER WARMTH

The winter has cast its cold, cold chill,
Locked in my heart the warmth of summer lies still,
The wind blows the driving sleet in my face,
But all I can feel is the heat of that summer paper chase.
That's where we first met, that Sunday in June,
The summer months have passed by so soon.
We were inseparable from June to September,
Clear across the world I wonder if you remember.
Your visa ran out and you had to return home
And now I feel so very alone.
I never meant to fall in love with you,
It just happened - what could I do?

Mid-December now, winter winds gust and screech,
Australia means it's summer and you can sun on the beach.
But as I close my eyes I can still feel the warmth we shared,
If we were together I wonder how our love would have faired,
Would it have blossomed like daffodils encouraging spring,
Or withered like leaves that the autumn can bring?
I guess I'll never know but deep in my love torn frame
Lies the summer warmth, calling your name.

LYNN SCATCHERD (MANSFIELD)

SUMMERTIME

Summertime is the time of the pretty butterfly
A time to let her beauty catch your eye
Time for lovely flowers big and small
So we can enjoy the perfume from them all
It's a time for barbecues, picnics and frolics in the sand
And a time for lovers to stroll hand-in-hand
It's a time for animals and birds with their young
To teach them how things should be done
And it's a time for colours, bright and free
To gladden the heart of you and me
A time for nature to burgeon on its way
To bring pleasure to each and every day.

LADY M (BOWTHORPE)

TO MY CHILD

Come take my hand, dear child of mine
And together we will roam
Across the meadow where wild flowers grow
Here on our island home.
We'll find a summer garden
Softly sheltered - bright with flowers
And listen to the songbirds sing
As we laze away the hours.

The winding lanes will beckon
As we travel mile on mile,
The beauty of the countryside
Whispers - 'Sat and rest a while.'

When the twilight hour is near
We'll homeward wend our way
Reflecting back upon the path
And the joys we found today.

The things we take for granted
Are a precious gift that we
Who love this land, dear child
Hold in trust for all to see.

EILEEN COMBELLACK (LOUGHBOROUGH)

SEASIDE

A sandy shore
Grey, green sea
There stands a child
In ecstasy
Brown, pale hair
Across her eyes
Small brown body
Sturdy thighs
Jumping every tiny wave
Showing Dad she's not afraid
Wanting not, the proffered tea
Enjoying space, sky and sea.

PAULINE HILL (LITTLEOVER)

Walking the Dog

St Mary's bells are ringing . . .
A happy song of praise;
A thrush is also singing,
Before the misty haze
As evening spreads its moisture
Refreshing all that grows
The trees have formed a cloister,
Soft grass beneath my toes.

The coolness of the evening,
So gentle from the day
When heat, quite overwhelming
Can burn our skin in ray.
My trusted friend and I will
Wander out together,
In silence and tranquil bliss
Delighting in the weather.

PEARL BURDOCK (WHITTLESEY)

Cruel Summers

Cruel summers, God's torment as they ravish from the sky,
Twisting the destructive hatred in the savagery of the needles' eye
Crashing the apocalyptic chaos of this Devil's tempered storm
Now the famine of misfortune leaves us lost and forlorn.
Millions left homeless in the carnage of defeat
Soul-destructive chaos
Lies in the mutilated bodies that amass under feet
No food, no water, only despair
You would think our God would offer us forgiveness
But as much as we pray
I'm left begging, does He really care?
Each year another disaster and we pray never again,
I'm losing faith in my religion as I call out once again.

SID (AKA STEVE ALLEN) (STOCKINGFORD)

Summer

We wake in the morning to the sight of the sun
And now we know our summer has begun -
The lambs are now turning into sheep
And the cows over the hedge at us peep -
The birds start to sing and are in good voice
Where to go for our holidays we have to make a choice

Apples and pears on the trees look very good fruit
The farmers and beaters are out on a shoot -
Bales of hay are ready in the field
Farmers are pleased with the amount of the yield -
Walkers go down sign-posted tracks
They look very loaded with bags on their backs

The chartered coaches call in the local pub
With elderly folk from the over-sixties club -
Grass in the garden has started to grow
Folk make quite a noise when they start to mow -
We get out the loungers have tea on the lawn
And bless the day that summer was born

EDDIE OWERS (STANFORD-LE-HOPE)

Raspberries

Strawberries are mighty fine,
With properties that clean the teeth,
But all the same,
They are a faff to hull, slice
And display in a line.

It is the raspberry that I prefer,
Dark fruits are the best
And raspberries are on their way.

With their tip-of-the-tongue sized hole,
Over my tongue
Each raspberry can roll
And be swallowed whole.

VIVIENNE BLANCHARD (HARLOW)

Contrasts

It's the rhythm of the steam train chuffing on its track
now out of hibernation, with the children on its back.
It's busy and it's noisy and it's smelly and it's fun
so they wriggle and they giggle and they are the summer sun.

But then . . .
look up into the lazy blue sky.
Softly, smile softly, see the swifts circle by.
Rest your gaze at the eaves of the thatch
as they flutter-by out and ballet dance back.

It's the squeal of the laughter at the picnic fizz pop
or maybe it's the barbecue with honey on top.
It's busy and it's tasty and it's smelly and it's fun
so they wriggle and they giggle and they are the summer sun.

But then . .
Take a breath as soft summer rains
faces, lift faces, feel the fresh free refrains
Rest your gaze on the late summer rose
where butterflies pause and bumbles repose.

It's the dancing on the grass lawn, lovers side by side
lovers who are mothers or grandpas or new brides.
It's hot and it's happy and it's lively and it's fun
so they wriggle and they giggle and they are the summer sun.

But then . . .
look up into the gentle moon sky
hands, hold hands, see a million stars shine
Rest your gaze on Venus' gold balm
where the twinkle lights cool night time's calm.

PATRISHA REECE-DAVIES (ORTON LONGUEVILLE)

Heartbreak Hill

He stood alone on Heartbreak Hill
His love he could not find
He did not know that she was ill
He thought she had changed her mind

He stood alone on Heartbreak Hill
For many months in vain
The autumn wind, then winter chill
Finally drove him insane

He ended his life on Heartbreak Hill
On a tree that held his rope
He sadly waited there until
He thought there was no hope

She stood alone on Heartbreak Hill
Her thoughts turned to the past
Thinking he would be there still
So sure their love would last

She stood alone on Heartbreak Hill
Her tears did make her choke
If only she had not been ill
Her heart would not be broke

She passed away on Heartbreak Hill
The place they both now rest
Although she never said, 'I will'
Their love was still the best

A young man stands on Heartbreak Hill
Where both his parents died
He never knew his father
Only the tears his mother cried

EDWARD ASHMORE (BURSLEM)

ROAD BRIDGE

They put a bridge over the road
To make it easy for us not to die
In the sift-shift multiplicity of cars
And lorries, buses and the like.
I've never seen anyone but me
Climb its height,
Walk over the speeding fleet below,
Feel it tremble with their impact
And then descend its metal stairs,
Safe now on the other side . . .
Even the old, the uncertain of foot, join the young
In the game of *cross without the bridge,*
Smiling their pride, on the other side
At having outwitted the motor traffic.

My mind, my life
Are faster than cars, a flash-past, crash-blast pantomime of speed
And I so love it
That I want to keep it
And need to protect it
By being careful
. . . and crossing the road-bridge.

EDNA HARVEY (WHITSTABLE)

PROUD SUN

The clouds above so greyly hung
Like shadows in a window
I feel each day my heart is wrung
My mind begins to spin, so
I gather my storms with lightning speed
And lift myself above them
And all is blue, the calm I need
To restore my equilibrium.
Gentle and fierce, the rounding sun
Beams light through cracks of cloud.
I look up and the clouds are gone,
Our star is young and proud.

CHRISTINE MICHAEL (BLIDWORTH)

GRANDMA'S MEMORIES AT THE SEASIDE

When I was young, I loved the sun
Now I'm old I feel the cold.
No matter though what my age
There's one place I always love to go.
Down by the sea and the golden sand
Watching the children in the sea.
Ice creams, kites, sandcastles too
Dogs, cooling down with a cup of tea.
Fish and chips in the evening for supper
Perhaps washed down with a beer or two.
Donkey rides, fairground rides
Watching the seagulls chasing the tides.
Enjoying the day, relaxing away
Reading the paper, books - the puzzles,
Watching the sun set makes me dazzled.
The glorious British seaside, a place to retire
Returning the deckchair I've had on hire.
Yes, now I'm a grandma of four, much older
I look forward to trips even more.
My favourite resort in Norfolk - Cromer!

CHRISTINE RANDS (KING'S LYNN)

THE MEANING OF LIFE

The warmth on my face, as the sun beats down,
The joy of your smile, replacing a frown,
The tickle of rain, as it runs down my back,
And see the hope, peering out of the black.

These feelings are golden, these moments untouched,
Like a beautiful painting, all coloured and brushed,
Like the wind in my hair as I stand and think,
Like the sun in my eyes as I stand and blink.

The meaning of life, if just this is enough,
It's moments like these, that smooth out the rough,
Simplicity is, simplicity does,
But more like my life, simplicity was . . .

JENNA GOODWIN (STOKE-ON-TRENT)

REGRETS

How many women I have known
In my carefree life
Not many, or maybe too many.

Vague memories
Gleaming like flesh under velvet
Disembodied voices, drifting
Like windswept clouds

Now, in the winter of my life,
A fashion parade of shadows
Passes before my eyes.
Why among the many should I
Remember one so vividly?

A sunny day. a secluded beach
The sea the bluest of colours
Tiny chattering waves
Chase after one another
In gentle motion.

A lightly red, shiny nose
A face with fawn-like grace.
Laughing and yet thoughtful eyes
That under trembling eyelashes
Reflect a dream
Of many summers to come.

That day, the months, the years
Have long gone.
Lost in the stream of time.
Often I thought of that dream
But then I was blind
And eagerness of youth
Left me no time to spare for dreams . . . !

VAIFRO MALAVOLTA (MAIDSTONE)

EPPING (LESS) GREEN

Before some ancient cottages
Of ivory and timber brown,
Set light amidst black conifers
Against a pastel sky . . .

There lies a fragile village green -
An island in a graphite sea
Of roads that, almost certainly
Are younger than the grass.

Upon this verdant isle, there grows
A tree - with shining berries clad -
And, next to it, a signpost points
To Epping (and away).

The rowan proudly rules its place -
All crowned with berries, burning red -
Yet fears its realm of no import
To human mind and eye.

For, this once-perfect triangle -
(Joy to behold midst sea of grey),
Is daily disappearing as
The careless few destroy.

Since o'er its apex every day,
Some unconcerned drive - oft times park -
Whose car wheels now have carved a ditch
And emerald's turned to mud . . .

SUSAN DEVLIN (EPPING)

The Smell of the Soil

Sandwiches and flask, packed in his bag,
Safely tucked by his feet;
He climbed aboard his tractor,
And made adjustments to his seat.

A turn of the key, and it burst into life,
His transport, for many an hour:
Plenty of revs to warm it up,
Relying on its power.

The multi-bladed plough was fixed in place,
Tested, to prevent any trouble;
The isolated field was his task for the day,
To turn over the harvest stubble.

His course was plotted, in his mind's eye,
A straight line, his guide for the day;
Ignoring the contours of the field,
As he proceeded on his way.

He edged the tractor to its starting point,
Lowered the plough, to rest on the soil;
Pushed the lever into a low gear,
And started his long, hard toil.

As he moved forward, the blades cut deep,
Angled, so it turned in his wake;
The dampness of the underlying soil,
Exposed, for the sun to bake.

It had been a long, hot summer,
No rain for quite some time;
Everything was dry on the surface,
Even now, the sun still shined.

Facing a fixed point in the distance,
He cut the first furrow in the land;
Checking over his shoulder, to see all was well,
A straight line - exactly as planned.

Pleased with his efforts, as he neared the field's edge,
He raised the blades into the air;
Rotated the heads for the return path,
Fixed his eyes ahead, with a stare.

As the blades sliced, through the hardened soil,
The wheels of the tractor, followed the dip of the rut;
Produced by the outward journey,
When he made the initial cut.

That first furrow is all important,
It's a template, for what will follow;
A straight line, as a guide, will start it right,
As the tractor glides over hillock and hollow.

The smell of the soil, so freshly turned,
Pervades the stillness of the country air;
Flocks of seagulls gather overhead,
Following the tractor, everywhere.

As he progresses, across the field,
What's left behind is quite fitting;
Row upon row of neatly turned land,
Looking remarkably, like a piece of knitting.

To finish off, the new ploughed field,
He skirts around the edges;
Making use of all available space,
Dodging footpaths, and driving round hedges.

The furrows will crumble in the next few weeks,
As the land begins to dry;
Then the farmer can rake it, to break it up,
Under the blue of the autumn sky.

A picture postcard, when viewed from afar,
The gulls, white, against a background of earth;
Rising and settling in the wake of the plough,
Preparing for a new crop's birth.

JIM BELL (CHATHAM)

Southwold

There's nowhere I would rather lie
Than under a tall, wide Suffolk sky;
There's nowhere I would rather be
Than down at Southwold by the sea,
With lovely church, where long I've tarried
And, forty years ago, was married.

Oh give me a Suffolk salt sea marsh
Where, though the east wind can be harsh,
You can hear the sound of the curlew's call,
The lapwing's cry, and see the tall
Grey herons, and best of all can hark
To the glorious, soaring song of the lark;

The lark, who knows that Nature's part
For him is to sing with all his heart
As if he's in his seventh heaven -
With a voice like his he deserves all seven;
His song ascends up, up on high
And away he soars in the tall, wide sky.

Oh give me a marsh of moss and sedge,
Where the reeds stand tall at the water's edge,
Where time stands still and you feel at ease
As the grasses ripple in the sun-kissed breeze;
Where the creeks meander but the drains run straight,
And your cares are lost in a blissful state.

A half mile on and then you reach
Beyond the dunes, the shingle beach
Where the spume-edged waves cause a constant jingle
As they swish and swash up the salt-rimed shingle;
And as you gaze at the grey-green sea
Your thoughts are lost in eternity.

At marsh's edge is Old Quay Inn,
With red Dutch gables, warm within,
Which my wife's ancestor* once kept
As victualler; and smugglers crept
Beneath a tall, wide starry sky;
For there 'the gentlemen' passed by.

Oh give me a beach where wild waves roar
And break upon an east coast shore;
Or give me a sheltered harbour wall
For fishing from where seagulls call.
Or boats that land a treasure that's
The best of all - a catch of sprats.

Oh give me a town with a lofty white -
Painted lighthouse and its warning light;
With seven greens and guns on a hill;
An ancient town, where time stands still;
A town that's graceful and, though small,
Is full of charms that never pall.

And none can find, how far they search,
A finer fifteenth century church,
With fleche on roof, whose porch and screen,
Whose font and pulpit must be seen;
And Southwold Jack, who knows full well
Has, every hour, to smite his bell.

Then after church and parson's tale
A pint of splendid Adnam's ale
Or, if you wish, a glass of wine
Is good to have before you dine;
The Swan's the place or else *The Crown,*
The pick of hotels in the town.

And, most of all, what I aspire
To do when I at last retire
Is to spend my days on the Suffolk coast
In that little town that I love the most;
It's there, beneath that tall, wide sky
Of Southwold that I wish to die.

* Sophia Smith d 1891

BILL SCHAEFFER (SEVENOAKS)

Recollections

A late summer's day, a few years back
Complete with cagoule and haversack
We walked the Southern Downs.
The views were fantastic - the air was keen,
Not many people to be seen
The day we walked the Downs.

Rabbits scuttled around our feet,
The sky-lark's song from afar was sweet
Welcoming us to the Downs.
Late summer, yes it may have been
Yet wild flowers in plenty were to be seen
The day we walked the Downs.

Time to go, with a sad farewell
To poppies and orchids and blue speedwell
Blooming that day on the Downs.
Bales of straw then caught our eye
Stacked gleaming and gold 'gainst the evening sky,
As we turned our backs on the Downs.

MARIE LEPPARD (LEIGH)

Twisted Emotions

Upon my shoulder
a whisper sits
speaking sweet nothings
in thy ear
is it you
my dear departed
come to watch me
never let me forget the
oh how I loved you
why did you leave me
so empty
help me
leave me
I must move on.

THOMAS BAKER (HIGH HALDEN)

THE WANTON LOVER

There was a silence between us that day
And she wore that dress, the one she wore the first time
That swung about her heels and fell loose at the shoulders
As we kicked up sparks that barely smouldered

But still no words arise from the wanton lover's breath
Who could never again love so passionately like the
First time . . .

Who dared to question what love is unlike the
First time . . .

And could never say those words replete
For every love declared that missed the beat

For her malign arrowhead resides still within this chest
And what remains of spirit wants none of the rest

For want of love and life will never cease
What fickle vanity pervades such peace

PETER LEE (RUSTHALL)

THE DARKEST DAYS BEFORE THE DAWN OF SPRING

While walking in the woods today,
Amongst the leaves, brown, crisp and dry,
With little light to lift the sky,
The darkest days before the dawn of spring.
But in the gloom my eyes can see,
Bright green shoots are pushing through,
Promising a fine display of bluebells,
And the celandine - with her tiny golden face,
Will bring back beauty to this place
And with these thoughts of new life born,
My heart begins to sing,
On this dark day before the dawn of spring.

CYNTHIA SHUM (YOXALL)

Ode to Summer

Oh, the joy of summer.

The air, heavy with the scent
Of flowers and new mown grass.
The warmth of the sun as we
Stroll along.
The bees busy darting from flower
To flower.
Butterflies, a joy to behold.

It's nice not to wear lots of
Jumpers and coats to keep warm.

I can hang out my washing.
It smells so lovely in the
Warm fresh air.

Summer is so transient, before
We know it, autumn has come . . .
Each of our seasons have their
Own character, and shape.
When winter arrives our foliage,
Our flowers, are mostly gone
'Oh dear,' we sigh, it's so cold
And damp.
Of course, next year, we await
The arrival of spring, then again
Summer is a-coming . . .

SYLVIA SMALLMAN (TAMWORTH)

BUTTERFLY

Where are you going as you flutter by
with your wonderful colours, oh butterfly?

What can you taste, what can you see,
with your rugby shirt on, you big bumblebee?

Are you really happy, can you tell us a tale?
Slug with home, slow slippery snail.

You're always around, do you ever get lost?
You're annoying and scary you stinging bad wasp.

Why do you buzz around at full throttle?
You're only a fly, you giant blue bottle.

Do you really eat soil, will you ever learn?
Slithery, slithery, garden worm.

Why can you carry things heavy and giant?
You're only minute, you small little ant.

What's it like as you climb over rubble,
in your hard suit of armour, shiny black beetle?

Can I watch you spin that web bigger and wider,
Mr hairy long-legged, wriggly spider?

They're all in our world around us each day,
crawling and flying, in their own special way,
we share this big place with every insect,
living their lives, so show them respect.

JONATHAN RHODES (CHESTERFIELD)

Through the Eyes of Scampy

I turned up on your doorstep, and you took me in.
My coat was quite a mess, and I was very thin.
You provided me with food, and saucers of milk.
Now I am beautiful, and my coat is like silk.
For me, the first of February is a memorable day.
I had no home to go to, I was just a stray.
I came through your cat flap and made myself at home.
Then for three or four hours a day, I would go and roam.

What was I looking for? Nobody knows.
I often heard you say, 'She comes and she goes.'
But now I have your heart, and you have mine.
I have a *purr-fect* life, everything is fine.
I know how to get your attention, by scratching a chair.
Then I start on the carpet and drive you to despair.
Then I often get called a b****r! but that is not my name.
I will only answer to Scampy, the name you gave me when I came.
Thank you both for your love and care.
For giving me a home for us to share.

Lots of purrs, Scampy.

BARBARA RUSSELL (TUXFORD)

Journey Through Summer

Winding paths through daisies, in leafy wooded glades,
Sunlight sifting through the trees revealing hidden shades,
Blues, greens, browns, yellows, all the eye can hold,
All the different colours are something to behold,
To sit awhile on tufted grass and feel the sun's warm glow,
Or splash through pebbled streams, as soft warm breezes blow,
Lazy days when snow-white clouds drift on soft blue skies,
Making different shapes appear before artistic eyes,
Wild flowers in their clusters, nestling in the grass,
Throwing out their beauty to people as they pass,
Capture all this magic in your heart and carefully tend,
For summer time is wonderful as nature did intend.

MAGGY HARRISON (MANSFIELD)

T-SHIRT DAYS

I saunter amongst grassland
Fluffy clouds move in
To ponder life's plan and when
Does it begin?
Summer's come back,
It gets under your skin
Jogging, skipping, trying to stay slim,
Back-to-school adverts
Before we broke up
Picnics, gardening
A borrowed library book.
Cyclists serviced their sturdy ride
Energetic enthusiastic go flow with the tide
Wimbledon strawberries
All mishmash caps
Lollies, ice cream
Food all low fat.
Salad days
Waterways attract tourists all day
Hosepipe bans, parade's noise and stands
Candyfloss evaporates away
Bobbing boats sprawl idle
We focus on the pool.
Squawky greedy gulls eat till they're full
Dotted wan cottages built around the hills,
Countryside, seaside this paradise thrills.
Daylight, sunlight so superior to me,
Happy days you lounge away.
Yet Mother Nature returns
Hot summer days
Our dreams unfazed
We tan and laze and burn.

ANGELA ALLEN (WESTON COYNEY)

Sweet Remembrances

This season
Our garden is wearing
Muriel's pink lacecap hydrangea
With a flounce of red peony from Betty
Ethel's Hebe is wagging
Gloved fingers of white lace
Which when scattered
Resembles confetti
Jean's honeysuckle
Trumpets the sun
Don's Virginia creeper
Spreads a radiant glow
Tom's fragrant rosa mundi;
Rambles on
Cyril's crown imperial
Reigns supremely yellow
Thelma's begonias
Flash an orange sensation
Iceland poppies from Alec
Wave cool pastel flora
Rose and Mick's Chilean vine, saffron-clad
Worships a south-facing corner.

Wilf and Clare are ever present
Around the herb garden
Memoried with parsley, sage, rosemary and thyme
Their notching minty green fingers
I fondly remember
Whilst I'm grafting
Dibbling and puddling in rhyme.

LUCY GREEN (BURGH-LE-MARSH)

Blue Skies

I sit outside just to watch
The beautiful blue skies
With clouds afloat
A flaming sun shining bright
The birds singing to me
In the trees above
Flowers in an array of colour
Bumblebees humming away
As they work
Blue skies every day
Oh what heavenly days
So sweet, so sweet
Is life
Blue skies every day
Help to pass the time away
Give them to me
This is what I pray

JUDITH MARY DRINKHILL (REDDITCH)

Clouds on a Summer Day

A bright blue sky, with clouds floating by,
Enormous balls of pure white cotton wool.
Clouds as soft and inviting as huge marshmallows,
Drifting endlessly onwards across an azure-blue sky.
Clouds high as the heavens slowly moving,
Clouds low and far away in the distance,
Clouds just peaking above the horizon.
Surrounding the pale green trees,
Blue, green and brilliant white,
The colours of an English summer day.

PATRICIA BISBEY (STOURBRIDGE)

Ode to Old Age

Next month I will be eighty-three
That's fairly old as you can see
The clock is ticking it never stops
Old Father Time is licking his chops
But wait one minute
Hang on there, don't rush
This old girl does not need a push
Life is unfolding God holds the line
He is the one who finally calls 'time'
Whatever he plans will be OK by me
I've had a good stretch
What will be, will be
But just for a minute, I've got a request
Could I stay a bit longer
Even though you know best
So much to settle so many to love
Perhaps then I'll be ready
To fly like a dove.

ANGELA MAGUIRE (SMETHWICK)

An End of a Perfect Summer's Day

Walking along the riverbank at the end of a hot summer's day,
breathing in the salty air while the breeze blows the cobwebs away,
throwing off the lethargy that the heat has left behind
while water rippling up the shore helps soothe your troubled mind.
The sight of the many seabirds landing on the beach to roost,
Lift your jaded spirits and gives your whole being a boost.
The setting sun sends streaks of colour marching across the sky
to be mirrored on the water as it slowly flows on by,
as the sun sinks and disappears, and your feet turn homeward bound,
the moon takes the place of the sun in the sky, casting its light all around.
How could one not be moved, by sounds and sights such as these,
how could one ignore the scent, carried on the evening breeze.
It's the perfect way to end a hot summer's day and to find some relief from the heat,
and to thank the Lord for being alive, to enjoy such a wonderful treat.

B M GREENWOOD (BARTON-ON-HUMBER)

Happiness

My favourite thoughts of summer
Are when we were kids
The tar so warm on our feet
Bottles of water and just a few sweets
Head for the woods and carpets of flowers
No coats in sight, we'd dance to the showers
Butterflies, bees, gnats by the score
We didn't care, as we rolled on the floor
Happy we were! Without any money
Everything said, was immediately funny
Laden with flowers we'd make our way home
No one to call us, there was no phone.
Muffins for tea, then in the tin bath
Did as were told, or we'd feel her wrath
Tucked up in bed, clean and content
All say our prayers, were all Heaven-sent!

E CORR (CORBY)

Dronfield Summer Morn

A butterfly rests on a chosen bloom,
Bees are buzzing their usual tune,
The sun burns bright in an azure sky,
And two calling birds fly swiftly by.
Strawberries peep 'neath their covers of green.
Whilst the bees gather pollen to present to their queen,
Princess of the garden, the beautiful rose,
Awakens, unfurling her red velvet clothes,
Oh beautiful morning, what more can I say?
Than praise be to God for this wonderful day.

MARGO RONDELL STORER (DRONFIELD WOODHOUSE)

The Desert

Amid the shifting sands of folded time
Unremitting contours redefine.
Abrasive winds, the rocks torment
Where heat and cold crack and rent,
Letting footloose grains of sand
Escape to vagrant dunes unplanned.

Landscapes with asymmetry all their own
Poised elegance released from stone.
Deserts sprinkled with volcanic sands
Transform to marbled magic lands.
Such visual delights full of surprise
Match the wondrous night skies.

Great pyramids defy advancing sand
With bases wide and inclines planned.
The Neza lines clearly display
Unsolved symbols of yesterday.
Hidden Petra desert's surprise
Oasis to travellers' eyes.

Reclusive sages have deserts sought
Where emptiness condenses thought.
With ego subdued and senses aware
Learning is etched with meticulous care.
Yet mirages will tease and try,
Create illusions, question why?

Answers exist, the Rosetta stone
Yielded secrets long unknown.
Wisdom like gold, does not rust
Yet often lies buried in the dust.
What designs once carefully planned
Are lost and abandoned in the sand?

H D HENSMAN (SIBBERTOFT)

OUR SUMMER DAYS

I sit here in my armchair,
And think of times long past,
When in my younger courting days,
Our journeys they were vast,
No coffee shops to pass our time,
We had to go for walks,
And we were very lucky,
As we had some lovely parks,
We've a glorious arboretum,
With its scenery so grand,
An enormous lake for fishing,
And it even had a bandstand,
We would listen to the music,
As we ate our picnic lunch,
What finer place to spend our time,
We enjoyed it very much,
It cost us not a penny,
To while away our days,
We looked forward to the weekends,
As we strolled in the summer haze,
It's still there in its glory,
For everyone to see,
I hope you enjoy your time there,
I know it brought pleasure to me.

MAVIS FRY (WALSALL)

SHARP AUGUST BREEZE

On a leafless branch
The willow tree
Swings the thin ghosts
Of summer.

DAVID R SMITH (LONGNOR)

Living in Ashford

I am living in Ashford, boy oh boy
With the river for a toy
Swimming, fishing and all the rest
A spot of poaching, yes oh yes.

I am living in Ashford, boy oh boy
We can watch cricket on Sunday while drinking beer
Who hit the ball last Monday night
That broke Jim's greenhouse roof not in sight.

I am living in Ashford, boy oh boy
How about a raft race in Wells week
Or making a wish in the well
Just be careful what you wish for I might tell.

KEITH L POWELL (ASHFORD-IN-THE-WATER)

Summer Flowers

With tender touch, she snips away,
Pruning here and shaping there,
Creating an image in her mind,
Planting bulbs with loving care.

In wet or dry, skies blue or grey,
You'll see her gently strive,
With little touches every day,
To bring her dream alive.

Her fingers stiff with passing age,
With shawl on shoulders, keeping warm,
She tends and weeds and gradually,
The masterpiece is being born.

Now, at last, the time is here,
Reward, for all the gruelling hours,
With cup in hand, she sits and smiles,
Her garden filled, with summer flowers.

CAL PEARSON (KINGSHURST)

MAY

Each day's getting warmer
Spring is slipping away.
Summer's standing in the wings
Not so far away.

Lots to do in the garden,
Clearing away spring flowers.
Making room for summer plants,
Soon fills in the hours.

Children thinking of summer days,
Exams a thing of the past,
Long summer days before us
Holidays at last.

God gives us the strength to do these jobs,
Let's be ready when summer comes,
So we can enjoy those long sunny days,
There's nothing we can't overcome.

HAZEL PALMER (SWADLINCOTE)

SUMMERTIME FOR ME

Summertime is a time of joy and fun,
Laughing all day long and baking in the sun.
A nice ice-cold beer while the BBQ is burning,
With all your friends around until the sun goes down.
A walk around Clumber Park, a dip in the lake,
You can stay all day until it gets dark.
To the pub we must go I'll buy the round
Drinking throughout the day not a drop of rain in the sky,
I love summertime.
But now it's nearly over and winter is on its way
So people will pack their bags and go away to somewhere hot.
Maybe one last BBQ while it's still light,
We will turn the music up and party into the night.
That's why I love summertime.

CRAIG STANLEY (MANTON)

BYE-BYE, BEAU BOGLES

(THIS WAS WRITTEN (IN APRIL 1991), AT THE REQUEST OF A FRIEND - THE MOTHER OF A SON AND DAUGHTER-IN-LAW WHO LIVE IN THE ORKNEYS. THEIR CAT HAD JUST DIED AND SHE WANTED TO SEND THEM A MEMENTO/EPITAPH. APPARENTLY, WHEN THEY WALKED DOWN TO THE SEAFRONT BOGLES WOULD FOLLOW THEM, ON TOP OF THE SEA WALL!)

'Farewell', alas, to dear old Bogles -
What will we do without him?
We've been like slaves of Eastern Moguls -
He had that air about him.

He'll be by wives and offspring missed,
So many share our loss.
The definitive polygamist -
To them he was 'The Boss'.

He had no need to seek them out -
His ladies came to call!
Of his appeal he had no doubt -
They loved him, one and all.

Though he welcomed strangers to his house,
He might say, *'That* chair's *mine!'*
But willingly he'd share a louse
Or give their shoes a shine!

'Whiskas' was his favourite food -
He downed it by the tin
But still he brought, when in the mood,
Dead birds and rabbits in.

His hunting prowess knew no bounds -
Sometimes his quest took days.
He caught more than a pack of hounds,
Such were his cunning ways.

He would, without much hassle,
Have jumped a fast jet liner
To play 'I'm King of the Castle'
Atop The Great Wall of China.

If there's a place 'up there' for cats,
We know that, by and by,
He'll reach his final goal, and that's
A harem in the sky!

STAN TRENT (COVENTRY)

JUST DREAMING

Their vocational days have passed them by,
Tomorrow they will have to fly
Back to a world of reality,
But refreshed with a new vitality.

They've bathed in the sea, lain on the beach,
Each to each other a perfect peach.
They've kissed and cuddled along the way,
Each to each other a perfect day.

They've climbed the hills, walked for miles,
Enjoyed the dales and rested on stiles,
They've dangled their feet in cooling streams
And refreshed themselves on lots of ice cream.

They've been to the races and backed each way
A horse still outstanding at the end of the day.
They've hired a car to go further afield
But where did they go to? Lips are sealed.

They've been to the cinema and to shows.
When you're on holiday anything goes.
In nightclubs they've danced the hours away
Almost to the break of another day.

But now it's all over, they're homeward bound.
Is it true love that they have found?
Will he be her Jack and she his Jill?
One day they might just say 'I will'.

PERCY WALTON (LEEK)

Summer 1914

In silver-gilt arrayed, the clouds float high;
Our boat glides gently down the golden river;
A swirl of starlings sweeps across the sky;
An otter surfaces: the waters quiver.

A timid vole peeks shyly from his lair;
A single leaf turns slowly on the river;
A lapwing calls; and in the fading air
A bumblebee begins her last endeavour.

Now, as the sun sinks down behind the hill
Swans hide away their heads beside the river.
A blushing stillness reigns: could human will
But make this tranquil moment last for ever!

And now a baleful crimson mars the sky:
It warns us of another, alien river -
In foreign fields we lie, my friends and I,
By folly sacrificed, to sleep for ever.

GRAHAM SAXBY (WOLVERHAMPTON)

Alone In My Thoughts

Sometimes it would be easier to disappear
so be no more, and have no fear,
what life throws at you sometimes is most unfair,
what can I do but feel despair,
yes life feels one big struggle right now,
I need some changes, but don't know how,
Thinking of sad events I can do nothing about
my mind's in a turmoil and I want out,
but when I feel low
which is more often than not,
I take a step back, to see what I've got,
focus on the good times not bad
then you'll feel happy not sad.

CHRISTINE FRANCES WILLIAMS (LOUGHTON)

A DAY AT THE SEASIDE

We went for a day at the seaside,
Caught the early morning train,
The sky was blue and cloudless,
Not a sign of rain.
With a picnic of pop and sandwiches,
We sat upon the sand,
Paddled in the sea, jumping the waves,
Tightly holding my sister's hand.
Scoured the beach for pretty shells,
Stashed them safely in Mum's bag,
Helped our brother build a huge sandcastle,
On the top we put a flag.
Dad snoozed in a deckchair,
A knotted hankie on his head,
Whilst Mum smothered us in suncream
(Cos our shoulders were turning red!)
Then a donkey ride, a trip to the fair,
Hot tasty chips to eat,
And a creamy ice cream cornet apiece,
Made a perfect day complete!

LESLEY PAUL (IRTHLINGBOROUGH)

THE LOSS OF A CHILD

My child, to me you are the world,
But sadly the world never got to see you the way I did.
You are the sun that never got to set,
The moon that never got to shine,
You are the story that's not fully told,
The unfinished poem that will never rhyme

I think of all the things we said and did
And all the times we laughed and cried
Although not in my arms today you are always by my side
My child.

COLIN O'REILLY (IPSWICH)

One of Several Possible Endings

The windows crack,
The plates start to break,
The wood, it snaps,
The room starts to shake.

The floor opens up,
As the trees overturn,
The cars are colliding,
While everything burns.

There's dust, so much dust,
As the motorways crumble,
The floor opens wider,
As skyscrapers tumble.

Until there's a silence,
Once heard long ago,
There's finally peace,
And nature can grow.

ED WATTS (KNOWLE)

Nature Is Industrious

Summer in the city
Changes what city means
For nature is industrious.

The block becomes a cliff;
The kestrels think so.
A dragonfly takes to the streets.

A goldfinch turns up
Greyscale to five-ton.
Foxes flash amber in the night.

So much more
Than nowhere roads
Running into infinity.

NICHOLAS ARIS (NOTTINGHAM)

FAST FOOD

My cats are thrilled with ring-pull cans
Cos food comes so much faster.
Their mistress with an opener
Was such a great disaster!
The handle broke or fingers bled,
The cats meantime a-cryin',
'Our tums are empty, we are starved,
Of hunger we are dyin'.'
Of course there are the times when now
The ring pulls off in hand,
The contents still in tin intact,
Such cruelty should be banned!
But all in all, it usually works,
Fur-clad meat loaf on floor
Is fed with meat loaf out of can,
In seconds flat, what's more!
So, here's to progress cat food wise,
Technology is fine,
Next thing they'll have a 'widget'
With their cat milk as they dine.

PAT WILLIAMS (WELLESBOURNE)

SUMMERTIME

What makes summer so special for me,
The sight and sounds of
Children playing happy as can be
Colours of flowers in full bloom
Waiting to be picked to brighten up a room
The village green looking very tidy and neat,
To have a picnic on is a real treat
Plan the day for a walk alongside
Of canal so peaceful and calm
As we stroll along arm in arm
Clouds slowly moving over the clear blue sky
Wishing it could be summer forever and ever
But it is just a dream,
As we have to have wet weather.

PATRICIA WHITTALL (CODSALL)

The Peak District

A hazy day of summer sun
Deer grazing in the parks
A walk in the country
Is there we'll go
To view the sights and scenes
We love to see
Perfect idyllic tranquillity
A babbling stream
Silver fish are jumping
Stepping stones over to the other side
Hills and dales
To climb and descend
And rocks and caverns
Above and below
Who needs to go far away
When a special place can be so near
In the Peak District
On a hazy day of summer sun.

J E WINFIELD (CHADDESDEN)

Beaches

I love to wander on the beach, strolling on the sand,
With the wind blowing, gulls calling, it really is just grand.
Picking the stones, that are so flat, to skim along the sea,
And smell the fish, on the trawler boats, fills my heart with glee.
Under rocks in pebble ponds, are different types of crabs and features,
Some bright coloured, some are dark, all wonderful living creatures,
When it's wet, the beach has charm and a charming feel of peace
It melts your heart, warms your soul, a feeling that won't cease.

COLIN GRIFFITHS (KETTERING)

My Local Church

My local church
In a leafy lane
Churchyard full of mossy gravestones,
In the porch a drowsy bee stings.
By the windowpane,
Door unlocked,
Smelt the musty church odour,
Up in the distance, glows a lamp of deepest red,
Board on the wall, shows church officials.

An old piano stands in the church,
It's been there since Doomsday,
Who knows?
It's a stand-in for the old organ,
Built by you'll never guess! Morgan,
As the old brass plaque shows,
The vestry locked to keep the sacred robe out of reach,
Down each wall tells a story,
Which grants us all a glimpse of glory,
On the stained glass windows,
I prayed to the Lord to keep me safe,
I dropped a coin into the dish by the church door,
Knew I couldn't hang around much longer,
I left behind just what I'd found there,
An atmosphere of prayer.

TERESA WHITFIELD (WESTON-UNDER-LIZARD)

Reflections in a Mirror

One day as I walked by the sea,
In a shop window I did see
A beautiful mirror, it took my eye.
I stood to admire it, by and by
I saw reflections of days gone by.
A beautiful girl so sweet was she,
Her laughter infectious, happy with glee.
Passers-by smiled at this lovely scene
Seeing themselves as they might have been.
The reflection changed a young man was there,
Together they made a wonderful pair.
The love that shone through their eyes so true
Paved a picture of happiness to a life so new.
The paths that they chose were like so many others,
Some bumpy, some smooth, like all young lovers.
But their enduring love for each other was sure
And together they journeyed through life evermore.
A magical scene still very upbeat.
Two babies arrived making the picture complete.
Times were changing, the babies now fully grown
Flew the nest to make homes of their own.
They in turn now their families extended
Made lives so full as Nature intended.
Dark clouds loomed there were days of despair,
Their daughter - an illness - was beyond their care.
The families rallied, the pain was so raw,
Life goes on but not like before.
As time goes on pictures ever changing,
Children had children, their ages far ranging.
The road had been bumpy now safe and sure,
Their love had been tested but was now more secure.
The circle of life nearly complete,
The youngsters, now old, unsure on their feet.
But their love for each other, a story now told
Had lasted a lifetime, more precious than gold.
As I continue to walk on my own.
Memories are there so I'm never alone.
Today is so beautiful, tomorrow who knows.
We'll meet again - that's how life goes.

ELIZABETH TIMMINS (WALL HEATH)

As Time Goes By

Long hours of daylight, short hours of dark
Allows the British summer to make its mark
Thanks to British summer time. We played
Outside as carefree youths. No duties weighed,
Even lightly, on our shoulders. The balmy nights
Meant disturbed sleep. A small price for the sheer delights
Of dawn to dusk sunshine. Did it ever rain?
Our memories don't recall it. Perhaps it's not in vain
That we're selective in our recall
Making memories of idyllic summers available to all.
But, with the passage of years, one's aged frame
Cannot stand the heat and one's main aim
Is to seek solace in the shade. The midday rays
Are far too hot on glorious summer days.
To stay out after tea is no longer a desire
As one eases aching bones before a welcome fire.
The rain is needed too for gardens dislike drought
Certainly Nature's seasons epitomise, without a doubt,
The many stages in the life of Man's ability
With summer coming between childhood and senility.

JOHN W SKEPPER (BURTON-UPON-STATHER)

Summer Beaches

The beautiful warmth of summer sets my heart aglow,
As I awake to see darting dazzling summer rays through my window
That warms the cockles of my heart.
To see breathtaking sun shining days
Which take my breath away.
As I begin my day with shorts and sandals to stroll down life's
Promenade as I see the sun as it goes high in the sky
Shining rays dancing on the seashore sandy beaches.
And time goes by to summer teatime tea.
As alas, the sun starts its journey towards
Evening's sleepy breezes
Till tomorrow,
As I hope in my heart that the good Lord grants me another day
To see sunshine summer beaches.

JOHN BRIAN WATKINSON (CHESTERFIELD)

Cornwall

Seagulls, fishing boats, Cornwall's rocky coast
Place names that start with Port, Saint or Tre'
Giant wind turbines slaves to electricity
High rolling waves crash against the ships' mast
White water pounds beats against jagged rocks
Along treeless coastlines lighthouses lifeboats
Caves below the cliffs images of pirates
Surfers rush to meet the waves fear they mock
Looking like seals in black rubber suits
Ride upon the white manes of wild horses
Claustrophobic meandering courses
Lead down to small fishing ports and hamlets
Each with their own collection of gift shops
Food outlets, Cornish pasties, clotted cream
With a menagerie of houses random
All clustered together white as snowdrops
Built from the black rocks and stones of Cornwall
A few clad in grey slate towards the lee
To hold back the ravages of the sea
A home on dry land to those the sea calls
Fishing trips sea safaris salt sea air
Holiday makers bright lights seaside fairs
All sit together on rocky outcrops
Staring vacantly into the cosmos
Akin to a colony of puffins
Soaking up the golden rays of summer's sun

DAVID M WALFORD (CLEOBURY MORTIMER)

MORNING GLORY

This flower is for you . . .

There are a number of different varieties
But the one for me is the heavenly . . . blue . . . it can take longer to bloom . . .
But when it does bloom, this flower has beautiful . . . blue . . . petals . . .
And it is surrounded by wonderful green heart . . . shaped leaves,
It needs a gardener's daily intake of patience,
But the wait is well worth it,
This flower is for you . . .

This beautiful flower is such a heavenly shade of blue . . .
I watch it bloom . . . in all its morning glory,
The blue . . . is so intense . . . with its yellow centre,
It seems to glow . . . as it opens itself . . . in bloom,
And then reach out to you . . .

The flower is almost saying,
Smell me . . . touch me . . . hold me . . . enjoy me . . .
While I am still alive,
This beautiful flower wants to survive,
It reflects your wonderful blue . . . eyes . . .
When it is in bloom.
This flower is for you . . .

Alas . . . this flower only blooms for one day,
And then it fades away,
You need to sow the seeds each year,
And plant in the month of May.
I will plant this flower for you . . .

DAVID WRIGHT (EAST HUNSBURY)

Hurt No More

The lights go out and I lay down,
Another night without you around,
You left me here sad and alone,
Just went right out, didn't come home.

I sat, I waited, I did not sleep,
I watched the clock, I counted sheep.
The hours passed and there I lay,
I watched the night turn into day.

And if I dare to fuss or complain,
Your anger fuelled by grape or grain,
There is a heavier price to pay,
So quietly again I'll hide away.

Oh please, just see what you have done
Your heavy hands and your vicious tongue.
This time you couldn't talk me round
I ran away never to be found

Years have passed and still I fear,
Nightmares still make me shed a tear
But now as I wake late at night
My body shaking from the fright,

The memories still vivid and real,
The cuts and bruises I still feel
I can reach out and know I'm safe
She'll stroke my hair and kiss my face

Her hands don't hurt but only hold
Her arms that take away the cold
All her energy used for loving
Not for pushing or for shoving.

For now a woman shares my life
We want to be each other's wife,
You broke my body and my mind,
But because of her my soul survived.

SAM SHINGLER (MAIDSTONE)

Picnic 1900

Not another picnic!
Lots of flies and gnats
Grandpa in his flat-cap
Grandma with straw hat.

Dried and curled up sandwiches
Bottles of cold tea
Now we've lost wee George
Wherever can he be.

Baby whining all day long
Cannot stand the heat
Little Willie runs to us
Cowpats on his feet.

Sister in her button boots
Climbing up a tree
Grandma soothing baby
Bouncing on her knee.

Father found our George again
Chasing flocks of sheep
Grandpa sits beneath a tree
Falling fast asleep.

Sister falls out of the tree
I hope she is not hurt
Mother tramples in the mud
Holding up her skirt.

I hate these ritual picnics
They cannot end too soon
One day I'll have a peaceful one
Sitting on the moon!

IRENE DODD (NORTHFIELD)

Summertime

Summer's here which with it
Brings delight
clear blue sky and the sun
shining bright
people out with family
on their countryside walk
children running and playing
while adults talk.
Afternoon picnics are displayed
all over the park
but all are soon home
the minute it turns dark.
Summer brings the smell
of a freshly cut lawn
and the sound of music
playing till dawn
people having barbecues
and cracking open the bubbly.
This is what summer's all about
lovely jubbly.

DIANA STOPHER (PEASENHALL)

Regrets

An invite to a party
I never attended
The photo of a friendship
Broken and never mended
A brochure for a course
On a subject never learned
The contract for an article
Showing the payment never earned
Directions to somewhere
In the life I never chose
A box filled with memories
I want to stay closed

ANDREW FISHER (SKEGNESS)

Summer Rain

The wind-swept, bleak embankment, washed with rain,
Knew no life . . . but for puddles splashing
Under the incessant pouring -
And the swaying canopies
Of trees, thick with trembling
Leaves upon shaking
Branches - and rough,
Sharp billows
Sweeping
Fast,
Past
Weeping,
Blown willows
Brushing 'mongst tough
Reeds as the rushing
River, pitted, surging,
Swirled 'neath the bridge, the eddies
Circling the billows . . . and riding
The water, two swans, graceful, gliding,
Impervious to wind and summer rain.

DIANE ELIZABETH MALTBY (CLIFTON)

I Dreamt of a Summer's Day

Through the winter I dreamt of a tranquil summer's day,
The scent of sweet lilacs and smell of new mown hay.
Enjoying my sunlit garden for endless contented hours,
Or lazily sitting in the shade amongst a host of flowers.

Warm evenings with close friends and meals outside,
While laughter and happy voices on the still air ride.
Or sit quietly with contented thoughts in the fading light,
Listening to a lone blackbird singing late into the night.

JOHN MITCHELL (THURLASTON)

Warwickshire - Enjoy

Enjoy each ventured green leafy Warwickshire lane
stroll, stride, plod and hike before brick houses gain
lung fill history laden air by river, canal, towpath alike
dust down, oil, clean weary shed-housed drop
handle bar bike

Seek remote paths to remarkable villages unseen
take roads and lanes to Cotswold's edge of dazzling green
to Warwickshire's highest point, of name, Ilmington Down
dropping to sleepy village of well earned renown

Admire lichen covered stone roofs atop cottages of mellow stone
in quaint, bow fronted, step-down shop, sample produce home grown
in Ilmington's 'Howard Arms' sup fine Hook Norton ale
partake of fine fare, crackling log fire and laughter of friends -
never known to fail

Replete, stride local lanes to St. Mary's fine Norman Church
seeking out 'Compton Scorpion' Manor, an immensely rewarding
search, grand home of Sir Adrian Beecham, son of maestro Sir Thomas
ending your day to Warwickshire's edge with Morris Dancers
most joyous.

CLIVE BOWEN (HAMPTON-IN-ARDEN)

Easy

A poet finds it easy to write in rhyme
Because he does it all the time
A flower, the sea, the sky
A poet does not have to try
A petal, a wave, a cloud
To a poet they speak out loud
The flower gives colour and a scent
A wave goes back from where it went
Clouds are like great balls of cotton wool
Sometimes dark like a raging bull
To other people this is just nothing at all
To a poet it's like dancing, having a ball

TREVOR BEACH (BIRMINGHAM)

Summer Morn

Hail to this lovely summer's morn
with its deep blue sky
where white clouds float slowly by
and leaves stir in the gentle breeze
to keep us cool beneath the trees.

The silence breaks with cuckoo's call
and skylark sings high above the heath
as we watch it rise and fall
back to its nest beneath.

Hail to this summer morn
where we can sit beside a stream
as it bubbles on its way to waters new
the place where we can sit and dream
pass an hour or two.

We hear the cry of sheep and cattle as they graze
and yonder rooster rouses folk from sleep
the sun rises o'er the hills above the mist
to kiss the gentle rose with drops of dew
and water turns the wheel to drive the mill
as back to the barn the night owl flew.

Hail to this summer morn
cottage gardens at their best
life is surely at its best
and flowers nod their heads to greet the dawn
on this gorgeous summer morn.

JOHN HEWING (SPONDON)

Special Summertime

Summertime picture the scene
Lots of trees different shades of green
Colourful flowers a wondrous delight
Summertime can be a beautiful sight

Summertime walk along any seashore
Sun out shining couldn't ask for more
Watching kids playing in the sea
Summertime is special don't you agree

Summertime with its beautiful sky
Or the beauty in a butterfly
I'm getting old, but my mind is like a boy
Summertime is special and brings out joy

Summertime most people seem content
A good summer seems Heaven-sent
Try to put worrying thoughts to the back of your mind
Summertime is special don't you find

RON DOVE (WEST HEATH)

A Day in the Park

Summer has come,
Time on my hands,
The park is nearby,
Where I can have,
An ice cream, and,
Watch the train,
Go by, while the,
Ducks float on,
The water, they,
Are not the ones,
Ready for slaughter,
While the men,
Play their cricket,
Not to hit the wicket,
What a lovely rest,
Like a fiesta.

BARBARA BROWN (CHESTERFIELD)

SWEET LIFE

Such a rush we are in to have lived and be gone
Destination so dark we're afraid of
In moments of truth do we stop, does it dawn
What on Earth is this life all in aid of?

So much to enjoy if only we could
Just to break from this race and be free
Nature's wealth at our feet if we realise
Endless pleasures in things we can see.

The contrasts in colour that each season brings
The flight of the birds in the air
The antics of insects, the pride in the trees
The appearance of flowers from nowhere.

Smell fresh ploughed earth, and new mown hay
Feel the soft summer breeze on your face
Taste the sweetness of fruit newly plucked from its bush
Hear the thrush sing his magical phrase.

Fall asleep in the shade in the heat of the sun
Paddle barefoot in a clear mountain stream
Climb gentle slopes of the hills all around
Fish in pools with their trout and their bream.

Countless things that abound costing nothing but time
All about us we have them so near
Life is so worth living if lived the right way
Without hurry, worry, or fear.

JOHN COCKBURN (BOTTESFORD)

SHERWOOD TWILIGHT

In a summer's tree-locked dell,
A dappled path I've Reebok'd well.

Often paused in reverence stood,
High on the nous of old Sherwood.

With instinct forest creatures have,
I arrived home safe without satnav.

There to savour new joys I sipped,
And long past dramas without a script.

Short trouser days, macho grazed knee,
No guardian ASBOs, kids went free.

Later carving two names, one heart,
First affaire d'amour, un-epic start.

Grace Kelly swans showcased for us,
Shy, sober newts hid, back row chorus.

Chrome-eyed rabbit, salivating fox,
Fuzz chase escape worthy of the box.

Kingfishers in swift motion Stuka'd,
Pool playing minnows grimly snookered.

Soggy crisp bags, cartons from KFC,
Ubiquitous cans, our designer debris.

The once pristine forest now bereft,
A paradox of takeaways people left.

Almost a Tate Modern in its layout,
Remote, distant, not so way out.

More drama, dark clouds were scanning,
A local builder given outline planning.

To clear the forest, new houses built,
Who was responsible for this guilt?

A rich man with his designs from Hades,
Or simply the hots for a cool Mercedes?

Fair dos he bought his Eden years ago,
Savvy thinking, then land price was low.

His plot grew, ah there's the pity,
Our Forest Town became Forest City.

Now I know why he sold that paradise,
They trashed his land we paid a price.

Now gone forever my summer den,
Its true first joys never come again.

At twilight now under streetlamp's flood,
Wistful, I muse, this used to be Sherwood.

PETER ALVEY (FOREST TOWN)

GIVING MY LIFE

Everyone takes a part of me
they drink me dry, how can this be?
I've always been strong, people rely on that,
all troubles they know I can combat.

My shoulders broad to take the strain
hoping my help will never wane
Everyone thinks I'm a woman of super strength
to ease anyone's pain I'll go to any length

With a smiling face and a healing hand
I'll challenge all illnesses and take a stand
facing all your troubles and pain full on
never giving up till all have gone.

Think positive, be strong all problems seem less,
smile at everyone, that takes away stress.
Look around the world there's trouble and strife,
in your world everything is alright.

I'll take on board your troubles and strife
mulling things over so they come out right.
When people are with me, they tend to say
all their problems seem a million miles away.

JOAN MARRION (OAKHAM)

Our Granny Trip

Each summer we rely on our Enid
To organise trips to the coast
All of us grannies with aches and pains
I suppose I have more than most!

Last year we all went to Whitby
Fish and chips, rock and ice cream
The Abbey was all we thought it would be
And Whitby was beautifully clean

The bus pulled into the car park
We all piled out with our bags
To have a good time was our aim
And not come home until dark!

The day started well - we were all on time
The driver was cheerful that day
The wheels rolled along and we all sang a song
But only the Whitby-wards way!

Three of our ladies went missing!
They wandered away from the group
Without the police searching for them
We'd all have been in the soup!

Restored to the fold we continued
To enjoy all the Whitby delights
Boat trips and whelks and big sticks of rock
Enid checked that we were all alright

Homeward bound with 'loo stops' we motored
Heads nodding in a sea of grey
Happy and full of the day's events
On our lovely Whitby day.

JANE DAY (BARROW-UPON-HUMBER)

JUST DREAMING

Sometimes I do a little daydreaming:
About the days in the distant past,
When we planned, did a lot of scheming,
In a youth that couldn't last.

I long to restore those happy days,
To live them just the same.
But there could never be a way
To live those memories again.

But first, I have to remind myself.
Why do I reason. Why oh why?
Just now, I get a flash back,
That urges me on, to try.

Yes! - It's coming back again.
My delight reached dizzy heights,
I see those people, alas, long gone,
They all seem just the same.

The many years now gone by
I compare them with today.
'Precious youth', is what we enjoyed.
Now all that has gone away.

I prepare myself for the coming years.
To swell the growing ranks,
With aging joints, and worrying fears.
After all, I give my thanks.

I have survived to a grand old age.
I am received with great respect
The things I say, the things I do
Gain more than I expect.

GEORGE S HIGGS (BIRSTALL)

THE GRAND OLD BEAR

He wears a button in his ear -
It's been there all his life -
For it proclaims to all the world
'This bear was made by Steiff'

His paws are frayed, his fur is thin,
His nose is rather battered
But many children loved him, so
These things have never mattered

Now he is worth a fortune
In the value of today,
So he sits there under a dome of glass
And is never allowed to play!

This grand old bear is very proud
(You'll never hear him grumble)
But he longs to join some children
In a game of rough-and-tumble

But now there are no children here
(His owner's grown quite stately)
She dusts the dome from time to time -
He's grown so bored just lately!

A little girl has come to stay!
With bright and smiling face
'Oh Gran,' she cries, 'what a dear old bear -
What's he doing in that place?'

'At auction, Sal, a bear by Steiff
Would fetch a handsome price'
But Sally wrinkles up her nose
And murmurs, 'It's not nice -

- He's all alone, he looks so sad
Oh, Gran, please set him free
He wants to be out here with us -
Let's take him out for tea!'

'Now, Sal, a bear can't eat and drink
He can't feel sad or lonely
It's make-believe to think he can,
He's a teddy bear and only -'

But suddenly Sal's Gran stops short.
And lifts the dome away
For she remembers when the bear
Was her friend of yesterday -

His paws are frayed, his fur is thin,
His nose is rather battered
He may be worth a fortune
But that too should not have mattered -

For Sally loves him!
In his eyes a smile begins to dawn
As Gran and Sally take him out
To picnic on the lawn!

JUNE OLIVER (LEISTON)

WATER-LILIES

The lily
awakens the new day
Heaven's soft light reflects in her eyes -
Like a mirror reflects the water, clouds, the sky
Nothing can intrude in this moment
Not a murmur or sigh
her beauty.

The lily
reflects gentle nature
an angelic pose, peaceful beauty
grace pondering a thoughtful silence, all is still
Nature's beauty all unfurled to see
Heaven and Earth collide
Still waters.

The blue sky
time to stop and wonder
Heaven's soft light reflects in her eyes
Like fairy boats - maybe they sailed in there towards
a peaceful haven, tranquillity
the artist paints beauty
Lilies float.

JENNY AMERY (SCUNTHORPE)

The Leaf

I take upon my morning stroll
In a woodland oh so green
The silence wakes up my soul
And the air it is so clean
The sun peeps through the treetops
As the clouds drift on their way
I sit upon a tree stump and marvel at the day
Just for a little moment I can look inside my soul
Or am I just between Heaven and Earth? For this I do not know
A butterfly flutters past me as it goes up on its way
Perhaps to find some nectar or does it only want to play?
There's a wind in the treetop
Some leaves have broken away
As they float down in the air waves my hand reaches out to save
I will place it in my memory book of events of yesterday
And recall of how it got there on some other distant day
This little leaf I captured it never reached the Earth
The entry underneath it will be its epitaph.

S JACKS (SHREWSBURY)

Times Are Changing

Arriving at the crowded station, we found our train was delayed
There was time for refreshments, our tickets we had already paid.
We saw people with badges, phones and laptops too,
We were conscious of age, as they don't look at you.
With fingers all tapping, they have no time to lose,
They listen with mobiles of anything they choose.
Their life seems so different to the times we once knew.
We had fun in our youth there was so much to do.
No such thing as computers, knowledge was kept in the brain
Mobiles had not been invented, so our ears took no strain.
Let's go back to the good old days, when people had time to talk.
Our ears not glued to mobiles, and quiet roads we could walk.
Life today is so different; it is a rat race we have entered.
It's such a pity our lives are all so technically centred.
But they call it progress, and progress we have to accept
Whether we like it or not, we will all be put to the test.

MARGARET MEADOWS (BURBAGE)

STAINED

The man in the coffee shop has fingers that
Nicotine so lovingly painted. Then he left her.
Those ornamental red flecks aren't masked by it,
Blood. (Or maybe dying his daughter's hair.)
You don't reach his age without a stain or two.
A stain or two. You don't reach his age without
Forgetting or regretting where they came from.
Until you're cupping coffee in those nicotine-
Stained fingers, wondering after red flecks.
Wondering after blood on your hands,
How it came to be there, how to get it off.
And though your fingers are resisting and
The coffee is slowly scalding you hold on;
Blistering through each bloodstain.
Like coffee to the oesophagus he's burning,
Searing through the recesses of his life:
For punishment, for penance, for purgatory,
For the sweet spot at the bottom of a latté.
The man in the coffee shop has fingers
Lovingly painted by nicotine. Blood burnt.

EMILY COTTERILL (ALFRETON)

SUMMER

The men are in their whites,
The cherry is shiny and round,
The green grass is cut finely,
And the stumps are in the ground.

The sun is warm and welcoming,
The opening bowler is not,
The silence reigns around us,
As the batsman plays his shot.

Wicket, four or six,
The crowd will give a cheer
To show their appreciation.
Cricket means summer is here.

LAURA DOBBINS (LOWER BROADHEATH)

THE GLASS BIRD

The little glass bird sat on the ledge
Looking out the window to the outside world
No cage to prevent it from stretching its wings
Just too afraid to fly and be bold

So the little glass bird sits on the ledge
As the folks outside strolled along
A melody flowed through the window
As the lonely bird sang his song

Then one day it heard a voice
Just above its head
'Why do you sit on your ledge and not fly in the sky?'
The little voice said

The bird looked up and saw the source
Of this quiet mellow sound
For above him was this little spider
Spinning its web further down

'I'm afraid I'll stumble and fall'
The little glass bird said
'I'm afraid I'll never recover and . . .
Then I'll never fly at all'

'My dear little bird,' the spider said
'How do you know this is so?
If you think this way, you'll never move forward
Your happiness will cease to flow

You cannot think this way and . . .
Shut your heart for ever more
Life is for the taking, grab it
Be proud and stand tall

Yes you'll stumble, you'll make mistakes
Sometimes you may also trip
But listen to me and I'll teach you
A very important tip

You have to take a chance
And learn to fly high
Because when you grow up, little glass bird
You'll regret that you never tried

Sooner or later, I'll cease to be
But there's so much that I will have gained
When I do go, everyone will know
The sky will fall with rain

But the worst rain of all
Is in your heart
If you make a stumble, if you fall
Learn, and then next time it won't be so hard'

The little glass bird realising his mistake
Thanked the spider and began to sing
His song was bright and cheerful
He felt joy in everything

The window was open, as he looked outside
It was a bright and sunny day
He thanked the spider once more
Then stretched his wings and flew away

LISA BURTON (WEST BROMWICH)

NORTHUMBRIAN MELODIES

Rippling and twinkling with flashing sunbeams
The river meanders slowly down the valley floor.
A small breeze flickers and dancers with the trees
Brushing the lush growth brought on by a fruitful spring.

It seemed that all the life danced to a haunting tune
As the breeze whistled like the Northumbrian pipes.
Each note seeking their passage through the thick growth,
Acting as if the valves of those magic pipes

It was a sound that hill shepherds everywhere recognised
Their loneliness broken with the soft call of the pipes
The wild becoming tamed just in that moment
And the eagles fly high and call as they hear that sound.

A sound that enables the loved ones to feel nearer
Bringing back those far distant memories of years gone by
Memories that had seemed lost by the passing of time
Like the tunes of the past that had been long forgotten.

BARRY SCOTT CRISP (GRIMSBY)

PASSING LOVE

She loved him forever.
Though he tested her so.
Even with such adoration.
He decided to go.

The new love was everything.
Satisfied his human joys.
So he left a wife.
And two little boys.

With all this she still loved him.
With all she had come to know.
She could not release him.
She would not let him go.

This near senior playboy.
Sporting a pony tail.
She could not believe with such arrogance.
Even her love could fail

TREVOR A NAPPER (PETERBOROUGH)

THE PLAY OF LIFE

As a child, we sit in the audience,
to watch the play of life.

As a youngster,
we are given minor roles to play.

As an adult,
we take on the leading role,
as we have learnt so much,
from the play of life.

In our twilight years,
we become an extra,
in a cast of many.

And because sometimes we are lucky,
extras are always needed, and wanted.

JACQUELINE CLAIRE DAVIES (DUDLEY)

SUMMERTIME

A yellow sun hangs in the sky,
The grass is tall and shining,
A lazy butterfly slips by,
On wings of velvet flying.

A haze of blue drifts o'er the corn,
See the pollen rising,
The swallows they come swooping down,
For insects are a-buzzing.

The cattle stand beneath the boughs,
Of trees that are a-spreading,
Their branches wide for all to share,
The shade that they are making.

Summertime is here once more,
The countryside is showing,
Its prettiest face to anyone,
With eyes enough for looking.

OWEN DAVIES (HORNINGLOW)

EVERY DAY'S SPECIAL

Today is a special day, for the rest of my life.
Every day's special, without any strife.

To get through the day, doing everyday things.
It's all special to me, as the radio sings.

Keeping house tidy today, keeping it tidy tomorrow.
Doing these things, are special without sorrow.

In the garden today, weeding and mowing.
Keeping it neat, my life is flowing.

Doing some shopping, buying food and clothes.
This is special too, there's nothing to lose.

So today and every day, is so very special.
Whatever is done, my life is special.

SHIRLEY LONGFORD (SOMERCOTES)

Harvest 1930s

As fields of corn sway in the breeze
Now ripened by the sun
No time for men to rest at ease
For harvest has begun

Labourers start with scythes held steady
And cut a track quite wide
When this is done, the field is ready
For the binder to move inside

Shire horses have the machine in tow
And set off round the track
Around and round the field they go
There is no time to slack

Sharpened blades slide to and fro
And cut the golden straw
Onward still the horses go
The machine cuts more and more

Although it's working at its best
And got through quite a lot
It's time for man and horse to rest
As sun is burning hot

The horses have nosebags of bran
Then drink from stream nearby
While men swig tea from Billy can
Or home-made beer they'll try

Refreshed, so now it's off they go
And start up once again
While men stack sheaves in row on row
To 'air' the ripened grain

And though there's still lots must be done
There's quite a 'buzz' you'd hear
As some folk wait with dog or gun
For rabbits may soon appear

A couple or so of weeks pass by
It's time to move the stooks
They'll make a rick about house high
When thatched how great it looks

With one stook left no one can glean
To do so would be trouble
But once removed we'd pick field clean
And just leave all the stubble.

DERRICK WOODING (MOULTON)

GOD'S HELP HEALTH-WISE

God tries to look after us health-wise,
If we are willing to follow His advice,
He knows if we have tried to work hard for Him,
So He will help us to keep going along.

I fell down quite a few times,
As I was walking along a road,
But I was lucky to have not been hurt,
Not even to have hurt my nose.

A woman once fell down,
And she also broke her wrist,
So I felt then that I was very lucky,
To have not been at that risk.

Twice when I fell down,
Two women were walking past,
They very kindly helped me get up,
So we were all happy at last.

So I felt that I was very lucky,
To have fell down and not be hurt,
I certainly was luckier than some,
To get up again and to walk.

IRIS COVELL (SLEAFORD)

THE LOVERS

Out in the woods where vines entwine,
I am hers and she is mine.
In dappled dewy glades we lay,
Sometimes by night, sometimes by day.

Time and space, and hate and fear,
Are nought to us, when no one is near.
We cling together, two now one,
And in that place our love is sown.

We are in a heaven of our making,
Truly lovers, there is no faking,
What is life about? We ask the trees,
We ask the flowers, the birds, the bees.

But no answer comes our way,
As in the dewy grass we lay.
One thing we know, but dare not tell,
We love each other very well.

Love alone is all we need
We breathe it, taste it, and we feed,
Upon the rarest fruit of all,
The one that made Adam sell his soul.

Angry voices from down the lane,
Tell us that her father; he is a pain,
Is trying to find us in the wood,
Thinking we are up to no good,
We do not answer his urgent shouts,
Hiding deeper amongst the roots.

If he did find us, the blows would rain
Upon my head, but what would he gain?
Our love is not for turning, now.
No matter how he shouts with furrowed brow.

Has he forgotten those days long gone,
When he loved, and lost, then won,
The sweetheart who he called his own,
He loved her and his love was sown.

And now he hurls abuse on us.
It makes no sense for him to fuss.
We do no harm to him, so why,
Can't he go home and let us lay,
Out in the woods in dewy glade
Happy, loving, unafraid.

T RAYMOND STUART (SKEGNESS)

MOTHER NATURE'S LARDER

It is time to start again and collect the fruit of Mother Nature's labour.
First are her apples so round and so fresh,
Next comes the plums so yellow and red,
Blackberries sweet and lush in their protective beds.
We gather them in to cook, make wines and sweet desserts like nectar on our tongues.
As the months get colder the smaller berries come,
And fruits for other drinks and food have begun,
The black sloes don't look like much,
But add your ingredients and get rich red wine!
Oh she still looks after us even after all this time.
We burn fir cones for a sweet-smelling hot fire, to cook our food on.
And the logs of old trees lit from the cones burn long,
And give your back ease!
The stories are told in the circle round the fire,
With family and friends we rest a while.
Thank you Mother Earth for all that you give,
As our Gypsy blood makes us roam through your larder.

JANET ANGELA BENDALL (ALFORD)

Anglia's Four Seasons

Anglia in early springtime, creates new landscapes of yellow, green and blue,
Forest glades carpeted by bluebells portrays splendour to our view,
Dogrose with blooming buttercup embellish serene woodland rides,
A soft shimmer of rainbow colour, reveals a fritillary butterfly's fluttering glides.
Anglia in warm mid-summer unveils, weasel and red fox prowling accompanied by birdsong.
Nature alive in peaceful harmony, paints her charm and beauty all day long,
A natural order of flora and fauna, stretches as far as our eyes can see,
A panoramic scene of tranquillity, creates a lasting vision for you and me,
Anglia in late autumn, a rustle of golden leaves as they fall thick and still,
A kaleidoscope of changing colours, endows a new identity to nature's will,
New hues and colours in great wild woods, announces a different day,
Completing a cycle of wonder, giving fresh sights of beauty along the way.
Anglia in mid-winter, white landscapes reflect noble conifers like sentinel on guard,
Copious flood waters stilled now as frozen ice, alongside land now solid and hard,
Creatures begin to hibernate, ferns of frosty filigree begin to blanket virgin ground,
A lapwing's plaintive cries, mingle with hungry rooks in a crescendo of sound.
Anglia you colour four seasons, giving an eastern promise of delights,
Heralding in a natural order, constantly thrilling us with new sights,
Across open fens an orchestra of reed beds, whispering sweet music to our ears,
Gentle breezes kiss still waters, while expanding ripples catch fallen tears.
Anglia in evening sunset, skies painted pink and red aglow,
Silhouetting circling wildfowl, soaring high in thermal currents they climb and go,
As we feast our eyes with wonder, as majestic pictures are created about,
We can sense from within this order, a hidden hand is reaching out.

JIM WILSON (WESTCLIFF-ON-SEA)

Summer

As the days grow longer, and the sun doth shine
That's when I become happy in this heart of mine
And as the sun shines down, and the world becomes bright
That's when the flowers from last year start to pick up and fight
Just as the daylight extends and the warm nights become longer
It's the time that barbecue smells start to become stronger.

The swift and the swallows, in their droves start to arrive
And also the magic of our bumblebees making honey in the hives
But before June is out, things start to get real busy
Hanging out our baskets, full with colourful bizzy lizzies
It's great to just feel the sun pulsing down on your skin
But make sure you put your sun lotion on, not too thick not too thin.

The sun shines on the good, or so they say
But, if you stay in it too long, then boy do you pay
Tons of people go overseas just to chase the sunshine
But me, I'd rather stay at home in this fair land of mine
So, in the end almost all would like to agree
Who'd want a fake tan, having to pay a small fee.

Later on we complain when the rivers run dry
Again, not enough water has the government put by
Not forgetting about the hose pipe ban that comes into play
And if you break it and get caught, a fine you will pay
A sun worshipper I am not, or likely to be
I am happy to spend my summer, with my wife and family.

KENNETH LYNN (DUNHOLME)

A LOVELY WALK IN THE COUNTRYSIDE

The misery of winter having faded away,
Gone are the clouds, bleak and so grey,
It's walking boots on, polished with pride,
For a lovely walk out, in the countryside.

We'll take in the magic of nature's own gifts,
Hearts and minds receive wonderful gifts,
Her very own paintbox with pallet of colours,
Warm and uplifting, so perfect for lovers.

The early sun rising over the hills,
As dewdrops shimmer upon daffodils,
Spiders repair, webs broken and torn,
Whilst field mice scamper, in young blades of corn.

Fresh earth thrown up, by a hardworking mole,
His glistening fur coat, as black as the coal,
Squinting against the light of the day,
He's happy at work, not wishing to play.

The rat-a-tat-tat, from afar can be heard,
Seems hard to believe, that it comes from a bird,
It's a woodpecker chiselling a hole in a tree,
Preparing the place, where his nest needs to be.

The fox returning, his eyes wide with fright,
With stealth he'd hunted, in darkness of night,
For chickens provided, a most welcome meal,
But now he can hear, those hunting horn squeals.

Huntsmen are coming, in coats red as blood,
Their horses both snorting and splattered with mud,
Ahead run the hounds, each searching for scent,
Eager to find out, which way he went.

Soon peace is restored, with a feeling of calm,
As butterflies flutter, adding colour and charm,
Ants hard at work, engrossed in their labours,
Envied yet feared by some of their neighbours.

Up high in the sky, some swifts whirl and call,
As a skylark is seen, to suddenly fall,
Like a stone he falls, after fluttering at length,
Why does he do it? Has he run out of strength?

The raucous cry of the magpie is heard,
An unusual sound from such an elegant bird,
Pure white on his breast, with black tail and wings,
Known as a thief, who likes pretty things.

Midges brought out, by the warmth of the sun,
Dance up and down, like they always have done,
But bats stay concealed, in the roof of the church,
Upside down clinging onto a perch.

Squirrels play aloft, in the branches of trees,
Free to scamper wherever they please,
Darting along, the branches and boughs,
Whilst beneath can be heard, the munching of cows.

These cows so contented, they rarely glance up,
Nibbling at grass and the odd buttercup,
Just a swish of the tail, or a flick of an ear,
Warding off flies, when coming too near.

After a long winters' sleep, in a pile of dead leaves,
Emerges a hedgehog, all covered in fleas,
Both are as one, each needing the other,
Months laid together, in the dark leafy cover.

High in a tree, an owl has a doze,
Snug in her nest, on eggs I suppose,
Soon they will hatch, into fluffy young chicks,
To be fed at length, on mice from the ricks.

With a shell for a home, attached to his back,
Leaving behind him, a silvery track,
Goes the snail at a pace, seemingly hardly to move,
Why should he rush? He has nothing to prove.

Bumblebees flitter, from flower to flower,
Collecting their pollen, hour upon hour,
Then taking it back, to the hive for the honey,
No prettier sight, on a day warm and sunny.

As fast as an arrow, and bright as a quiver,
A kingfisher darts, from bank to the river,
Returning with fish, he passes the vole,
Nervously venturing from out of his hole.

Out on the pond, a lily leaf floats,
Supporting a frog, who persistently croaks,
Extending his cheeks, till fully inflated,
At last the spring, that's been eagerly awaited.

PETER BRAMMER (SHIREOAKS)

About Living . . .

The spiritual poetry of life . . .
Is it sleight of hand what we don't see?
Is it all down to trickery . . .
Or - and here's the essential juice,
truth is magic, on our world loose?

Illumination of perpetual beauty - all about,
this world.
In diamond spiritual and glorious sparkling shout . . .
Where the incredible rises,
Everywhere
with spectacular surprises . . .

Life evolves in physical wonders,
the universe flows . . .
From cells and atoms filled with living light
each soul grows.

In the space between what we hold known,
Something more underpins it all, is grown.
Of reality, what seems - our journey alive in time
Humanity, spirits vessel, our souls,
illuminating God's rhyme . . .

Mystery holds true sway.
In its enfolds we awake our way . . .
Glimpse in moments what's realer still;
and know inside,
it's magic stirs our will.

All is one energy, life's growing light.
Souls expanding through space the infinite night . . .
We are so much more than we seem.
For more so yet, eternity can still dream . . .

PAUL HOLLAND (STOKE-ON-TRENT)

TATTERSHALL

It's a magical place
With so much to see,
You need to look carefully
So you have to follow me.
It starts in the market place
That's where there's proof
It's Tom Thumb's house
Up upon the roof.
Of course it's only little
But it's a proper little home.
He lived by himself
In his lovely little home, alone
If you visit Tattershall church
Alas you must behave,
As inside the church
Is Tom Thumb's little grave
Not far from that's the castle
Across the bridge, over the moat
Sometimes we get ducks and swans
And lilies afloat
Then we have the castle
With the peacocks in the grounds,
So much mystery and beauty
It's a treasure we have found.
So inside the castle
Up the winding stair
Lots of rooms to explore
But please take care
It's a long way to the top
And it could be tragic
But it should be very special
A place full of magic.
Imagination is a toy
So use it wisely and enjoy!

STEPHANIE LYNN TEASDALE (TATTERSHALL)

Thoughts of Jackie, a Precious Daughter

You left a void when you went away
That no one else could fill
For three long weeks, we waited for the day
To see you walking up our hill
When you did come home we cried and cried
We were so pleased to see you
But never mind how hard we tried
The days you stayed were but a few

A 'mod' you were when you went away
With dark brown locks framed round your face
But what a change, what a price to pay?
To have shorn blonde hair which looked like lace
That day we left you at the station
You seemed so young and alone
To leave you there gave us no elation
And we both sobbed all the way home

We'll never forget how you looked that day
A case in each hand and a pack on your back
We'll never forget you're going that way
We were losing a loved one - our only Jack
We couldn't accept that you wouldn't come home
We'd try anything to make it all right
We fretted and worried, like a dog at a bone
And lay totally sleepless night after night

Had no way to contact you, only by letter
Each day met the postman, but you never replied
Your very rare phone calls made us feel so much better
They were all we had left of you, on them we relied
We came up to see your first flat - horrified
At the squalor and dirt and decay
We bought you some paint, put it on, really tried
But how could you put up with living that way?

You came home more often. You seemed ready to give
Us more of your love, we loved you in return
We accepted the terms of you not here to live
Even though that was what we really did yearn
You moved once again, to another town
You lived in a house, three up and two down
We came on a visit, on the way we broke down
And you made us so welcome, you deserved a crown

While you lived there, you telephoned every week
You seemed settled enough, even going to work
But it appears something more you were trying to seek
And you didn't tell us of your wedding, which hurt
Then you told us you'd moved, again what a shock
You had a new boyfriend, what was his name?
You stopped coming home, stopped contact, the lot
We had started to settle, now things weren't the same

Then home once again, you had a new flat
Told us of new friends, but of your old, hid your hurt
Twelve stories up, new paper, paint, and a cat
It sounded quite nice, no fuss, mess or dirt
When Nana died and we wrote to you
You came right away, via train and bus
The days you stayed again seemed so few
But we let you return without any fuss

It's been almost three months since we heard from you
And it's breaking our hearts once again
We'd love to get to know our new son-in-law
Can't you possibly drop us a line?
No matter what you do to us
Your life is your own, not ours - never
We don't want to make any bother or fuss
All we want is to love you forever and ever

CAROL TEMPLEY (HARLOW)

Only One Summer

Every year in summer
The gardens burst into bloom.
The grass is green, leaves on the trees,
The air filled with perfume.
Nature always renews itself,
Ever since time began
And summer comes round many times,
But not in the life of Man.
In our life span we get one summer
(We get no second chance)
When in our prime we have the time,
To lead a merry dance.
Our summer will not return again
Once our autumn and winter have fled
So make the most of your given time
We are a long time dead.

SYLVIA R A SOUTHGATE (FELIXSTOWE)

The Turn Of The Tide

Slowly and silently, barely perceptible,
As the low tide in the estuary turns,
Oozes through mud-flats and dances in rivulets -
So comes the truth for which honesty yearns.

Watching a tide as it flowed to the estuary
Filled me with dread at the long wait ahead;
Would such a flood really halt and return again,
Cleanse and refresh once more whence it had fled?

As by the river I stood when the tide had turned,
Down on the beach came a sight to amaze:
Filling each castle moat, where once was fortress strong,
Waves crumbled ramparts that took hours to raise.

So, once the wall is breached, small though the crack may be,
Each single drop meets and joins in the dance;
Truth, like the waves rolling forward inexorably,
Casts wrong aside - none can halt its advance.

BARBARA WILKINSON (LONGFIELD)

JOY AT LAST

Gone is all the hurt and pain
No more do I cry in the rain
All so sunny my life is again.

Not feeling depressed all the time
At last can see, feel the sunshine
Knowing that everything will be fine.

Don't think about I want to die
Now it's tears of happiness I cry
With wings of love I'm flying high.

Can now say goodbye to the past
And say 'hello' to peace, joy at last
Once again I can smile and laugh.

Still like a little girl so very young
It's time to really have some fun
Now that my life has just begun.

Out loud I do want to shout
That I have my life sorted out
Being positive, optimistic no doubt.

Finding my way it all feels so right
Dark no more, now my life is bright
Each day I'm walking in the light.

It is so great the path I am on
Always contented no more do I long
Living in the 'now' yesterday is gone.

You can tell just by looking at me
That again I am so very happy
And my life is magical in harmony . . .

LINDY ROBERTS (WORLINGHAM)

GOOD MORNING SUNSHINE

Waking early to the birdsong
Feeling keen to start the day
Eat breakfast on the patio
Is there any nicer way?

With no clouds on the horizon
Lovely sunshine wall to wall
Blue skies seem to stretch forever
Did I hear a cuckoo call?

I'll just do a bit of housework
This behaviour is the norm
I flick around with my duster
Long before it gets too warm.

Looking forward to my next task
This one always takes some time
Some can't understand the reason
Why the pleasure is all mine.

I'm off out into the garden
Often I am there for hours
Snipping and clipping or weeding
Or just deadheading the flowers.

Neighbours call by for a cuppa
Passers-by stop for a chat
Everyone's in such a good mood
It's thanks to the sunshine for that!

SUE REILLY (KINGS CLIFFE)

A PROPOSAL

'So what do you reckon?'
And down on one knee,
Longing and honesty
Sealing each part of me.

Vast mountains of meant to be
Surrounded in four corners.
Rivers reflect a moment of contemplation -
And then I can see.

'Of course,' I flutter.
My breath is caught
So to our ever after.
No more need of thought.

He always asks
'Why did you not cry?'
The truth? A moment.
Too perfect to cloud my eye.

The secret of a marriage
That'll withstand all?
I do not yet know - mine
Starts with a proposal.

LAURA GORDON (BENFLEET)

Our Summer

Well summertime is here again
It comes round every year
And so do all the silly people
Who burn from ear to ear.

Well summertime is here again
And out comes all the flesh
I've had enough of muffin tops
And boobs not at their best

Well summertime is here again
The barbecues alight
Do you mind a bit of dirt in yours?
Never mind it will taste alright

Well summertime is here again
Let's all go to the seaside
That is of course unless you're stuck
In a traffic jam on Teeside

Well summertime is here again
Bring on the wonderful tourist
All they ever do is queue
Hang on they weren't before us

Well summertime is here again
What happened to the heatwave?
Better get the brolly out
And the plastic Mac from cheap save

Well summertime has been and gone
But it won't be forgotten
Lots of happy memories
And pictures of us sodden

LYN SULLIVAN (CHATHAM)

CHILDHOOD SNAPSHOT

A child of the riverbank born to be
Sat in the arms of an ancient tree
To feel the surge of an ancient tide
And seek to follow the river wide.

To paddle and pause through the flowing deep
Past water dykes where the lilies creep
Then watch the dance of the duck weed go
Where the waters ebb and the waters flow
And bankside grasses wildly spawn
In meadow dew of early dawn.

A child of the riverbank born to lie
Among tall reeds of a mud bed dry
To watch the sway of their feathered heads
As the wind its idle whispers spread
Or hear the bittern sound its boom
And all around bog flora bloom

And chance to see a reed warbler hem
Its tiny nest amongst the stem
While peppered moth and southern hawker
Flicker and feed around birch water

Oh child of the past will your daughters care
How nature's balance flourished there?
Will dragonfly and water boatmen
Still survive the waste and flotsam
Of so many who would share
The jewels of nature hidden there.

DINAH WILLIAMS (LUDHAM)

Picturesque

Golden fields of barley
Rich golden seas of corn
Dark green trees of mystery
These golden fields adorn.

Tracks that lead to nowhere
That never seem to end,
Fenced in by thorny bushes
Shall do their best to blend.

Tustled groups of ragging weeds
Claim their patch of ground
There they grow unhindered
On which the farmers frown.

Raggy wooden posts, so dry
Which once were oh so high,
Lay gnarled and brittle twisted
Beneath the summer's sky.

Lanes that twist and turn
Then end in tiny hamlets
Inhabited by people
Never to return.

Cottages that tumbled down
Thatched roofs their tops awry
Windows blown wide open
In invitation to the sky.

Crooked ivy covered chimneys
Offer up a sigh
As they lean in sad remembrance
Of summer days gone by.

Someone's pride and joy
A broken flower pot,
Claimed now by Mother Nature
Its owner quite forgot.

A garden shed so lonely
Once heard a cheery song
Echoes of a melody of happy
Times long gone.

Graceful trees intertwine
Then caress the road
They whisper tales of long ago
Standing there alone.

Dappled light and golden glow
Light this magic scene
Hiding many secrets of an
Endless dream.

Birds that fly forever
Float across the sky
Drifting on the summer breeze
In Heaven surely lie?

Houses peer, and poke their roofs
Just above the corn -
Then stand in dreamy silence
And wait to welcome dawn.

Rabbits pop a startled look,
Then run away to hide
As pigeons coo and rustle by.

A lazy cat just sit and stares
Sleepy from the heat
He can see what we can't see
Hiding in the wheat.

Lazy streams and willow trees,
Rustled by the breeze
Present a perfect picture of tranquil
Lazy ease.

As warmth and sunshine fan the land,
I should reach out and take God's hand
I'm certain that He cares you see,
For He grows the wheat for you and me.

JEANNE YVONNE SIMPSON (SUTTON-ON-SEA)

Summer

Another long summer with such stifling days.
Too hot to work in bright sunshine rays.
The worker bees drone, as they nuzzle the flowers,
Whilst we sit under trees, which over us tower.
High in blue sky, there's a white vapour trail,
And out on the water, a billowing sail.
A butterfly sits on a wild bloom nearby,
Whilst a dragonfly hovers high up in the sky.
With no work to do and nowhere to go,
I move my position but do it quite slow.
Does one read a book, or take a short nap,
Or just play the fool, with a girl on one's lap?
Hush now, I know, we'll have a cold drink,
It'll be so refreshing, to hear big ice cubes clink.
As we swirl round our glasses, all topped up with gin,
And Martini, quite dry, with an olive stirred in.

COLIN HUBBERT (SUTTERTON)

River Swimming

Everywhere seems still under stiff summer heat
Only distances shimmer where field and hedgerow meet.
The river's sheen glides amongst rinsed sunshine
Drawing curious kids close in a line.

Their parents waver by this water's edge
Before lying a blanket over grasses or sedge.
Soon they doze; statues before some moorhen's cries,
Oblivious to a shoal of fish snatching flies.

Those children saunter, splash where it's shallow,
Clothes heaped by the stubble field set brittle yellow.
Somebody tumble-wades deeper than the rest,
A hesitant chill closes, sluices up to their chest.

This weight displaced, smoothes off skin,
Gawky awkwardness cancelled by this first river swim.
We saw this by the pebble-pool and willow trees,
Caught in lost currents, washed by with the memories.

CHRIS TODD (PETERBOROUGH)

April Cottage

The cottage stood in solitude
Upon a country lane
Where hearts were filled with utmost joy
Enhanced by birds refrain.
Sweet honeysuckle stole the scene
Entwining with the briar
Of fair wild rose, whose gentle pose
One only could admire.
I gazed beyond the rustic gate
Towards to old gnarled door
And seemed to view a thousand things
I'd never seen before
The roof was thatched with golden straw
The knocker gleaming brass
And flowers of every scent and hue
Now edged the soft green grass.
I longed to walk that zigzag path
Where puss lay in the shade
And rest upon the peaceful bench
As rambling rose displayed
Her crimson shower like setting sun
To grace the garden wall
And nowhere else upon God's Earth
Could sunflowers grow so tall
A fountain shed its crystal tears
Where flowed a gentle stream
Cascading through the rockery stones
Reflecting sunlight's beam.
A purple buddleia old and proud
Reclined 'neath clear blue skies
And drew like magnet to herself
Those bees and butterflies
I stood in awe upon that scene
For I was so aware
That I had never known before
A cottage quite so fair.
This was of course in summertime
Upon that day I came
But *April Cottage* never could
Have had a sweeter name.

JULIET C EATON (ALLESTREE)

THE YELLOW DOLL

(MEMORIES OF AN EVACUEE'S FIRST CHRISTMAS AWAY FROM HOME (1939)

She woke on Christmas morning
Her thoughts still in a daze
She rubbed her eyes then saw me
Her face in shocked amaze

Gingerly she picked me up
Then clutched me to her breast
'Twas then I knew she loved me
And I loved her no less

We quietly lay together
This five-year-old and I
Her heart beat loudly in her chest
So much, I thought she'd die

She tweaked my golden tresses
She smoothed my yellow dress
She pulled a little at my legs
And still I loved her best

How brief our friendship was to be
How soon our joy was vanished
For my young friend then wet her bed
And forever, I was banished

Some fifty years have passed now
Yet still I can't forget
That five-year-old who loved me
And grieves for me still yet

Perhaps we'll meet again one day
Now wouldn't that be grand
My little friend, I wait for you
In Never Never Land.

JOAN BURGESS (WEST HEATH)

WHAT WE MISS

The sky's now full of feathers white
The cirrus clouds sail by,
This golden autumn evening
Make spirits float on high.
The lichen on the mountain ash,
Whose scarlet berries wait,
A welcome larder for the thrush
On some cold winter date.
Please watch a spider's web in sun
Its iridescent strands,
What work it took to fashion
Such glorious coloured bands.
The sweetness of wild blackberry
The last rose on the bush,
The first crisp snow on garden path
Before it turns to slush.
We're not consumers of this world
But part of Nature's plan,
To take some time each day to see
The needs of fellow Man,
It seems to me that many now
View life from plastic screen,
Just images computer locked
Where landscapes should have been.
The tragedy of life is not
What we suffer most,
But what we miss and fail to see
When real life's just a ghost.

MARY LEFEBVRE (STAFFORD)

Summerscape

Pollen sated, in soft-bellied flight
The worker bees, a scrum of whirling wings,
Weave like dowager matrons to their queen.
Along the hedgerow, intertwining tight,
The dog rose briar gleams and climbing clings
To the steep banks of twisting coils of green.

A half-grown vixen pauses, paw in air,
Under the shadow of a hawk hung high.
Fieldmice freeze at this double jeopardy.
The stillness breaks. The fox slinks to its lair.
The hawk wind-swoops, then hovers in the sky;
A speck against the blue infinity.

The soil bakes warm beneath the midday sun.
An adder curls upon a rocky ledge,
Its entwined bootlace young soak up the heat.
Far off, the echo of a hunter's gun
Drives a young hare to shelter in the hedge,
Girdling a field of slowly ripening wheat.

I watch a frog puff out its goitered throat,
Perched on a pebble by a drought drained brook
Eyes closed, it croaks its own brief requiem
Oblivious of a predatory stoat
And deaf to harsh cries from a warning rook
That counterpoint this final brief amen.

DON NIXON (ALBRIGHTON)

GLIMPSES OF HEAVEN ON EARTH

I love the sigh of the wind in the trees,
The crunch of the leaves, 'neath my feet:
The sound of the birds as they fly through the woods -
The sight of a deer, swift and fleet!

The sheep with their lambs on the side of a hill,
The wide open spaces between:
I love to breathe the pure clean air
As I gaze on this peaceful scene.

I come to a stream winding gently along,
Its surface all dappled with sun:
The sky glows brightly with red and gold
When the last lingering sunrays are gone.

The hoot of an owl as he wakes in his tree
While the night sends most creatures to sleep:
The moon floating over treetops
Shines on the cool earth beneath.

Whenever I think of these beautiful things
Which our God has so graciously given,
I praise Him for letting me have just a glimpse
Of the way it will be in Heaven.

JOAN MOORE (GRANTHAM)

THE BEACH BOYS

Volleyball on the beaches, surf-riding the waves,
Blonde beauty, dark brunettes that joyful youth craves;
Semester has ended, east coast and west-bound
Free passions, throbbed rhythms, The Beach Boys own sound.

Stretched blue skies, shrieked laughter, white, sleek, powered boats,
An imaged tanned goddess in musical notes;
Moonlight on the dancers, and parties in caves,
California, high summer caressing lapped waves.

Dreams, kisses, new yearnings, the decade went round,
Brothers word-strumming, who sought and then found
Descants, soft trebles and harmonic staves,
Unique and enduring on magical waves.

Soul-firing encaptured, a flashing fast train,
And happiness echoes in every refrain;
Bound but not fettered, times rhythmical slaves,
Starbright is the summer on lyrical waves.

CHRISTOPHER ROTHERY (UTTOXETER)

COUNTRYSIDE LOVING

Summertime in the open countryside where I live has a loving tide
of happiness and pleasures while watching the birds and butterflies flying around
the flower gardens and happiness trees
Afternoon walks with diamond gold
Mum and Dad and the black Labrador Queenie feel the tremendous explores
With the butterfly breezes which enables us to walk around these 2 fields
When we cross this stream with the sun beaming and shining down we all feel
like the happy warm A-team
As we are nearly home we can feel almighty fond while sitting by the fish pond
Where we can enjoy our fruit drinks and cream cakes
While we happily and warmly chatterbox away this lovely poetry day.

STEVEN PEARSON (HEMPNALL)

STOURPORT-ON-SEVERN

The snowdrops, at the first snowfall,
The crocus, narcissi, daffodils tall,
The flowers of May, the April skies
Then, June in bloom, what a paradise.
The blossoming trees, the birds that sing,
To herald the wonderful morns of spring,
They lift my heart, make life worthwhile,
I go about with a sunny smile.
And, so it goes, through all of the seasons,
Giving my heart a thousand reasons,
To bless the day that I landed here,
Tho not a local (and I fear)
I didn't appreciate at first
This one horse town, with language queer
That didn't appeal, to my Welsh ear.
But 60 years on, most yearnings gone,
I count my blessings - on and on.
I'm settled now, with families - many
And constantly think - there isn't any
Place that I relate as Heaven
Than dear old Stourport-on-Severn

JOAN WHEATCROFT (STOURPORT-ON-SEVERN)

MABBS MUSICK

In shady nook 'neath wooded glen
The fairies dance now again
Their wings of pearlescent light
Give fright to mortals such as we
But through a child's eye we can
See their beauty as we once
In childhood did.

ROBERT WALKER (SHIRLAND)

Summer's Song

Summer's river lies cool and inviting
Dappled by dark drape of trees
Marigolded margins of rushes
Sway in soft summer breeze
In the blue high above, a hawk hovers,
Silent swift killer on wings
And the bulrushes stir
With the scattering
Of unseen and silent small things
A pair of pale yellow shoe button eyes
From the opposite bank watch me pass
Then the water rat dives for his future
With a barely discernable splash
The mute swan is nursing its offspring
A promise of beauty and grace
Whilst a coot, biding time in the reed bank
Is betrayed by white splash on her face
Still, amid river reeds lurking,
Patient pike waits for its chance
Its teeth a saw's edges inviting
Swift death in the current's dark dance
I am caught in the thrall of the river
In the dance that beguiles with its spell
It's lament for lost summers that linger
In each ripple and eddy and swell
I am nothing compared to its story
Its words hold more power than mine
For its song holds an echo of Heaven
In a ballad far older than time

JESSICA HEAFIELD (KEGWORTH)

KNICKERBOCKER GLORY

Walking quickly to school without touching a crack
And ambling and rambling on the way back
To the warmth of the welcome which love does inspire
And the warmth of the kitchen and tea by the fire.
A strict lesson from Dad on finding a ring.
No 'finders are keepers' for this pretty thing.
Just a trip to the cop-shop and handing it in,
A pat on the back and a chuck 'neath the chin.
When it's time limit passed then his dad he could thank
For a spanking new scooter and cash in the bank.

Watching the world and absorbing its cries
With hair blowing back and young eager eyes
Front-seated atop the adventurous buses
Or down-gazing to tracks where a steam shunter fusses,
Sorting its stock of clattering trucks
Like a drake with a harem of chattering ducks.
And should it be dusk and the Pullman was due
He thrilled as pure luxury swept into view.
All chocolate and cream and ladies in sable;
Curtained windows aglow with a lamp on each table.

But *his* life was best for the sun shone each day
And his best friend was living just three doors away.
With a bat and four stumps and an old tennis ball,
His sister, his friend, friend's brother and all,
He'd set off for the park and his favourite pitch
Which was way past the bandstand and over a ditch.
They'd a batsman, a bowler and one to keep wicket,
And friend's brother to field for this Jimminy cricket.
Then when it was teatime back home they would crawl
With the bat and four stumps and the old tennis ball.

JACK LE C SMITH (OCKBROOK)

Summer Fun

A soft breeze whispers through the trees,
There's colourful flowers and bumblebees.
A red-hot sun and creamy ice cream,
Just lay back, close your eyes, and dream.

Or there's sandy beaches and the cool blue sea,
Like holidaying in Blackpool, the place to be.
With the pleasure beach and the evening shows,
At the top of the tower, where everyone goes.

There's woodland walks and the country scene,
Picnics in the park, now that's just serene.
A day out at the zoo or a good theme park,
Just be out with friends, it's late before it's dark.

Summer is freedom, the chance to have fun,
Be out and about and enjoy the sun.
Autumn is slowly coming and winter is too,
Then it's time to stay indoors with nothing to do!

LADY SANDIE SMITH (MEIR)

Life's Jungle

'Life is what you make it' people used to say,
But no one knows what is in store for them today,
Life is so very hectic and such amount of stress,
Sometimes you wonder how you got into such a mess,
No one smiles, they don't have time,
If you talk to children it is a crime,
What has gone wrong with the world today?
Somehow, somewhere we went astray,
Do we put it down to greed,
Ever wanting things we don't really need?
Years ago it was make do and mend,
You had someone to talk to a real friend,
Life means nothing no matter how much wealth,
The biggest fortune is your friends and health.

DIANE YOUNG (SPALDING)

NO FLIES ON THIS BANANA

Brrr, brrr.
The telephone rings.
Hello.
Is that Mr Robinson?
Mr David Robinson?
Yes.
Congratulations,
You have won a free holiday.
To claim it you must answer three questions.
First question?
The answer is always Spain.
Second question?
More often than not, Greek Islands is winner.
Third question?
Where would you like to visit?
Derbyshire.
Pause . . . then
That is where you live.
I know, aren't I lucky.
The phone goes dead.

DAVID ROBINSON (BELPER)

CHOICES

The choices we make are not always right
Sometimes we struggle to survive when others
are rolling in the high life
Sometimes we allow ourselves to make the wrong
choice and we suffer when we find ourselves
on the wrong pathway
Sometimes life hurts but we have to learn to live with it
When life pushes us to the limit we have to
Hold on or go crashing faster and faster into despair
Sooner or later we have to get to grips with it
Although mistakes will be made whether we
make them on purpose or without realising it
Once opportunities are lost there is nothing we can do to bring them back.

CAITLIN KOVACS (ETTINGSHALL)

Summer in Colchester

The season of sun and lack of rain.
Summer has returned again.
With picnics in the park or at the beach,
All life's pleasures are within your reach.

Castle Park is free to all.
Showing remnants of the Roman wall.
The swings and slides for children to enjoy the freedom of play.
While parents watch and wonder how time, so quickly, slips away.

The town of Colchester is an ideal place.
Catering for every age and taste.
Steeped in history with a castle as well.
What wonderful stories the Roman walls could tell.

London is not too far away.
For newcomers to visit for a day.
While Clacton or Walton provide a great beach.
Both of them within easy reach.

There are so many places you can choose to eat.
With vegetarian choices if you don't eat meat.
Costs vary so suit every pocket.
No need for holiday costs to rocket.

The castle museum is very interesting to see.
Enjoyed by both adults and children, but unfortunately not free.
Everything is explained so all can understand.
It helps you visualise the history of our land.

The summer passes much too fast.
I wish these happy days would last
With freedom to enjoy the pleasure.
That gives us memories we all can treasure.

CHRISTINE WARD (COLCHESTER)

His Final Summer

His final summer was glorious,
With cerulean skies from horizon to horizon,
Occasional flecked with wispy white clouds.
Mature leaves in verdant colours darkening.
Yet new greenery springing from twigs still.
Whilst the brook which ran deep in spring,
Now runs shallow, gurgling melodiously,
As it runs over stones and polished pebbles.
Quicksilver light scattering over the surface,
Having long forgotten the winter's rain.
Birds hunting manically in the herbage.
Within the garden trees and shrubbery,
Feeding fledglings or succeeding broods.
Instinct driven, but finding time to sing.
The air humid, yet balmy, calms him,
Rather than being too hot to please.
Everyone talking about why go abroad,
When nothing compares with old England,
In the verdant glory of high summer.
Barbecues rather the traditional picnics,
Fashions over the decades had changed.
All his childhood memories flooded back,
As he recalled days and folk long passed,
And sheds a tear for those dear ones,
Forgetting the austerity and the rationing.
The sheer hardship of day-to-day living.
Truly the neighbourhood was friendlier.
Will these memories be replayed again?
He deems this summer day truly blessed.
Dozing as day diminishes to a violet haze.

JOHN PEGG (MEIR)

SUMMER SEASON

This the season to savour,
For better the weather,
For better the hours of light,
For better the sunshine to cherish,
For better all outdoors to do.

Time flows on, the most to be made,
By all time that is,
Of work or leisure
Opportunities there season by season
To latch onto, to utilise.

Back or forward, some doting of summer delights,
The fruits, the crops,
All add towards requirement,
Deprived of holds no thought
A year without a perk.

A safer reason by all that's good,
As carefully to opt, like moral code,
Prioritising season by season
By such a season beams much
Glory be to God, for all things bright and beautiful.

He knows and cares by love renown,
To spend and be spent,
Whatever the time, let gratitude flow,
Blooming in that glorious season,
A perfume of His spirit to possess.

RACHEL TAYLOR (WINTHORPE)

Summer 2010

What summer, I ask.
A season, a climate, weather.
Long awaited for in anticipation,
Evenings to outsit the sun.

Summer season, only a name.
It's the weather we enjoy.
Season of sun long awaited,
odd day has been our luck.

Dreams of trips to the country or seaside,
Oh, the fuel we've saved.
Reluctant conservers of energy.
Someone has it all planned.

Autumn, winter, spring, summer.
Not much change, only the fall of the leaf.
Nature confused as ourselves
bloom when you can. The order.

So outlive the season.
Plan your day as it comes.
Pay the heating bills and dream,
next year may be even better.

So let 'summer'.
Be in your heart,
Sing, dance, whistle and praise.
Bloom, be a creator of love.

RALPH A WATKINS (WELLESBOURNE)

Me Old Banger

Our holidays, we leap in car.
No four by four, no Jaguar.
The wife and I, three kids in rear.
It's an old Ford banger, that I bought last year.
We got it through its MOT.
Three hundred quid it has cost me.
No worries now, we raise a cheer,
As I rev up, engage first gear.
Two miles down the road a shout,
'I'm feeling sick, let me get out!'
Another ten I'll make a bet,
Are we nearly there Dad yet?
Now, on the motorway, it's clear
Then what all us drivers fear
Ahead I see a braking light,
An ambulance dashing to the sight,
Policemen cleaning up the wreck,
Whilst I crawl by with rubber neck.
The wife reminds me, 'Do take heed,
Be alert and watch your speed.'
The kids all shout with one accord,
'The journey's long, we're getting bored!
For half an hour, we've played I-spy
And fifty red cars have passed us by.'
'We want to eat.' 'I need a wee'
'I think me mom wants a cup of tea.'
'I'll have a burger, I'd like a scone.'
'Buy us something Dad, go on.'
'The price of food in here's too high,
Just have an ice cream then let's fly.'
In half an hour a shout of glee,
'Look over there I can see the sea'
I lay me down upon the sand,
Say to the wife, 'Love this is grand
Who would have thought, we'd get this far,
In that little battered old Ford car?'

ALBERT WATSON (HODGE HILL)

TIME MARCHES ON

In the early morning of life
The sands through the hourglass of time
Do so slowly seem to flow:
Energy levels are high; tasks are few
Thus time is that delay waiting for:
That next meal of the day
That next chance with friends to play

By late morning
Learning has occupied our time
In preparation
For our adult role
And in the expectation
Of having with another
A loving and rewarding
Inter relation

The early afternoon sees a task escalation
Family responsibilities are now our lot
And tasks now take on a toll of time
And energy levels suffer quite a drop
'Tis then a glimpse is caught of that upland green
From where the chains of care are shed
And where a loving mother and wife
May now - at long last - relax instead

'Tis now the evening of life
The loved one is lost
Energy levels are low
Tasks fill the time left
For those who are bereft
Time marches on - regardless

VICTOR WILLIAM LOWN (LOUGHBOROUGH)

Autumn

How I love an autumn morn
Wreaths of mist a watery sun
Prelude to a halcyon day
The fruitful circle scarce begun.

On every shrub, tree and holly
There's evidence of the spider's folly
Tinted leaves begin to fall
So catch them, happy months for all.

Chimney pots the mists adorn
Like a goblin's hat of fun
The golden sunflowers tall and gay
Droop whilst waiting for the sun.

To smile on them and make them jolly
Then autumn with his bounteous trolley
Doth give to creatures great and small
The lovely fruits of tree and wall

IVY GEE (OADBY)

Summer

Summer now has come at last
Mowers going over grass
Shears at hedges snip away
Hanging baskets on display
Swallows soaring in the sky
Catching food as they fly.
The blackbird gives a warning call
A predator is on the wall.
A cat or magpie it might be
But it soon goes off
When it sees me.
The wildlife is a joy to see
The pleasure it gives to you and me.

ZENA BROWN (RADFORD)

ALL CHANGE

The rain - it has fallen,
Being heavy at times,
And by many a holidaymaker,
Charged, with committing a crime,

Dust-covered pathways and byways,
Have now been washed and cleaned,
By the turning on of nature's tap,
While brook courses, struggling to
Survive, in summer's heat,
Are jubilant, at being given
The chance, to make a comeback.

Flowers and leaves on the trees,
Battered - by the storm,
Now raise their heads to the sky,
Refreshed - as they welcome a new day's morn.

The sun returns, to its rightful position in the sky,
Having taken a short rest,
And once again with its warmth,
Another summer's day is blessed.

Happiness - reigns - once again,
For one and all in the land,
What more could one wish for,
Than the joys - given for free,
To be shared - by all -
Courtesy of the Creator's hand

BAKEWELL BURT (BAKEWELL)

TILIKUM

(IN MEMORY OF DAWN BRANCHEAU, (HER JOB SHOULD NEVER HAVE EXISTED) RIP)

My floppy dorsal fin is a testament
To this unfit world I exist in . . .
I am *not* a performing circus poodle
I do not *want* to perform tricks
I *need* the open sea
I *need* it to be there for me
I *need* to be free.

In order to feel true love for something
You also need respect.
Shouldn't 6 tonnes command respect?
30 years old, imprisoned in a tank.
I'm going to die in this pool.

You were in the wrong place at the wrong
time on that dreadful day.
People told their children to look away.
I did not *want* to do my tricks.
No matter how many performances we had given together
you could never give me a workout, like the wild sea could.

On that terrible day, I just felt so bad
You got in the way . . .
I'm sorry that I temporarily relieved
my frustration on your fragile body.
Desperation sees no friend clearly.
Take your hands *off me. I am no pet.*

I am an orca
A killer by name
It is in my nature
The way I was designed
It is the open sea that is right for me.

We are intelligent individual beings
How well most of us bear our confinement
What was our crime?
We were not made for mankind's entertainment.
We want to be in the open sea
free and at peace.

N BROCKS (GEDNEY DYKE)

Summertime Bliss

Endless rays of golden sun stretch over hill and dale
Dancing across the crystal stream nestling in the vale
Migrating birds sail on highin skies of azure-blue
Hilltop gorse sways in the breeze emitting summer hue

Shadows lengthen as darkness descends and the sun begins to fade
Moonlight flickers through the trees in the cool of the evening shade
Gentle mist shrouds the land lingering until first light
Then drifts away as temperatures rise dismissing it from sight

Sunshine glistens on early dew erasing it away
Leaving behind fields of green overlooking the bay
Golden sand spans far and wide as the sea pushes gently to shore
Gulls shriek in the midday heat as up above they soar

Rippling waves break on the rocks as the tide ebbs slowly away
A gentle wind carries granules of sand entwined with foamy spray
Distant clouds drift along carrying summer rain
Then disperse in the humid air as the sun appears again.

PHILIP O'LEARY (REDDITCH)

Where the River Lyn Flows

The narrow river Lyn courses through this park!
And at one time the peacocks' cry would have been heard at the gate!
But now it is the time of the swallows . . .
They are back at the barn again!
Skimming and dipping as if they'd never been away!
A lone harebell grows
Where the swallows fly!
And tiny tormentil flowers creep along the sun-baked ground -
Four-petalled yellow flowers
Amongst the white crosses of the heath bedstraw.

VERONICA TWELLS (GROBY)

Summertime

Summer is a wonderful time,
Makes every day feel fine!
The sun, birds, flowers,
Long light nights seem to last for hours.

You see some folk fishing,
They sit there just wishing,
Hoping they get a bite,
That would be a delight.
The water's so still,
They probably will.
Then it's time to leave the park,
Before it gets dark.

When you're walking along,
You'll hear birds in song,
People strolling with pets,
Don't ever forget.
This is all down to our Lord,
Pleasure we all can afford.

You see the odd butterfly,
Then flies past the bee.
Seems like the trees,
Are dancing in the breeze.
God is our maker,
He made them all.
So let's thank Him,
For summer, the season for all.

CAROL ANN ELSMORE (OLDBURY)

AFTERNOON TEA

Blink and you'll miss it; my special place.
Its beauty without there isn't a trace.
Go softly my dears; down the winding back lane.
Past a white-faced cottage with lead windowpane.
Hear nattering brown hens and a cock's mighty trill.
See lowing fat cows on yonder small hill.
A combine so busy; its harvest to gather;
Crows and a jackdaw flapping round in a lather.
An ancient old bark bows just near the stile,
Its shade begging travellers to rest for a while.
Over the rill; through the paddock so green;
Rabbits and hares are frequently seen.
Down past the spinney red fox has his lair;
He has lived for some years now that hunting is rare.
Skirting the meadow; with wild flowers a-sway
Dance butterflies, bees and insects at play,
Through the gate; cross the yard to the farmhouse I tread,
Good friends made welcome with tea, jam and bread.

DEAN BUFFIN (NUNEATON)

A COUNTRY EVENING

A gentle breeze blowing
like a whisper through the trees
The peaceful sound of a stream
flowing over its stony bed
In the quiet meadow
little creatures come out to play
When the twilight falls
and stars come out
The hoot of an owl
can be heard round about.

M SIMPSON (OAKWOOD)

The Mermaid of Mablethorpe

A glimpse of circus dome
To a giant ice cream cone
Standing on the street
As you walk on past

To vast kaleidoscopic rays
Of sweets and treats on displays
From jars of humbugs and drops
To stripy, sticky sticks of rock -
Lettered through
Numbered with e-numbers
And too hard to chew
And dummies and lollipops
That stick to teeth like glue

Through the shell curtains
Of a souvenir shop door
Golliwogs and voodoo dolls
Doll houses and dolphins
Shelves on spells
And shelves of shells galore

A myriad of the mystical
And mythological;
Fairies and mermaids
Witches and wizards

Fridge magnets;
Sea horses
Crabs and lizards

Then through the
Jingle jangle jungle
Of electronic jumble
Competing beats
From amusement arcades
Along the streets

Cartoon character caricatures
- Giant, garish and grotesque -
Grin at you from inside arcade desks

Past the funfair
A crocodile ride up in the air
A carousel
An empty ghost train
Giant teacups
And toy planes

Prizes to win if you dare
While jazz tunes, soft rock
And hard metal blare

A pirate ship hangs off a cliff
Where crazy golf is played
While back on the sand
Sandcastles are made
And donkeys parade

Past the stripy row
 - A rainbow of huts -
The *'Bathing Beauties'*
to be hired and admired
Bright and bold on show
And a puppet theatre
For a *Punch and Judy* show

Climbing over the shoulders
Of sand dunes . . .
Leaving behind the spectacle
Of the staged seaside sets

To stretch of sky
And stretch of beach
And stretch of sand
Beneath your feet

To the gentle hum
And murmur of the sea
Inviting me

To starfish
On the sandy beach
In dangerous reach
Of children's hands

And the skulls of baby shells
Cracking underfoot as you walk

To the squawking and screeching
Of seagulls in the air, tracking
And trailing a fishing boat sailing

And beware of jellyfish beached
Invisible blobs on land
And nippy crab claws
Nipping bare feet

Clusters of clams
And shingle of
Razor-sharp razor shells . . . and . . .

The local mermaid washed ashore
Waiting for the sea to collect her
So she can ride the waves once more.

JANE AIR (MABLETHORPE)

A SUMMER'S DAY

The long grass swaying
in the breeze
The green leaves
waving on the trees
The blackbird sings
his merry song
The nights are short
and the days are long
The flowers are in bloom
and looking their best
And all birds are young
and fled their nests
The earth is dry and parched
from the hot summer sun
and is waiting for the rain to come
and quench its thirst
And make it lush and green again

M LOVESEY (STONE CROSS)

OUR SPECIAL SUMMER SEASON

Four seasons, what a privilege,
Each bringing great delight -
Winter's white robe, with gems, is spread
Spectacular and bright.

The youthfulness of spring brings cheer,
Activity is seen,
Lambs play, birds build and ev'rywhere
Buds open fresh and green.

Summer brings welcome breaks and we
From time-tables are free!
There's tennis, cricket, country walks
And visits to the sea.

Here in my town of Shrewsbury,
The Flower Show delights
Huge crowds, that come from near and far
To see its splendid sights.

Parades and choirs, bands and the tents
With floral art displays.
Outstanding fireworks mark the end
Of two exciting days!

Autumn replaces summer with
Rich colours, russet gold
Those who visit Shrewsbury Show
Such happy thoughts will hold.

MARY LACEY (SHREWSBURY)

God's Creation

If you stroll across the meadow
And find the old-fashioned stile,
Slowly gaze around you
Then sit and rest awhile.

There are scabies and buttercups,
Golden ladies' fingers,
Down by the hedgerow,
Fragrance of honeysuckle lingers.

The blackbird's never-ending day,
Collecting insects by the score,
Open mouths of the fledglings
Still calling out for more.

The skylark soars way up on high,
As if to disappear,
While the cuckoo sings oe'r yonder woods,
Its call so loud and clear.

A storm thrush sits on the highest twig,
Singing to the world,
The rustle of the tender leaves,
So green and just unfurled.

Now you have rested for awhile,
Close your eyes and pray,
Thank God for all these precious things,
And another peaceful day.

PAULINE VINTERS (TATTERSHALL)

NIGHT SONG

The night is long when sleep won't come and so
I sought the coolness of a summer breeze
And gentle comfort of familiar trees
Through open window - but the night was dark
And still, no moon, no form below, no sound.
I sadly turned around, no comfort found.
And then I heard one single, timid note -
I turned again to hear, as if for me alone,
More notes, full-throated and magnificent,
A song of joy, of hope, of life. Its end
Brought back the still, dark and silent night.
I breathed in deep and caught the scent of mint,
Rosemary, lavender and just a hint
Of roses and the new-cut grass. I smiled.
That little bird had sung his song too soon
For dawn, but in the singing of his tune,
Reminded me the nights, though dark and long
Only gently cover the beauty of the days.
Familiar paths are there - and well-loved ways,
Though out of sight. That fearless little bird,
He knew his day would come, but couldn't wait,
So sang his song for this unlikely mate,
And blessed me, truly blessed me for I found
My spirit lifted and my heart was eased.

JUNE HICKABOTTOM (SCUNTHORPE)

My All-Time Favourite Boxing Stance

Coaches may give you various alternatives
but you can scour the index list
of any boxing manual and still not find
my all-time favourite boxing 'stance'.

They can exhort, "Left hand up,
right hand near the chin,
come in at an angle
shoulder up, chin well down,"
even recommend the crouch arm-crossover
à la Frazier or Foreman as defence,
but none of these are my favourite boxing 'stance'.

Because my admired stance
is not a stance at all
more an attitude to Fate,
more the true meaning of 'daredevil'
more a case of 'going out on your shield'.

Groggy, battered and bleeding
he rocks against the ropes
beckoning his rampant opponent onward, inward;
the chief second wants to stop it
white bloodstained towel ready for launching,
but my hero curls his lip and says, "No!"
He even has a pursed grimaced smile;
did I see him wink just then?

He knew he was in for a beating,
but his 'stance' spoke volumes,
it said, "So what."
He can go on taking it forever and ever - Amen.

Yet still he returns the punches
dizzily matching fire with fire,
as he embraces
my all-time favourite boxing 'stance'.

His legs are wobbling now,
Ringside commentators compare it to "a silly dance"
Not realising that to my hero
Such a movement makes perfect sense.

He's out on his feet
"One good blow" the commentator says,
"Would finish him off";
but he takes that good blow
and then invites another one,
always banging back!

Why does this image always draw me in?
Why do I compare myself to him,
my life to his?
Why, in short, is this my all-time
favourite boxing 'stance'?
This gravitational pull must say so much,
about the two, him and me both: we like that approach.

He's leaving the ring now - another sad defeat,
broken but unbowed, though the towel is still in the
cornerman's hands! (And that's what counts).
As he turns away, hooded in black satin robe,
for the first time I see, boldly embroidered
on the back of the gown, in white,
a few words he wants to say to me, personally;
an old Eighties slogan clichéd but true - it goes:
'Life's a bitch and then you die'.

TYRONE DALBY (BOSTON)

PICNIC AREA

It is a lovely place for a picnic, secluded, yet with pleasant views.
It was the middle of May and time for Molly and I to visit our favourite picnic site.
The early weeks of May had had cold winds blowing most days,
but the 18th May was a perfect day for a picnic.
Spring flowers were in abundance, magnificent trees in all shades surrounded us.

We happily sat on our picnic bench enjoying jam sandwiches, iced cakes and lemonade.
We had been careful to carry our food in our picnic basket, covered with a red and white checked cloth,
just like our friends Noddy and Tessie Bear cover their picnic basket
It was great fun.

When it was time to go we picked up litter, repacked our basket and set off home.
Our journey was pleasantly short!
Just a few steps from our garden seat and indoors,
but what an adventure for Molly and me!

THELMA ROBINSON (CLARBOROUGH)

A SUMMER EVENING

Rind of a moon,
Fields with folded wings
Sleeping twilit
Under a fading dome.

Slow wisps of silence,
Streams dissolve;
Insects, suspended, dart -
Erratic particles
Testing edges of the dark.

Evening settles like a dust,
Levelling the landscape,
And sighing hills subside,
Relinquishing their thrust
To safely hide
Where slow light lingers,
And only stiffened fingers
Of the rushes write,
Pencilling in charcoal
Long fingers of the night.

MICHAEL COTTON (KETTERING)

LAST SUMMER

I remember well last Summer, your eyes of sapphire-blue.
Fond memories I recall of when our love was new.
The nights we strolled beneath the stars, moonlight shimmering in your hair.
Entwined within each other's arms, a love beyond compare.
But sadly with the Autumn our love began to fade.
With the snows of Winter gone were all the plans we made.
I still recall last Summer although it gives me pain.
For what we shared together will in my heart remain.

JOSIE RAWSON (SELSTON)

Sunset

As I look through my window
And see the beautiful sunset
I give thanks to You Lord
As You bless us with this

Your creation is wonderful
Help us not to abuse it so much
To appreciate our free gift
And give thanks in prayer

You love us so much Father
Your Son died for us
Help us to remember this
We must love others as He loved us

BRENDA CHARLES (SHERWOOD)

Dreams

Who's that woman in the mirror? Surely it can't be me,
I really can't be that old, I'm only thirty-three!
It only seems like yesterday I danced the whole night through,
I had such boundless energy, my aches and pains were few.
I may be older outside, but inside I have dreams
Of things I'd really like to do, I could write reams and reams.
I'd like to achieve an aim in life before I grow too old
To be a success at something, if I might be so bold,
Not just someone's mother, not just someone's wife,
But to be someone special who got herself a life.
I love my family dearly, they mean the world to me,
But inside is a person, not just an entity.
Maybe one day I'll reach my goal, time alone will tell,
I'd better get a move on before the final bell.

YVONNE POWELL (THORPE SATCHVILLE)

My Favourite Subject Is Me

My favourite subject is me . . .

I can sit and talk about this constantly.
Ain't a mountain I haven't climbed
And a river I haven't crossed,
I can deliver this to you naturally,

My favourite subject is me . . .

I might as well study it like it was a degree.
My appalling behaviour needs someone to save me,
Before I cause myself more tragedy!

My favourite subject is me . . .

Me, me, me, me, me, me, me!
Is there anybody else out there?
Because I haven't stopped and stared,
I'm like chalk to the average one's cheese,

My favourite subject is you guessed it . . . ?

There is not a real world outside me?
Don't talk you just listen,
Mine is your own vision,
And I thank you for just letting me be.

WESLEY ALCINDER (DUDLEY)

Solitude

Solitude is heaven-sent,
Solitude - a blessing
Release from tension with
Time to savour the present,
Energised with the spirit
To flow into the future.
Solitude yesterday has
Silently merged through
Hours of night
Into another day.
Ceaselessly flowing into eternity.
Solitude supports and strengthens
Determination to face the future.
From quiet moments of reflection
Grows the confident awareness
Of trust and hope and surety.
Solitude of sunlit moments
Or raindrops falling softly
On the grass.
In shower or shine
Solitude is mine.

SISTER GREGORY FEETENBY (MATLOCK)

Summer's Delight

Awakening to bird song, summer's delight,
Gardens all smartened, sunlit and bright,
Bees busy pollinating, humming their tune,
Soft summer rain, and fresh morning dew.

Powder-blue skies, milky white clouds,
A shaping new moon in a clear night sky.
Stars twinkling and winking up on high,
Summer's a love song, a sweet lullaby.

A time to be busy so much to see,
Oceans swell in a gentle sea,
Children's laughter joyous and free
This is what summer means to me.

The smell from a barbecue,
Fresh scent of the flowers,
The dances of butterflies,
And longer light hours.

BETTY JOHNSON (DERBY)

A Summer's Day

We walked by the river, 'twas such a lovely day
The birds and ducks had all turned out to greet us in their way
The sun shone bright, no clouds around
Pathways cleaned, no litter on the ground
Hedgerows blooming such lovely wild flowers
Everything's shining, the countryside all ours.

Wild roses nodded as we passed by
There were butterflies, bees and a sweet dragonfly!
Children's laughter rang out from a boat passing by
And the sun shone down from its place in the sky
The warmth touched my face, my heart it took wings
Cause summer had come with such wonderful things.

GOLDAH JANKIEWICZ (MANSFIELD WOODHOUSE)

A SUMMER'S DAY

What does summer mean to me?
Scones with jam and cream for tea
Earl grey served at half-past four
Friends and family at the door
We count our blessings and be glad
We have this life which isn't bad
Our guide dog lying in the sun
Resting from a day's work done
Stretches out and gives a sigh
As the hours slowly saunter by
Grandchildren playing laughing and happy
Time to change the baby's nappy
The gentle hum of people talking
Little Amy's started walking
The sun sinks quietly in the sky
Nearly time to say goodbye
All too soon folks drift away
The ending of a perfect day

MARILYN BLOOMFIELD (GLASCOTE HEATH)

MORNING LIGHT

There is a stillness not a sound
As morning dew, begets the ground
Climbing high the misty shrouds
Float towards the moving clouds
An echo now of the cuckoo's cry
As wings take flight into the sky
Seem to herald dawn's first light
To start the day and end the night

Then changing clouds turn silver-blue
With golden lights breaking through
The rising sun in a misty haze
Creates an aura to amaze
Sparkling amid the glorious blue
Shimmering rays, fall from the hue
Sending down warmth and light
To wake the world with delight.

EILEEN HENDERSON (NOTTINGHAM)

Memories and Dreams

Long winding roads, slow meandering streams
Stars in the sky, memories and dreams
Mountains so tall, oceans so deep
Walks on the wild side, awake or asleep

Tropical forests, deserts so dry
Bluebells in woods, birds flying high
Clouds slowly drifting, leaves in the trees
Warm sunny days, a soft gentle breeze

A beautiful rainbow, showers of rain
And everything's fresh when the sun shines again
The old village green, leather on willow
Sometimes I wake with tears on my pillow

Dark clouds forming lightning and thunder
Children growing up their eyes full of wonder
Bicycle rides, long lazy days
All nature's wonders never cease to amaze

Classical music, poetry to write
The moon shining brightly in the sky at night
A garden of flowers, fields of corn
All of these things since the day I was born

Wonderful creatures, forests so green
Flora and fauna like I've never seen
These are the things that bring pleasure to me
But the best thing of all is that they are free.

DONALD LINNETT (WIGSTON)

THE PARK - REFLECTIONS ON A VISIT

The air was warm
The skies were blue,
The day I strolled through
The park with you.

We watched the children
Playing on the swings,
They looked so mischievous
And as happy as kings.

The boating lake glinted in the sun
While the people boating
Seemed to be having
Lots of fun.

On reaching the pavilion
We bought ourselves an ice cream
To cool us down.
For the weather was hot,
And for a while,
It was a relief to be out of town.

From where we sat down
The flower beds we could see,
They looked so delightful and colourful,
They brought to the mind such tranquillity.

Soon homeward bound were we
Feeling quite refreshed,
And just in time for tea.
But memories they linger on
Although just another summer's day had gone.

MARGARET A STONIER (KIDSGROVE)

Peeling Dreams

Lazy summer haze
infects the pathways and alleys of this town
a yearly disease, and our cue to come alive.

Photo-shoot sky, backlit clouds
stumbling slovenly across the pastel-blue
like unruly schoolchildren idling their days away
as we did, content with being
who the world told us we couldn't, intoxicated on freedom
at least for the sun-bleached weeks
life's haunting pressures were just children's stories
designed to make us care
about our actions and consequence
but we re-wrote the rules and revelled in the present.

Muggy, August evenings
with midnight fire-lights
burning beacons casting faces
in soft orange, we would lay on our backs
gazing into the charcoal slab of night sky
and pretend we could touch the stars.

Too long in midday heat
gave way to sun-drunk blisters
peeling away, like the last days of summer
and our childish dreams gone with them
leaving skin curling like the edges of old photographs
revealing pale surfaces
clean slates
on which to etch our futures.

JACOB PARKER (RUGBY)

In Summer Once

In summer once
We dreamed a heaven world
Of everlasting sunshine,
Endless birdsong
And unfading flowers.

Summer is born of spring,
In bluebell time
When trees are new in leaf,
Hawthorn rich in blossom,
Hedgerows in lace.

Midsummer brings the rose -
The frail wild rose
In country hedges,
Honeysuckle, meadowsweet,
And foxgloves in the grass.

Earthly summers fade
Into a wealth of golden leaves,
Orange and russet,
Scarlet and crimson,
To delight the soul.

After the fall
Summer is but a memory,
Trees stripped of leaf
And branches writhing
In a bitter wind.

DOROTHY BUYERS (OSWESTRY)

Sitting On A Cloud

An amazing vista up here
So quiet, peacefully tranquil
Doves fly by like gossamer in the air
Ghostly shadows high on atmosphere

Unruffled mist hangs lightly in the air
Magically floating in the valleys
Treetops grey in the mist
While peace in the valley

Sunlight tripping over the mountains
Swirling clouds heavy with snow
Frost sparkling across the land
Eagles soar over timeless space

Rivers shaping the land
Oceans caressing the Earth
Trees a blanket of warmth
For all enjoy these riches

Mystical Earth, with mimesis of Man.

CAROLE A CLEVERDON (NORTHAMPTON)

One Night In Autumn

No moon, no stars, just heavy cloud that night,
House and street lights fail, darkness is profound.
Instantly we have lost the power of sight,
In blackness we grope and searched around,
A candle, a match, anything to give light,
Is there not a torch with batteries sound?
Each Stygian second fuelling greater fright,
Imagination, passing minutes crowned.
In modern times this darkness is not right,
We start to feel our hearts begin to pound
In daylight we know this would all seem trite -
Our feet would be more firmly on the ground -

A flicker, then returns that steady glow,
The power's back and things are as we know.

R L COOPER (RADCLIFFE-ON-TRENT)

LOVER'S SONNET

My newborn eyes open and regard their lover,
Her scarcity reclines in mid-morning sun,
I brush skin smooth as a Sunday in summer,
And her glimmered smile leaves me undone,

I sense it in the air when she's . . . almost . . . there,
Her breathless body surrenders to my touch,
And she curls a smile and whispers a swear,
As I wrap up her warmth in a tight clutch,

Amid our scattered underwear and wine
Spent time falls away with every caress
And within each burning moment we find
The soft ebb and flow of a lover's breath

She's my feminine complement, never alone,
Cos my heart beats at the same time and tone.

NATHAN THOMPSON (WARRINGTON)

SUMMER DAYS

At last summer is here once more
We'll have some fun like before
We will go away for week, maybe have some chips
Or just go out on day trips.
We can play on the sand
With bucket and spade in hand
Or we might go to the zoo
See some animals old and new.
There will be mums and dads, children too
Aunts and uncles, grandmas and grandads to name a few
There will be lots of treats
Lots of ice cream, lots of sweets
We could go camping for the night
Sit around a fire till morning light
Whatever we do, we'll have lots of fun
Especially if we get lots of sun.

E RIGGOTT (HOLMEWOOD)

Meditation

Bed of nails or an Indian carpet
But a rag will do
Peacefully aware of the countryside
Silence all and green
Removes all the frustration - distraction
No more physical tension, mentally
And spiritually and helps strengthen the mind
Relaxing automatically with rhythm off the heart
Mind gradually comes to rest in the breath
Peace, relax, freshness mooring moistness
No more dryness and boredom
Teach us to focus the mind and control our breath.
When nightmares pound the brain
Their confusion and despair
Totally honest and powerful ways
Seeking the treasure in this field
Re-balancing the body's energy levels
Meditation removes all frustration - distraction
Act of contemplation relaxation into
Meditation erase all the inner-pain
So get yourself a bed of nails or an Indian carpet
But never mind a rag will do
Beyond light and beyond darkness
Do a bit of meditation today.

RANJIT SINGH (DERBY)

THE LITTLE THINGS

(TO MARGARET FROM IAN. WITH ALL MY LOVE AND BEST WISHES FOR A VERY HAPPY DAY.)

You are all the little things.
That mean so much to me.
Just like asking me to dance.
Or taking you out to tea.

You smile you laugh you hold my hand.
As we dance round the floor.
I just want to be with you.
For I ask nothing more.

When I came to this ballroom.
I was a stranger all alone.
You came to me and danced with me.
And made me feel at home.

I'll never forget for what you did.
Was wonderful to see.
You made me feel like ten feet tall.
For what you did for me.

I don't need a four leaf clover.
A charm or lucky star.
You are all the luck I need.
No matter where you are.

Please stay with me and the little things.
That brought me close to you.
Will bring you closer every day.
For Margaret I love you.

Please stay with me my whole life through.

IAN PROCTOR (BIDDULPH)

I'D LIKE . . .

I'd like to be a pirate and sail the seven seas,
Going back and forth to any place I please,
I'd travel far and wide across the vast ocean,
Taking care of my lady with the greatest devotion,
She polishes up nicely and the galley does shine,
And all the sailors wish for a ship as good as mine.

I'd like to be a dancer and tip tap across the floor,
I'd do it so well the audience would beg for more,
My little shoes would tap on stages far and wide,
With the music softly playing always at my side,
I'd let the music carry me as softly as a cloud,
As for those that I love best? I would make them proud.

I'd like to be an artist and paint the world's best views,
And hang it in a gallery where art lovers come to muse,
What a delight to live off my love,
For me and art fit like a hand in glove,
I'd have paint and brushes a plenty for me to paint my dreams,
To create a world so pretty in which you can believe.

I'd like to be a pilot and soar across the sky,
With the engine roaring as clouds go steaming by,
I'd twist and turn and whizz around,
This way, that way upside down,
And on the ground everyone would see,
That the best pilot in the world, is me!

I'd like to be a spaceman and walk across the moon,
But it's pretty far away and I'd want to come home soon,
I wonder if it's made of cheese? I think I'd take a bite,
But right now I feel sleepy and it's time to say goodnight,
But one day when I grow up I'm sure I shall be great,
But until then, I guess I'll have to wait.

ADELE RAWLE (RUGELEY)

FULL ENGLISH BREAKFAST
(ISLES OF SCILLY 2000)

Bed and breakfast by the seaside. Wonder what these people do
when at home in Milton Keynes or Weston-super-Mare or Kew.
Silent couples eating grapefruit. Watchful landlord, feigning chatter,
makes a joke. There's no response. He drops a knife! Resulting clatter
brings us all to sharp attention fending off the next attack.

Apologies, with clicking heels; and then we hear him round the back:
expletives roar in sheer frustration, while his patient little wife
who organises all the business side of things, just wipes the knife.

Mushrooms, bacon, eggs, tomatoes, sausages, on plates so small
that crispy bread with oozing fat sits balancing on top of all
those calories that no one is allowed at home; - just toast and fruit.

Seagulls watch outside the window; plan to carry off the loot
they scavenge from the kitchen waste. With beady eyes they make their choice
to satisfy a wanton greed with wild aggression, raucous voice
and cruel beak. Now, guests are threatened from the window and the door.
Hungry birds or Sergeant Major? Who, I ask, is feared the more?
Landlord reappears to wipe the tables. *Have a pleasant day.*
Sunday breakfast eight-fifteen or grapefruit will be cleared away!

Dare we breathe or scrape our chairs or should we simply run outside
to feel the wind and salt sea spray and watch the surf on rolling tide.
To hear those seagulls' mournful cries, to see them low across the sand,
wheeling, swooping, gliding, snatching trophies from the cluttered strand,
to catch the smell of drying seaweed. This is all we need, it seems,
to make the perfect holiday we knew was hiding in our dreams.

BARBARA YOUNG (HEREFORD)

NATURE'S WONDERLAND

Tiny dewdrops - crystal pearls
Glistening and glinting there,
Oh what beauty meets the eye
When you've time to stand and stare.
Look how spider's web is spun
Fragile, delicate and sheer,
Trace the rainbow's fading hues -
Radiant colours there appear.
Butterfly with wings a-quiver
Velvet, iridescent sheen,
Flitting round the summer garden
Midst the flowers serene.
See the busy honeybee
Deep inside a flowerlet gay
Gathering pollen, drinking deep
Here and there upon its way.
Nature's beauty new appears
To eyes that seek and see,
Catching glimpses all the while
Of a wonderland so free.

FREDA SEARSON (RIPLEY)

A VILLAGE AFFAIR

As the colourful barge pulls into the marina,
The shouts are heard saying, 'I've just seen her,'
The band is playing, all the dignitaries are there,
Everything is done with such pomp and flair,
Looking and acting so regal and grand,
The lady steps out onto the dry land,
The crowds line the streets in anticipation,
As her carriage goes by there is such jubilation,
Bunting, banners and floats galore
All kinds of fun events are in store,
The procession of people weave their way to The Green,
For the annual crowning of our village Rose Queen,
I view this gathering and feel privileged to be,
A part of this rural community.

BRENDA REVILLE (WHALEY BRIDGE)

AHH SUMMER

When I was young and the summer came round
We'd play all day till nightfall came
Life was simple and times were good
All day, every day, was just a game.

The sun would shine and the air was warm
Sandals, shorts and a flimsy top
It's all we ever really needed
It seemed like summer would never stop.

School was out and holidays were in
There was fun and happiness all around
The noise was laughter, we laughed all day
No more teachers saying, 'Don't make a sound.'

But now I'm older and it's different somehow
Summer comes but not like then
It's here, it's gone, it's autumn so fast
Ahh summer . . . summer was way back then.

LINSI SANDERS (BARTON GREEN)

A SONG OF RHAPSODY

The wind in its weakest fear
Keeps the heart to a rose very near,
Frightens the storm with a spear,
Closes the mind's eye to hide the autumnal tear.

The windy garden blows the Cupid's shore
Upon which I murmur and roar,
Seize a love I walk and run for -
I cry, laugh and ask for more.

The shady flower comes and goes,
And this is the first year my land love sows,
Pleasant and fruitful the sunshine show;
Surrounding my country doth the spring vow.

DANIEL SONG (ARUN BUDHATHOKI) (NORTHAMPTON)

LINCOLN CATHEDRAL

We come from the flatlands
And rolling hills
Of Lincolnshire
Your might and authority
Calling us to account.

Grand matriarch.

Mother-ship to the county.

You sit in state.
Knees bent,
Stone feet anchored firm,
While rainbow eyes
Register the changes
Of a people.
Their haste and loud mistakes.
Their folly
And quiet success.

Deep within,
Limestone limbs
Endure Imp and Devil,
Where once rose up
A Heaven-bent arch of oak,
Beneath whose bounty
Wars wrought hardship,
Fear and loss.

And reconciliation.

Gargantuan marbled fingers
Lead us on a jewelled journey
Of grand architect
And simple man.
Vainglorious lives,
And humble hand.

Deafened by centuries of trumpeted triumph
You bear witness still
To small secret joys
Whispered by the soul.

And within the safety of your wall
We face our fallibility
And know greatness.

THERESA RICHMOND (WINTHORPE)

SUMMER ON HER WAY

Dawn has come and with her light
Says goodbye to the fleeting night.
She stops to linger on the hill,
Quiet and peaceful, almost deathly still.
She brings with her the warmth of day
And golden summer on her way.
Gone is the snow and the winter rain,
Gone till the sun goes to rest again.
She will draw her warmth into the sky,
So that cool and peaceful she may lie.
But now, the summer is here once more
To knock again on nature's door.
The tiny flowers will open wide,
No longer from the cold to hide.
She will cover the trees in leaves of green,
And lay for us, a joyous scene.
So all the Earth may realise
Summer again is riding the skies.
How long will she stay and fill our days
With fun and laughter from her ways?
How long shall we nestle in her arms,
To be captured by her unending charms?
Oh sun and summer, please stay long
And sing to us your friendly song.
So we can laugh and our hearts be gay,
For we know, summer, that you're on your way.

DIANA WALTER (CALVERTON)

THE LINCOLNSHIRE LASS

I am going back to Lincolnshire
It's where I long to be
There are things there oh so rare
That I just long to see,
It's not considered beautiful
To some I know it's true
But they just don't know where to look,
They just don't have a clue.

For Lincolnshire in summer is a treasure to behold,
The tulip fields of Spalding and the rapeseed fields of gold.
I know where the rabbits play
in countryside, at close of day,
where bluebells nestle in the wood
and squirrels play along the way,
where seabirds stalk the estuary
in moonlight on the ebbing tide
and have often watched in silence where urban foxes bide.

And when I stand on the shore
Looking out to sea,
With the wind in my hair
and just a trace of salt on my face
I'm sure I hear the sea say, stay with me
Then I know I am home and where I want to be.

SHIRLEY ANN SMITH (CLEETHORPES)

HAIRDRESSER HORSE

Horse is a hairdresser and
does not barber the grass.
He moulds it with his lips and tongue,
designing styles and shaping
shades that blend desire with dust
like dancing hair that plays at
hide-and-seek with laughing eyes.

The hairdresser is horse-like:
he grazes selectively
and gallops over the earth
with his tongue, stopping only
at fences erected by
his customers, who must be
carefully cultivated.

Scissor quick, earth-kicking hooves
ripple gloss from the flanks of
hairdresser horse as he moves,
tossing hair through deft fingers,
speech-feathered and supple, like
harness, close-moulding styles in
each hair that grows on our heads.

ANTHONY WEEDON (NORTH SOMERCOTES)

SEA OF DREAMS

As I peer towards the horizon
of the sea,
I visualise an ocean
filled with hope for me,
Carrying me to a land beyond uncertainty
and a universe with no fear
beyond there, is beautiful relaxing music
And that is all I can hear
I absorb the comfort of my dream
of wishes to come true
I feel the warmth of the sunbeam
As it shines down upon me
And when the ocean splashes
Gently up at me
I'll know there is some magic
Coming from the sea
Even in my dreams
Then everything will be
Just as I had hoped and dreamed
And all so magically

THERESA HARTLEY-MACE (CALVERTON)

SUMMER RAIN

Dark clouds, thunder, heavy showers,
The sun shines as the raindrops fall.
Sunlight and raindrops on the windowpane,
Delicate wet flowers in the rain.
In the sky, the rainbow colours flow,
A double arc of colour, mirrored bow.
That cool soily scent, of sweet wet earth and clay
In the wetness of a garden, on a summer's day.

VIOLET SINCLAIR (BEACHDALE)

ONLY DOG ROSES - BUT I CANNOT FORGET

Remember, remember - oh yes! I remember
Those days now long dead, with their pleasure and pain
The long days of summer, the kisses, the promise
The kisses now ashes, the promise in vain.

I bring back to mind our first meeting of summer
The sky's piercing blue and its light on the hill
We talked as we wandered, alone with each other
Of things that could not be, and now never will.

I think with delight of the joy of our greeting
In sunshine we walked and gave each our own heart
Secured with our love in its tangible splendour
Two lives became one and were never apart.

We kissed in the face of the high vault of Heaven
Held hands along lanes where the dog roses grew
We laughed as we shared the sweet joy of each moment
Through years that are finished, I think now of you.

A lifetime has broken the tie of our promise
And you are in dwellings where I cannot go
With time ever-present, no memory's needed
To live with those roses that I do not know.

And many long summers have brightened that hillside
The dead all together where spent roses lie
Your love colours all things that I shall remember
Till summer is over, and memories die.

ROY JOHN HUMPHREYS (RUSDEN)

My Favourite Walk

There is a very special walk that nature held in time,
A stroll for every season in rain, wind or shine.

Trees of every species such an interesting delight,
Giving shelter to the myriad birds, their songs of joy delight.

A rushing stream alongside the path seeks for a ruined mill,
In days gone by its happy task the water wheel to fill.

In spring vast sheets of bluebells beneath the canopy of trees,
Wild garlic wafting gently on a welcome summer breeze.

A group of copper beeches stand majestically and bold,
Their fallen leaves in autumn create a carpet of pure gold.

Most times this walk's deserted, its peace no soul disturbs,
The deer sometimes come to drink, a thrill surpassing words.

The river now has become quite deep, my favourite walk must end,
I allow my dog his longed-for swim, my faithful and true friend.

With joy I leave this peaceful place to wonder on creation,
So complete and perfect was God's plan, in wisdom and perception.

OLIVE BEDFORD (BURTON-ON-TRENT)

Sunshine Love

Muggy head rests
on thump-thump chest;
up down, up down
your pulse thrums in my ears.

Face grazes my cheek, gentle-gritty
while the summer wind outside marvels,
moaning through the reeds
and whispering across the water-top -
and I know it knows,
showing the wind as I sigh
into your kiss.

Low, summer-death sun
dusts the floor by our side.
Deepens into heady dusk,
then star-swilling night,
On and on, over and over.
Fingertips touch to touch
and the world runs by for right now,
we are eternal.

Time courses through young summer lovers.
And so it will always be.

NAOMI PORTMAN (WORCESTER)

THE FLOWING OF THE TIDE

In the mighty roar stretching far and wide,
As the waves surge in on the restless tide
Submerging the rocks as it rolls and sways,
Spitting furious froth in a million sprays,
Nothing is spared, nothing to save,
The waters so deep under each massive wave.
A power, that no one can fathom or find,
Vents its feelings on all things
And all of mankind.
Insatiable longing for multitudinous prey,
Swallowing everything that gets in its way.
After engulfing all of its fill
It begins to recede at its own speed and will,
Leaving behind in a trail of destruction,
Thrown aside and discarded
The flotsam and jetsam,
To lie there in peace under sun's soothing rays
'Til back once again comes the tide's rushing craze.

DORIS BAILEY (SHEEPY MAGNA)

MY KIND OF SUMMER

As summer is here, I'd like to share with you
All the things I like to do.
A day out to Alton Towers just does it for me,
Strolling in the gardens, then having a picnic for my tea.
Having a go on this new ride though, I'm not very keen,
I can't remember what it's called. Ten? Twelve? Oh no, it's Th13teen!
If I want peace and quiet, Shark Bait Reef comes to mind,
Where I can wander and view the sea life of all different kind.
Relaxing outside with a horror book can be rather exciting,
Wanting to know how it ends can be rather nail-biting,
I like biking in the Peak District when the sky is blue,
Just going along slowly, admiring the view.
A little bit of retail therapy never fails to impress,
Whether I'm buying shoes, trousers or a new dress.
So when autumn has kissed the summer goodbye,
I know I've got my memories - that I can rely.

RUTH WARRINGTON (CHEADLE)

ESSENCE OF SUMMER

Steady throbbing
toy aeroplanes
ploughing deep blue.

Chugging mowers,
shadows dappling
fragrant cut grass.

Motoring bees
busy buzzing
bloom to bright bloom.

Jewelled butterflies,
on gauzy wings
fluttering flight.

Light dazzled sight
warm reddened skin
heat tossed sleep.

Slow afternoons
hushed somnolence
drooping stillness.

Capture - crush - distil - pour into expensive gold-stoppered bottles

LINDA JENNINGS (BILTON)

NATURE'S PRAISE

The grass whispers God's praise
in the gentle breeze
Birds sing praise as they perch
in the trees
The leaves rustle as they join in the chorus
Welcoming the day that's before us
The sun peeks out on the horizon
bringing light and warmth to everyone
These gifts from God, glorify His majesty
are ours to treasure and enjoy for eternity

JAYNE SANDERS (BELPER)

Where the Sunset Meets the Sea

(MY FAVOURITE AREA IN NORTH WALES, I AM YET TO MOVE THERE!)

Where the sunset meets the sea, is my place of destiny, where I long to be
Where the beauty all around, is there daily, before my eyes to see
Where the air is fresh, to the body - uplifting
Where the land is open - being able to feel free

Where a degree of peace is there to be found
Where sunsets come and go, ever changing the skies' daily picture
Where mountains, at times, disappear under the rainy mist
Where trees change with seasons into colourful hues

Where the sea, one day calm, blue another, stormy and grey, the surface being tossed about
Where the sand can be flat, seen for miles, another day, in the formation of sandy waves
Where the cries of seagulls fill the air, showing off their fishing flair
Where, if you are quiet, willing to listen, to see, all manner of nature will come into your life

Where the tiniest of flowers in colourful contrasts spring up side by side
Where, out of season, you can listen to silence or the falling of the ocean upon the boundary of the sand
Where you can see, miles out, the perfect roundness of the horizon
Where, porpoise, seals, fish, pop up for air above the surface of the sea

Where, in reflective moments, I think about a lifetime of visits
Where, at times I can cry and the wind catches and dries my tears
Where, at the sea edge, God hears the cry of my prayers
Where my soul feels at peace

Where, the sea to my heart calls
Where the mountains never move, they, only watching the 'come and go' of life below
Where birds gather, in their family flocks, practising their strength of wing, for the migration journey up ahead
Where the 'baa' of lambs and the mighty bulls', 'call', fills the air

Yes, with affection, the place I long to be, where the sunset meets the sea.

BARBARA FLETCHER (TIPTON)

Summer Breezes

The summer sun is so temperamental
And when it shines it needs to give off heat
And hit the tattooed man
Standing on his feet,
He does not need to absorb its rays
Only feel its power and be amazed,
The crowd that flocks to the park
Will burn in its glows long before dark
They'll eat their ice cream with cold intent
And meet the trees in their green lustre of foliage and growth
And be swamped as the trees talk to each other,
But that's only on the summer breezes,
A girl runs by and she freezes
Just for a moment of summer breezes,
It chills her body as the sky grows cold,
A cloud blots out the whispering sun
Another day has to run
A shower will surely seem to fall,
A temperature drop,
The people in the park a heart will stop
You cannot hear nothing but the whispering trees,
Who talk to each other
The birch, the beech, the sycamore and the yew,
A rainbow suddenly appears in view
Its colours a radiance bright
The sun is strengthened by its plight
And the people in the park are amazed
At nature's creation
And away to the right a distant rumble
Everybody knows that's thunder
The rain will fall now and the sun has given up
People head for the exits before the rain comes
And summer now is oh so wonderful
And I rejoice
The tattooed man has found his voice.

T McFarlane (Wavertree)

My Special Children

They wake in the day with joy in their hearts.
They roll back the duvet as this day newly starts.
They stroll to the bedrooms where children sleep sound.
With love in their hearts, no comparison found.
They all look so perfect and wonderfully made,
But people would say they are tattered and frayed.
They say such things as they are all such freaks
They are all just so nerdy, a bunch of weird geeks.
They say they are stupid or social misfits.
Or simply they are your common eccentrics.
They say they are ignorant and so very rude,
And parents are neglectful when they run round in the nude.
They are told they are clumsy or babies or bad,
These people all make me so terribly mad.
It makes me so sad that they can be so cruel,
It's ignorance that helps to give this fire its fuel.
People don't know what a wonder it can be,
To love a child who's Autistic, Dyspraxic or ADHD.
If they did then they'd see how blessed that we are,
And how they are angels that fell from a star.
The wonderful world they show you each day.
And humour and illogical things that we say.
And they are all so truthful when things aren't quite right,
We all respect truth, this quality we'll fight.
So why is it wrong when it's born in your soul,
And you're told with an ASC you're not perfectly whole?
The truth of it is we are blessed with our kids,
And no more will we listen to your lies and your fibs.
We'll fight for the right of our kids on the spectrum,
Because someone out there needs to support and protect them.
Not from themselves but from people like these,
From people who like to judge and to tease.
We are so blessed with our kids from above,
With all their joy and honesty, truth and their love.
I wouldn't change my children for one minute or day,
For these children I give thanks as I pray.
Please Lord don't you change them they are wonderfully great,
Just be with them when they get in a state.
And help them to be the best that they can be,
For now and always for all people to see.

Shelley Whitehouse (Kettering)

A DAY OUT TO LLANDUDNO

I saw you in the pouring rain,
I felt you in the wind.
I knew your hands alone
Had made all these things.

The blossom on the May trees,
Yellow-gold of rape,
The trees all in new green today
Not one from my eyes did escape.

Then a vast carpet of bluebells,
Against the bracken still brown
The flowing gorse upon the hills
Looked almost like a crown.

So then the clouds did gently part
The sun came bursting through.
To light up the myriads of diamonds,
Upon the surface of the sea.

O, yes our God made all these things
Just for you and just for me!

SHEILA TAYLOR (KINGSWINFORD)

OTHER DAY BEGINS

Once again it's daylight
The sun is radiance bright
Not a cloud in the sky
Happy birds sing and fly
Time like a rolling stream
Ticks away like a forgotten dream
A day of joy and light
As it's followed by the night

ANN THOMPSON (LEDBURY)

A Walk Down a Country Lane

Walking at leisure in the cool clear air
I heard a sound, from I know not where.
'Twas the sound of a skylark flying on high
Up above me, somewhere in the sky
It sounded quite thrilling to the human ear
With its endless trilling, filled me with cheer.

Over the hedgerow, on the right-hand side
I spied a horse, which I'd like to ride.
With magnificent tail and polished coat,
The sight of him brought a lump to my throat.
He was running and jumping all around,
Everything shook as his hooves hit the ground.

A bit further on, where the lambs run and play,
I say, to myself, what a wonderful day.
The sun is shining, the skies are blue,
Keep saying to myself what else can I do?
The cows are all grazing, their noses to ground,
In fact the world's peaceful, serene all around.

I came to a stream and paused on the bridge,
Something flew by me, thought it was a midge,
But no! 'Twas a dragonfly, beautiful thing
With bright blue tail and gossamer wing.
Silently flying away in the air
A marvellous sight for people who care.

Journeying on, a fox crossed my path,
It was hunting a rabbit, which filled me with wrath!
No notice it took, as I walked on by
Because a fox on the hunt is terribly sly.
There was nought I could do to save poor bunny
Except keep on saying that's not very funny!

My walk down the lane came to an end,
The sky grew darker, rain began to descend.
I spied a main road where I might catch a bus,
Which will take me back home, without a fuss.
After a leisurely day in the countryside,
I can relax in my home, with a feeling of pride.

WILLIAM THIRKETTLE (DRAYCOTT)

SKIES

(Chorus:)
Oh may my eyes see sunlit skies,
And skies with stars and moon;
Oh may my eyes see sunlit skies,
To chase away the gloom!

I've lived long in the valley
Admired its mountain wall;
But cursed its constant shadow,
That hangs above us all.

(Chorus:)

I've heard of angry, leaden skies,
That turn day into night;
Of thick black rolling thunder clouds,
With shafts of burning light.

(Chorus:)

And I have heard of starry skies,
That calm the worst of fears;
With harvest moons and shooting stars,
That move one's eyes to tears.

(Chorus:)

And there's a so-called mackerel sky,
With clouds you scarce do see;
And other skies have candyfloss,
Or so it seems to me!

(Chorus:)

But where are those vast clear blue skies,
That stretch for miles and more?
For these are those to lift my eyes,
Beyond the valley floor!

(Chorus:)

DAVID E ANDERSON (WALCOT BY FOLKINGHAM)

Portsmouth Point

The hypodermic needle of heat
Pierces our bodies. We asked for it,
Tired of the cold normality
Of grey skies. Now we are hooked,
Energy lost, seeking rest
In anti-depressant shade.
This sluggard Pompey crowd
Sprawls in the life-giving breeze
At the restless harbour mouth,
Drinking thirstily at the Still and West
Or hugging the cool of Spice Islander.
At Gunwharf Quay they crawl like ants
Making for the sugar in the shops
But, anchored safe at their mooring,
'Victory' and Nelson greet the morning
With arrogant and sublime indifference.

PAUL NORRIS (KENILWORTH)

My Stolen Joy

Today's the day I lost my smile and that will never cease,
No matter what the future holds my heart has lost its peace.

All songs have lost their meaning and my ears will hear no more
Instead I'll sit in silence, staring only at the door.

I have no care for food or drink, for now they have no taste,
So what's left sat upon my shelves can all just go to waste.

I dare not enter the room where we laid side by side,
Because our dreams they haunt me and from them I cannot hide.

The sky will be forever grey, my mood forever blue,
I cannot even contemplate a life that has not you.

DICKON SPRINGATE (GILLINGHAM)

FLOATING IN MY MIND

I often sit and let my mind run free
Seeking answers to the questions that concern me
I ask myself who, what, where, when and why
Hoping the answers will help me to clarify
The thoughts which are floating in my mind

What are the questions which are concerning me?
One concerns the kind of world that I would like to see
I know it is a world where peace reigns supreme
Where order is established, and chaos is contained
Those are the thoughts floating in my mind

Is there any hope that this could ever be?
Is peace something that the world one day will see?
What is preventing my dreams from coming true?
Is there something that all of us could do?
These questions are floating in my mind

Before peace can come we have to eliminate the causes of war
Not just in this country, but on every foreign shore
My question is, 'How can this be achieved?'
I know the answer will be difficult to find
In the meantime the questions go on floating in my mind

How can the causes of war be eliminated?
After all these can be very clearly stated
It could be power-seeking, jealously or greed
Or from the under privileged crying out in need
These reasons go on floating in my mind

Sitting here and letting my mind run free
Fails to bring any satisfaction to me
For unless there is some means of eliminating war
The world will carry on much as it did before
And the same thoughts will keep floating in my mind

RONALD MARTIN (BULWELL)

THE SEASHORE

I walked across the sandy beach
So warm beneath my feet
The golden sand down near the sea
Seemed to shimmer in the heat.
The pebbles and the pearly shells
Newly washed and clean
Twinkled in the sunlight rays
Near strands of seaweed green.
The ripples of the outgoing tide
Left patterns in the sand
Whilst further out the bigger waves
Rolled back to far-off land.
The seagulls' cries as they circle high
And the scent of salt and sea
Filled me with a surge of joy
And made me feel so free.
Across the turquoise sea far out
Beneath the azure sky
The white sea horses rose and dipped,
The passing boats cruised by.
Upon this quiet deserted beach
Away from the distant crowds
There was a sense of heavenly peace
Away from life's dark clouds.

ENID HEWITT (GRANTHAM)

Poppies Glow

Poppies glow red and bright
bringing sleep through the night
to those that choose,
too much, you lose,

then face the Grim Reaper
he becomes your keeper,
taking from you
the inner blue

but take care and choose wise
see poppies with your eyes
do not wonder
or face thunder

the syrup so tempting
will leave you with nothing
except trouble
and no bubble

see the red not the dream
then keep your self-esteem
love the idea
don't live the fear
don't smoke poppies my dear.

GARTH (CRANWELL)

Summer To Me

Barefoot splendour,
pushing into warm blue and green.
Life bursting with growth,
a picture to be seen.
Trees and their tendrils
and sashaying style,
Flowers forcing forward
watching a while.
Clouds flowing across and around,
naked dancing,
warm rain refreshing
in summer's blessing.
Houses unsecured,
at one
with the dusty smell of corn
a playground on the lawn.
Hums and buzzes, high then low,
life leaking in all directions,
passing fast and slow,
knowing where to go?
Rigid thorns, nettles, bobbing,
sharpened wasps, a fly, a bee
Uplifting hope, freedom,
summer is calling on me.

PAULA JOHNSON (WICKENBY)

THE GREEN MAN

Malevolent spirit of the wood,
no concept of evil or of good.
His deeds and doings neither
right nor wrong.
His voice can be heard in the
cuckoo's song.
His sight as sharp as the
Fox's stare,
The wind it blows in his
willow hair.

His skin as gnarled as
oaken bark,
He stalks the forest
after dark.
The ability to shift between
reality and myth,
If you have the sight
you will receive his gift.

Legs long and lithe, as the
silver birch,
Fingers outstretched on which
birds do perch.
His arms strong and regal
as the elm,
Beware his lore if you
Walk his realm.

KEITH DEELEY (SOLIHULL)

Long Distance

I wish I could ring up my dad,
And have the conversations we never had,
There's a lot of things I'd like to say,
But sadly long ago, he passed away.

Loads of thoughts come into my head,
So many things, we never said,
Lots of things, I would ask about,
And he could always work them out.

To him I was a special son,
Memories I have, are full of fun,
As a dad, he was just ace,
In my heart he has a special place.

I know one day, we'll meet again,
In the future, on a distance plain,
Where we will both share eternal rest,
Because to me Dad was the best.

Time we know makes all things right,
God we all know, as special might,
There's nothing at all, that he can't do,
So I hope one day, my dream comes true.

JEFF HOBSON (LUTTERWORTH)

THE GIRL WITH RAVEN HAIR

I used to watch them from afar
Dancing around the fire under the moonlight
I would sit and listen to the jingle of the coins
Their magic of dark and desire

The one that hypnotises me the most
The girl with the raven hair
Her emerald eyes draw you in
Then you fall under her enchanting spell

The sailors come and never want to leave
Just one smile and their hearts belong to her
She tells their fortune and takes their gold
Ready to tell her stories at the meeting

I want to be just like her
With raven black hair and a smile to charm
She teaches me to dance the same under the moon
And chant the spells to steal your hearts

She smiles at me in a different way
One that leaves no spell for me
She was the gypsy girl with the raven hair
To me she is just my mother.

SHARON ATKINSON (STANFORD LE HOPE)

Autumnal Feelings

Deep, deep, silvery blue sky above,
lazy breeze moving leaves
some already tired, rustling,
the odd one flying high.
The last blooms withered;
they graced all summer in colour
like rainbows, feeding bees.
Slowly green vegetation yellows
on its fringes, like old age!
Greeting another season,
it's autumn in their lives too.

The beach, a dazzle of lacy white
gingerbread and sun-struck
shingles peer over the cliff, as
a grand brow, tired, frowning.
Spinning in aimless circles,
the honeybees, stitching
their endless looms above the grass.
Rows of chairs along the seafront,
each as empty as a faithless heart.

The starry night lit only by a
transparent slice of moon
on a velvet tray of cerulean sky.
A fractured memory teases
at the edge of our minds
reminding nature of the slip-
sliding universe, that made perfect,
irrefutable sense of a flaming forge
of life, changing the seasons
new for old,
bringing on its wings autumn
in multi-coloured gold.

ANNA ELLIOTT (FAVERSHAM)

MY BODY SANG IN MAY TIME

My body sang in May time
Refreshed by the gentle breeze,
My mind rejoiced as through my eyes
I saw beneath a canopy of trees
With never-ending surprise
New life burst forth, in May time.
My blood races cool beneath the skin
New vigour stems from deep within,
Love, laugh, run like the wind
Shout and embrace the magic clime
With never-ending surprise
Renewed each and every May time.

My body sang in May time
Under the sun and moon,
Through the trees the sunbeams
Danced merrily to the tune.

BRIAN C GAMAGE (SOUTHBOROUGH)

SUMMERTIME

When the sun comes out, we want to shout
'Hip hip hooray,' we will say
Ain't we glad for sunshine today

We'll go to the seaside with buckets and spades
Find lots of things to do
Build sandcastles by the shore
Have candyfloss, ice cream too
Pick shells of all shapes and sizes.
To make many disguises, have a lovely day
With lots of fun and sun.

JENNIFER REEVES (RUSHALL)

Reflections of a Summer's Day

Summertime to me means the early light of dawn, sitting in the garden listening to the sounds
of birds singing in the arrival of a brand new day.
The silence of the morning, no traffic on the way.
There is no busy daytime noise, the world is still at peace, I sit there with my cup of tea,
Smelling the clear blue sky.
Bees buzz around, birds soar past and butterflies flutter by.
The day has yet to begin its shift, it's still starting to awake, flowers stretch and open, the sun begins to glow.
Today is just coming alive, it's time to get up and go.
I head to work and watch as the daylight slips away, carrying out my office duties as is duly done.
I wish I could be outside sitting in the sun.
Then another day is over and the working shift is by, I make my way looking forward to welcoming my home.
My garden is full of colour, a peaceful place to roam.
I sit and watch the hot air balloon travelling overhead, people small within the basket, gliding gracefully in the sky.
Now and again the flame sends its jet shooting way up high.
Then we have the summer rain, afterwards it's so clean and fresh, watering the flowers helping them to grow.
The mixture of the sun and rain causes a rainbow.
The evening brings its own charm, sitting in the cool night air, relaxing after the hard day, taking in the evening pale.
Solar lights begin to glow, like in a fairy tale.
Summer means a chance to catch up on the way of life, to go to the beach, have picnics in the sun, sit in the garden enjoying the day.
Before the winter sets in and summer fades away.

FIONA HOLMAN (ASHFORD)

PLEASE PICK A POSY

Please pick a posy, a sweet old-fashioned posy?
Please pick a posy and give it to your dad?
Please pick a posy, a buttonhole or nosegay?
Please pick a posy for a poor old lad?

Though you may rather, bring flowers to your father,
Or send to him a grand bouquet.
If he were made to choose, he would rather hear the news
That a bunch of real wild flowers was on its way.

Is it too much to ask? Is it such a daunting task?
Is picking flowers a real lost art?
Is it something from the past of which we have seen the last
Or will it linger on to cheer the heart?

You may move him close to tears as you roll away the years,
And re-create those golden days gone by.
When you proffered your first gift in a grubby little fist,
With such love that might well moisten any eye.

Please pick a posy, for somebody who knows he,
Would rather take a daisy from your hand,
Than an orchid or gardenia, that suffers from anaemia,
And was raised in some far-off and foreign land?

Please pick a posy, a sweet wild posy?
Please pick a posy and give it to your dad?
Please pick a posy, a buttonhole or nosegay?
Oh please pick a posy for your dear old dad?

(Please note: it is now an offence to pick wild flowers so
Please grow a few in the corner of your garden and pick them.)

BERNARD NEWTON (CHESTERFIELD)

Ripe for the Falling

The farmer's almanac may predict
A rough winter with biting winds,
But now do not think of crisp snow,
Instead the glorious reds and ambers autumn brings.
Let the baking begin!
Filling kitchens with sumptuous smells that linger
Whilst whispering of happy childhoods
And rose-tinted dreams.
Let there be cinnamon-spiced apples cooked in pastry nests,
Or fresh bread rising like a beating heart,
Turning golden-brown off the flickering flames
Within the ebony hearth.
Hear the crackling of first fires lit
And watch the small plumes of smoke
Rise from chimney breasts.
Yearn for dying leaves to line the cobbled streets,
So I and other young-hearted souls might
Make them airbound with our kicks.
Good friends must gather round my card table,
Sipping hot toddies and clutching
Thick-rimmed mugs close to our chests.
The air will be filled with laughter
And ephemeral energy that dances amongst
The moonlight of early darkness,
As sparklers whirl around the air
Tracing their glittery trails upon the black,
Evoking fond memories of idle youth.
Let sheep nestle between scatterings of mist
Cast flavescent by rising soft autumnal sun
Whilst children with sticky hands might
Scoop Jack's russet brains upon the porch
To light the space behind his eyes with glee.
Our bellies must be filled with comfort food that
Restores our souls to good,
Whilst mouths are propped open with fine cigarettes
And elbows search to find their usual grooves
Upon the table's wood.
We will listen to loving strumming of guitar or uke
And tap a rhythm with toes readily turning blue.
We will sing some soft caressing song
That makes us all remember

Times of old and friends forgot.
We will be grateful for all these things and more.
Let's not yet think on Christmas
For autumn to ignore.
It is by far the happiest time
Of that I am sure.

OLIVIA KELLAS-KELLY (STAMFORD)

PICNIC ON FOLKESTONE BEACH

Rain, rain go away . . .
my umbrella turned inside out today.
I'm soaked, splashed - cross as sticks,
Seeking shelter from your perpetual drips!
I know you're needed, a force for life -
however, today you have just given me strife.
So wanted, a sunny day by the sea,
gentle sea breezes - but elements are playing with me -
Listen to my sneezes . . . !
Now gulls are mocking, laughing out loud,
looking skywards - there's a break in the clouds,
waves pebbled-growl, isn't quiet so loud?
Distant kite-surfers at speed, hurl themselves high.
I watch intrigued, courageous to do or die!
Sun's sudden smile, reflects on my flask,
raised teacup toasts, the picnic I asked . . .

JOANNE MANNING (HAWKINGE)

Boat Number 65

Boat number 65
On the River Avon
In Stratford-upon-Avon
Motorboat number 65
I hired with my cousin, Jordana
When we went on a day trip
On 3rd June 2005
We had a great day
Looked all round Stratford-upon-Avon
Jordana was an angel, as good as gold
She wanted to go on a motor boat
So we did, we hired a boat
I had a drive
Then Jordana had a drive
She loved every minute
I loved every minute
I filmed Jordana with a camcorder
I took photos and Jordana driving
Jordana driving boat number 65
On the River Avon
In Stratford-upon-Avon
Down the river we went
And back again
The hour we had for our trip
Jordana was good at driving
I was very proud
The day was mostly lovely and sunny
With odd drizzle of rain
The great time in Stratford-upon-Avon
On the River Avon
Aboard boat number 65
The date, 3rd June 2005
When I took out for the day my cousin Jordana
We had a good laugh and lots of fun
Jordana was an angel, a treasure
Me and Jordana aboard boat number 65
Boat number 65
On the River Avon
Stratford-upon-Avon.

DAVID J HALL (BIRMINGHAM)

Sunflower

I came across a field
Of glorious gold
Oh what a splendid vision
It was to behold

Stood to attention
Their heads held high
Graceful and proud
Under the cornflower sky

With their beady eyes
And golden crowns
From lofty heights
On mere mortals look down

They are crafted lovingly
In the image of Mother Sun
And worship her adoringly
Each and every one

At the break of dawn
They raise their heads
Cheerfully greeting
The day ahead

And as the sun fades away
It's time for them to rest
'Goodnight Mother Sun
Sweet dreams. God bless.'

ANNE MORGAN (TUNBRIDGE WELLS)

Hidden Burton

There is a view of Burton,
That Constable should have painted,
But you can only see it from a canoe,
Three miles upstream from where I put it in,
Up by the Leicester Line.

The left frame rises from dark waters,
Excluding pylons and power line,
Through purple loosetrife and bank of green,
To summer's cumulus galleons,
Sailing an azure sea.

The right rises from the other bank,
Including waving osiers,
Before a stand of prim Lombardies,
Green tower holding up the sky,
Hiding the Trent as it bends.

The washlands stretch, an unbroken plain,
No sight of road or bridge,
Nor street, nor houses
As the great dome that is Winshill,
Rises verdant, pristine and pure.

There is only one building to be seen,
Nestling in the riot of trees.
A perfect golden mean, between left and right,
Between ruffled water and burnished sky,
Saint Peter's white stone, filigreed tower.

Shines by its own ethereal light,
Beneath the midday sun.
Nature lifting her veils, the glorious gift,
To those who venture off the track,
And take the time to stare

ANDY BIDDULPH (BURTON-ON-TRENT)

THE MAN YOU SEE

He goes to work each morning
often before it's light
Careful to remember
The things he must get right.

The traffic is often heavy
The sky is often grey
But he has to make the best of things
To get him through the day.

He goes back home each evening
Sometimes after dark
Too late to see those he loves
And take them to the park.

He feels a little weary
With nothing much to say
And slowly drifts off to sleep
Too tired to save his day.

But deep in the heart of the man you see
Lives the man he wants to be
Free to live life, his own way
True to himself, every single day.

A man who can make dreams come true
a man like me, a man like you.
A man who can set his spirit free
to be the man he wants to be.

He goes to work each morning
The sky is often grey
And it's just another day,
Just another day . . .

TIM KITCHEN (BEESTON)

White

White is an angel, superior and mighty
Hosts and symbolises the meaning of purity
It is a woman so chaste and holy
The flaky snow that coats all over the grief
Esteemed, a majestic victor

White is an innocent newborn child
Herculean and a milky cream flowing from the fountain of Ishtar
It is a cloud that showers serenity, indulgence and harmony
The perogitive captivating the soul inside you
Especially a frost-bitten shroud of death

White is a turgid world of melancholy
Heinous sorcery that leads to a crematorium
Ignites the spiritless remembrance of misery, torment and agony
The ruthless, grieving old man that bores and ails
Endless sorrow and hostility is white
Heavenly, magnificent and virtuous is white.

AMBREEN AKHTER (BIRMINGHAM)

Holiday

I felt the need to get away
So I booked myself a holiday
Smart little chalet by the sea
I wondered what joys awaited me

The days sped by as I had fun
Plenty to see and lots of sun
I travelled here, I travelled there
Content and happy, free from care

Did you have a good time? Was the weather nice?
'Yes,' I said, 'but here's some advice
Travel north, south, east or west
You will always find that home is best.'

MARY SHEPHERD (NOTTINGHAM)

MY GO KART
(WRITTEN FOR MY GRANDSON, RYAN DEAN RUSSELL)

my go-kart, what can I say
it's well smart - I play on it every day
it's red and black and lives in the shed
when I drive it I'm full steam ahead
I go down our garden path with such force
If the garden were bigger I would make it a course
I would drive through tunnels go over cobbles
Ride over hills and make my wheels wobble
Through Mum's washing hung on the line
This would be so funny and sublime
Through the patio doors and into the house
Scaring my mum, sister and pet mouse
Screaming and yelling for me to 'Get out'
I'm only five there's no need to shout
My steering wheel turns, my wheels turn with it
'OK, I'm back in the garden, give me a minute.'
Out of my way you silly dog
That was too close, you jump like a frog
I'm going so fast - I'm sliding in my seat
Pedalling so fast I can hardly feel my feet
Just like Uncle William when he was a boy
His go-kart was his car - never a toy
If my go-kart breaks I know I can rely
On Uncle William to mend it when he pops by
Out with the toolbox to mend my car
Off I go again like a shooting star
Not in the house, I'll only get told off
Not through the line to dirty Mum's wash
Going like the wind, causing vibrations
Me and my go-kart - such adorations

ELAINE A BROCKLESBY (BRIGG)

Summer Love, Joshua And Ella Rose

So many wonders I have seen
Such beauties that are evergreen
The sea that turns hour upon hour
Each garden with the prettiest flower

How lovely the blackbird calling time on the day
Then waking to dawn's chorus in such a sweet way
All this through the summer is priceless to none
Except the sound of my grandson's summer fun

His laughter at play fills my heart with a song
The hugs and kisses when the day has been long
Sweet smiles from his sister only eight months old
Will live in my memory all the days I am told

All the wonders of the summer will never compare
Of the love of my little ones whose love with me share.

SUSAN ROFFEY (LONGFIELD)

Sunny Days

When I was small
Sunny days were fun,
Mum, would take me with my bucket and spade to the sea and sand,
Daddy was a sailor and was away at sea,
How I wish he could come and paddle with me,
One day Mum said, 'We can't go on the beach, because our world is at war
And concrete blocks cover the sands,' where I played before.
Now I am much older with a home of my own,
And a lovely garden all around.
Sunny days are still fun.
When the sun comes out; I take a lounge chair into the garden:
Sun hat, books oh bliss, housework abandoned not a care,
Sleep overcomes me
I dream, of fun days on the beach,
Did someone speak?
'Mum! Is it time for tea?'

JOAN MARGARET WALLER (SIDCUP)

SUMMER

The sun rises in the east and sets in the west,
Between these two is summer, the time we like the best.
At dawn the air is fresh and still,
Birds perch and trill and sit upon our window sill
Telling us time to rise and take our fill.
Now we are ready to face the world at will
We drive to the riverbank,
Swans glide along its glistening silver flow -
Cows in the meadow are free to graze and low.
Silence is perfect as we wend our way
Until we reach the object of our delight,
A little church and house perched upon a hill,
Trees and blossoms make it a wondrous sight
To be in the country today makes it feel so right.
We wend our way to a country pub,
Where they serve such special grub.
The interior is cool and bright.
The food and drink of which we partake
Is all fresh and of a country make.
Reluctantly we leave and say farewell
Of this day there is much to tell.
The countryside in summer belongs to you and me
I beg you all go and see.
Summer comes but once a year
And gives all so much cheer.
So accept it and let it cast its spell.

CARL KEMPER (LICHFIELD)

THE MEETING OF PERSONALITIES: MADAME TUSSAUD SCULPTS NAPOLEON'S LIFE MASK

'How flattering to hear you say, Sire,
That though the English cannot fright you -
Posing for Madame Tussaud can!

'Yet it is I who face the challenge of your life mask,
For however practised at the technique one may be,
There must be no obstruction to your breathing.

How will you take in air beneath the plaster?
Why, through these straws pushed up into your nose -
Like this . . . permit me . . . thus . . . and thus!

'Oh pardon, Sire, I was too rough, perhaps?
Your need to breathe imposes this indignity,
For which I crave your Excellency's kind indulgence.

'You say there is a question you would like to ask?
Then I shall answer to the best of my ability:
Mm . . . mm . . . why, yes, it's really true -

My expertise in waxen images did save my life
Throughout the terror when my revolutionary gaolers
Had me mould the death masks
Of their victims' heads they brought me
From the guillotine - hideously warm still, bloody to the touch -
Turning my prison cell into a waxwork studio of death.

Being of use to them, my life was spared. My crime?
For teaching drawing to the sister of the King - oh pardon, Sire,
I quite forgot - no longer must we think of him as royal,

But just another citizen by name of Louis Capet . . . yes, yes,
I held that head between my hands . . . those soulful eyes in prayer;
While Marie Antoinette's stared back at me in stark surprise,

As if they saw in my grim task a friend's betrayal.
Instinctively we value our own heads,
Discover nerves of steel we hardly knew we had.

Your living head is now my chief concern, Sire:
I'll take you through each stage - first lay the ground
With plaster . . . press into it the clay . . . then wait
Until the plaster's cold and set. Lift off the mask!

Behold the mould! Fill with the hottest wax and cool
To chip away the outer shell - your noble face disclosed.

It's then I'll crave a further sitting, Sire, to add
The finer points of nature that a scalpel and my brush
Dipped in the flesh-tints of my colour box may bring out your complexion.

Now courage, Sire, for your ordeal's about to start -
While mine's to face my greatest challenge - Buonaparte!'

GLORIA SMITH (CANTERBURY)

WILL YOU BE MINE?

I have left the Tyne, with a girl, for a mine,
I have left the Tyne, for a mine.
The girl isn't mine, and the mine isn't mine
but my prospects seem fine down the line.
Here, the summer's divine, and the wine is benign
so we left that cloud-covered clime,
to live in a sunny, faraway land
where the crickets shake heliotrope wings,
and anteaters dance in the dark and freeze
when they harken the jaguar's whine.
The hills host a choice, and echo the voice
of big game just naturally free,
which you never expect, with the greatest respect,
in the depths of our great northern city.
The girl isn't mine, and she may have a mine
but she lured me with rod, line and net,
A plausible soul, with beautiful eyes
which I noticed the day that we met.
I noticed a lot on the days after that
when her eyes seemed to mirror the sun,
They helped her a lot when she wound in her line
and I gladly fell into her net.
So I have left the Tyne with a girl for a mine,
I have left the Tyne for a mine,
The girl could be mine, but could the mine too?
I'll leave the conclusion to . . . *you!*

ALAN SMITH (BROMLEY)

COUNTRY HOLIDAYS YESTERYEAR

Sunny Suffolk meadows
Poppies in the corn
Drawing water from the well
Dewy grass at dawn
Thatched cottage gardens
Geraniums in pots
Uncle always digging
In his veggie plots
Busy aunt in kitchen
With her rolling pin
Rooster in the barnyard
Making such a din
Collecting eggs from hen house
While they still felt warm
Dodging past the beehives
Fearful of a swarm
Sitting by the village stream
With a fishing net
Trying to catch a tiddler
To keep it as a pet
Oh! The joys of country life
How I loved them so
Happy were my summers then
Long, long ago.

MARION WEBB (BROMLEY)

TIMMY

Timmy was a tabby cat,
A frightened, fighting, skinny cat
Whose mistress now had gone.
His tawny eyes were smouldering
With mistrust and with fear.
He wouldn't mix with other cats
And missed his home so dear.
He also missed his daily feed
Of salmon, rich and red -
So wouldn't look at Kitekat
Or other cat foods spread
On dishes for his dinner
No wonder he grew thinner!
Well, when I heard of Tiny Tim -
For that was then his name,
And saw him at the cattery,
I volunteered to claim
That sad, unwanted tabby cat,
So took him home with me.
- From Tiny Tim to Tiger Tim.

MARIA MOLLER (ROCHESTER)

A SPECIAL TIME

Changes of seasons,
What have we here?
Summer upon us with a tear,
Hayfever season with this comes sunlight,
Showers, rainbow bright
Insects, changing into wonderful colours
With children we can explore the wonders
That the seasons bring.
Running, laughing, playing together
Families enjoy the heat of the sun,
Water splashing, giving drops of rain,
A rainbow appears again and again.
Colours are changing the rainbow disappears.
A wish for all to explore,
Summer is fun be safe in the sun,
Before we know summer is a glow.
Autumn is here.

GWENDOLINE WOODLAND (GILLINGHAM)

PEACE

Peace, pax, paix, shalom
Whatever language we use
It's what we all want.

MEG NELLIST (UPMINSTER)

MY BEAUTIFUL BRITAIN

Often I take a look at my maps,
As there are many places I would like to see,
So naturally that also means, where I would also really like to be.
But of all the lovely and beautiful counties that I actually want to truly see,
Are Cornwall, Devon and Somerset, for they seem to awake a need in me.

Of course I've seen others more than once or twice,
And I know they're actually very nice
Especially the Old Kingdom of Powys, and other parts of Wales,
Well, I like them because I hear many old tales.

Yes just like Cornwall, their stories are ancient and old.
Yes of minstrels and kings and of course the very bold.
Though if the truth is known, I love all this land,
For green hills and forest, are far better than sand.

Yes old castles are better than any gold sands,
Though we have both, in these sweet lands.
And we have many a famous city and really busy towns,
Though personally, I would rather walk on our beautiful downs.

Yes probably that is why I often seek and search all the maps of mine,
But you see, for me there's just one Britain,
And again its enchanting scenery, looks perfectly fine,
Yes I know all the countries on this Earth are all very nice
But there's only one Britain, so that's been precise.

RHOWEN-MARGOT BROWN (SCUNTHORPE)

DAY TRIPPER

Venice retreats through diesel vapours
a living Canaletto.
Translucence burst on either side
San Marco hidden by water wash.

Passing the cemetery
the dead sunbath silently.
The boat groans slowing.
A mythical boar
foraging the forest of the lagoon
beneath our feet.

Coolly accelerating
the boar lanced by the throttle,
convulses, screams and lurches forward.
Buffeting against the water, we shudder
into Murano gently thudding
the contended death throes.

The hues of Murano's glass rape the eye.
Gaudiness bombarding the senses.
A sculptured head
three dimensional Mondigliano.
Trapped bubbles within
play with the light.

Sweating glassblower at the furnace.
A rearing steed with flowing mane is born.
A masterpiece of frozen motion,
until placed with identical others,
its beauty diluted,
its uniqueness dissipates.
The pilot,
passengatas with Italian arrogance.
Manoeuvring into the lagoon.
Onto quieter Burano.

As Murano is to glass shards
Burano is to softer lace.
Wandering the canal sides.
Breeze gently lifting filigreed lace
around windows.
At the restaurant,
the warmth of the afternoon sun.
I clean my fish bones, finish my wine.
My mellowness is complete.

Evening's chill,
thrusting hands deep into pockets.
Last light of day
silhouetting posts in the channel.
Far off
the sodium lights of Venice
reel us back home.

KEVAN TAPLIN (THUXTON)

ABBEY GARDENS

A walk in the park
Be home before dark
Pass under the arch
To the river march
Buy ice cream to eat
Goes down like a treat
See the ducks waddle up
Babies try to keep up!
How lucky we are
Do not need a car
It's right in our town
A jewel in the crown
St Edmund started it
But we all play a part in it
I am lucky to live here
Hope for many a year!

M TURNER (BURY ST EDMUNDS)

A COMPENDIUM OF SUMMER

Flowers explode, colour cascades
From pots, patios, baskets and balconies,
Spilling from hidden nooks and crevices
On sun-baked walls,
A feast for our eyes, their fragrance
Sending senses reeling.

Delicate butterflies dance in the air
Darting and dithering graceful and free
Leaving footprints on blossoms no one can see,
Clouds overhead silently drifting, glide
Pale against the blue,
While some grey tumble together,
A summer storm to brew.

Picnic baskets, sunhats and cream,
Beach balls and buckets down to the sea.
Building sandcastles, digging with pride,
While the restless sea watches and waits for the tide,
Scrounging seagulls scream and wheel above.

Luscious, ripe, red berries like jewels,
Nestle among bright green leaves,
Fingers juice-stained reach for these treasures
Again and again.

Warm summer nights when the sky
Is on fire
And the orange, red sun god slips into
Golden liquid.

J HUBBARD (DISS)

PARTY TIME!

The ripe fruits
Of high summer
Are well
And on the way
They decorate the hedgerows
And brighten the cloudiest day
There are glistening dark berries
Of elder
And clustered blackberries
True
There are rosehips fat and crimson
And plums of every hue
The birds rejoice
In plenty
They sing on the wing
On high
And the sun shines bright
In the heavens
That we may bask
In this glorious
Life!

LYN SANDFORD (ST GERMANS)

Song of the Teacher

Fling the windows wide! Begin!
Tell them now. Let knowledge in!
Hurry! Hurry! Half-past ten . . .
We shall not pass this way again.
This can change the world, you see . . .
Or so it seemed at twenty-three.

In daily wind of words
The chosen seed is tossed
About the changing heads
To set . . . to fruit . . . be lost.

And now when all is done
With father so like son
At term's end know
What seeds to sow.

A stranger says, 'You taught my son.
He loved his school. Had lots of fun.
He often spoke of you . . .' Oh then!
Fling the windows wide again.

GWEN DUNN (HADLEIGH)

Information

We hope you have enjoyed reading this book - and that you will continue to enjoy it in the coming years.

If you like reading and writing poetry drop us a line, or give us a call, and we'll send you a free information pack.

Alternatively if you would like to order further copies of this book or any of our other titles, then please give us a call or log onto our website at **www.forwardpress.co.uk**

Forward Poetry Information
Remus House
Coltsfoot Drive
Peterborough
PE2 9BF
(01733) 890066